# Suburban Warfare

A cop's guide to surviving a civil war, SHTF, or modern urban combat.

## by Don Shift

# Introduction

This book was conceived as a sort of appendix to *Suburban Defense*; a collection of many of the topics I couldn't include in the first book. Here I deal with topics that are more related to warfare often found in domestic conflicts and discuss what more tactically minded neighborhood groups can do. So while it's not an offensive operations guide, it is more proactive than the first book. *Defense* was focused more on mobs in an anarcho-tyrannical state and *Warfare* looks at a world without the rule of law (WROL).

The series is a thought experiment on how average people, with no military or law enforcement skills, who haven't been steeping themselves in the prepper/patriot movement for years can defend a modern American suburban neighborhood. Most folks aren't going to be a guerilla in suburbia. Instead they want to know how best to protect their neighborhoods. Unfortunately, most of the works I've read deal with operations in the woods or how to go on the offensive.

I anticipate that a lot of readers may pick this book up once things in the country get so bad that the police aren't doing their jobs. At that point, average citizens will be belatedly getting in the mind set that many of us have already been in. These people aren't going to be insurgents, guerillas, or be able to form some paramilitary force.

My non-fiction series adapts military and law enforcement techniques for average, untrained citizens who have to protect their homes, families, and neighborhoods in a crisis of civility. The ideal situation is to have a group of people who are all on the same page as to what's happening in America and that individuals will need to be responsible for their own safety. These sort of mutual defense groups were how people protected their towns and villages in the past. We will have to do it again.

I don't subscribe to the idea that anyone will have much success going around to their neighbors and asking them to join such a group pre-crisis. In the previous book I suggest just meeting people organically in your city or county with similar interests. I met my non-law enforcement friends at shooting matches and through ham radio. Together we have a small group of wide backgrounds, from tech, military, to law enforcement. Unfortunately, we do not live in the same neighborhood.

The average person reading this book in a crisis will probably have the interests, temperament, and ability to implement the suggestions here. In doing so he may find others who are more than just scared yuppies motivated to do something. This is to whom I've written this book, although for readers who are getting a rude awakening into the tactical world, I've kept it simple for you as well.

I've used military field manuals, law enforcement training, and a variety of other sources to use as a framework for civilian defense. Again, I'm coming at this from the perspective of the average man on the street, capable and smart, but not necessarily military minded. Infantry tactics aren't my strong suit. I also haven't lived through the fall of a city or survived an economic collapse. I'm not a gunfighting instructor or a civilian tactical trainer. I'm just a cop who has some ideas on keeping suburbanites safe.

With what is on the horizon for America, literally the specter of WWIII as I write this, an economic collapse, a border crisis, and civil war, a world without police and civil order is coming. The question is not if, but when and how bad will it be when the shit hits the fan (SHTF)?[1] As I said in the prequel, my intent is to provide suggestions and hope for those stuck in cities. What follows is just a cop's ideas and counsel on surviving urban warfare in modern American suburbs.

---

[1] I do not bowdlerize the term but this is the only instance of profanity here. Note that some of my fiction works do include profanity for the sake of verisimilitude.

# Unarmed Drone Usage Post-SHTF

At the end of the world, anyone who isn't crazy is going to want a friendly eye in the sky. Helicopters are out of the question, but an off-the-shelf consumer grade drone, or small Unmanned Aerial Vehicle (UAV) can be a large force multiplier for friendly forces. The advantages that they can give defenders could make the difference in a defensive situation or even an evacuation.

Drones can provide real time intelligence from "impossible" perspectives that someone with a pair of binoculars in a tall building or on a hill can't see. The area that one can actively surveille expands with the drone's height and mobility advantage. They allow loitering and tracking of mobile targets. Ground units can be supplemented or supported by aerial observation.

## Capabilities

Various models exist, including large-scale remote controlled fixed wing aircraft. Here we will focus on consumer drones, which are usually quadcopters. These are the cheapest, most ubiquitous, and easiest to fly. They are sold and owned in large numbers.

Consumer drones can reach altitudes of up to 1,500 feet, speeds 20-50 MPH generally, have a range of up to five miles (depending on the line-of-sight to the controller), and loiter (endurance) times of up to thirty minutes. Remote control aircraft are more capable, as will be modified or homebuilt drones.

Please note this data varies from model to model. Manufacturers may have set a 400/1500ft altitude restriction (depending on location) in the firmware, but some models do have the capability to fly at altitudes of conventional aircraft. Firmware restrictions can be removed by the end user.

Some versions have modes that can be pre-programmed to travel a pre-set path (user defined pattern) or even be set to autonomously track a moving target. Cameras can be in ultra-high definition, extreme zoom, see at night, and utilize thermal vision all while transmitting the feed back to the operator in real time.

Virtually all drones are capable of audio and visual surveillance; video can be day/night/thermal although audio will likely be degraded due to distance and the hum of the rotors. Camera quality depends on the model; larger drones can loft telephoto lens equipped cameras. Typical consumer cameras that can be used with drones typically lose video quality at distances in excess of a quarter mile or more (1,320 ft).

Payloads can be carried by drones, up to around five pounds maximum in some models. 1.5 pounds (half a kilo) seems to be the most common safe maximum payload. Homebuilt versions could be made to carry far more. Note that carrying any payload decreases range, speed, and endurance. This capability could be used for offensive purposes (see "Armed Drones" section).

Note that all of this will vary depending on the exact model in use, however, these are very rough parameters that can be expected of drones that are commonly sold commercially.

## Advantages

Some of the advantages drones can provide to neighborhood defenders are:

- Perimeter surveillance.
- Reconnaissance (scouting).
- Threat awareness.
- Real time route advance reconnaissance.
- Unarmed overwatch.
- Deterrence/suppression/distraction.
- Battle damage assessment (BDA) and casualty confirmation.
- Secure communications delivery.
- Small package delivery.
- Short term airborne radio repeater.
- Inspecting suspicious packages or vehicles.
- Tracking a moving target (person or vehicle).

I feature the use of drones being used to the advantage of good guys post-SHTF in my EMP series of novels.

## Perimeter surveillance

Some uses of drones for perimeter surveillance seem obvious, like artificially giving a defender increased height for greater observational distance, but they are much more than highly placed eyes in the sky. Drones:

- Have the ability to look straight down and see around visual obstructions versus line-of-sight only for a static observer.
- Can maneuver around terrain, structures, trees, or other visual obstructions affecting your line of sight.
- Create time-lapse videos to identify any sign of intrusion on your perimeter or property.

Drones are not restricted to observations from an aerial static location, as an observer in a high tower or on a hill is. Nor are they bound to a five to six foot high view from the ground that a person is. They can go behind obstacles, fly over buildings, and fly very low to inspect things behind obstacles like fences. They can easily inspect dangerous or denied areas.

Drones can be programmed (depending on model) to "patrol" a geofenced loop. By watching this video over time or using software to analyze it, changes can be detected over time. Perhaps a camouflaged observation post has been constructed just outside your fence line.

Threat awareness is about monitoring for potential dangers beyond your immediate perimeter. This is an indefinite distance but assume that it is the maximum range your drone could fly, or the distance you could walk in an hour. An example is scouting a nearby major intersection or roadway that attackers or refugees may use for activity. Put most simply awareness via drone is getting to a high position, looking down, and seeing what's going on.

## Reconnaissance (scouting)

Reconnaissance is more specific than general surveillance or awareness. I use the term to mean targeted inspection, observation, or study of a particular event, activity, location, or persons/people. In other words, you want to know something specific. This also includes preparation for an attack or defense.

In my book *Hard Favored Rage*, a drone is used, flying at high altitude and partially concealed in low clouds, to create a detailed map of an enemy camp and gather valuable intelligence. A drone can perform pre-attack survey and also support the attack (or defense) itself by providing real time updates on enemy movement.

Spy planes often fly over wide swaths of territory photographing everything beneath them for later intelligence analysis. Drones can do this too. Firmware modification to override any restrictions on distance from the user could allow you to program a flight plan that takes the drone out of line of sight communication to perform a reconnaissance mission. Of course, the drone would be on its own and midcourse updates or evasion is impossible. This will require a functioning GPS system.

## Route monitoring and overwatch

In Iraq and Afghanistan, vehicle convoys and foot patrols often had helicopter or Predator drone support to alert the soldiers and Marines what was happening around and in front of them. One could remotely clear intersections, curves in the road, behind hills or obstacles, for ambushes. Imagine that instead of having to send a team on foot to check out some wrecked cars in the road, your drone can simply do a fly-by to see if guys with guns are crouching on the other side.

Overwatch support was vital to American troops in the last thirty years. Even without the ability to fire on the enemy, eyes in the sky passed on timely tactical intelligence that often saved the day. For instance, unarmed overwatch could allow you to detect and respond to an ambush or flanking maneuver before it occurs. A checkpoint could be given advance warning of a breach attempt. Unfortunately while consumer UAVs can pass on warnings from what they see, they cannot provide fire support like helicopters or

Predator drones can.

## Communications and delivery

Like carrier pigeons, drones can deliver written or recorded messages securely to allies across contested or inaccessible terrain. Messages would need to be encrypted in the event the message is captured or the drone is shot down.

Another use is as a flying short term airborne radio repeater. A ham skilled with a soldering iron could rig up a lightweight repeater that could potentially cover a 50 mile radius from a height of 1500 feet (depending on terrain). This would enable long-range line of sight communications if a grid-down disaster (or sabotage) has rendered conventional repeater towers out of commission. Its utility would be limited by the duration of the drone's batteries.

Small packages of urgently needed material could also be delivered via drone. Large consumer quadcopters can carry up to five pounds in some cases (with a severe range/endurance reduction), enabling emergency delivery of critical goods. When American troops were surrounded by Germans in a battle in France, empty leaflet shells were loaded with desperately needed medical supplies and fired on the American position. Unfortunately, most of the supplies were damaged on impact.[2]

Drones can take this idea and deliver things a bit more gently. Isolated homes may be resupplied in a number of drops. A fighter trapped behind cover might get needed ammunition or water dropped to him. Drones could even drop smoke grenades in the open to provide concealment to ground forces.

## Drawbacks

Some of the drawbacks to drone usage are:

---

[2] 30th Infantry Division at Hill 314, Mortain, France, August 1944.

- Their usage can draw unwanted attention.
- The characteristic buzz is now immediately recognizable as a drone.
- If you are trying to remain as clandestine as possible, a drone may negate your other efforts to remain undetected.
- They can be followed back to their point of origin or their landing spot to identify the owner.
- Interest in a location can alert an enemy to a potential attack.
- Regular surveillance patterns can be exploited.
- Firmware limitations.
- Potential unavailability of GPS.
- Need for electricity to charge frequently/limited range and endurance.
- Potential unavailability of repair parts.
- Can be shot down, hacked, or jammed.
- Limited flying in low-visibility conditions (rain, snow, fog).
- They are not a replacement for patrols, observation/listening posts (OP/LP), surveillance cameras, or general situational awareness.

## Firmware limitations

Many commercially available consumer drones are easy to fly thanks to firmware that uses AI and other advanced features. The downside is that many manufacturers have placed restrictions on their products, from geofenced restricted areas to altitude limitations. Drones may require an Internet connection before launching or regular updates to remain functional. Certain flight behaviors may be prohibited.

To overcome this, a user serious about unconventional post-SHTF use needs to look into disabling these limitations and restrictions. There are ways to "jailbreak," or circumvent, the firmware or overwrite it entirely. Doing so will likely void the warranty and may constitute a criminal violation in some areas. At least purchase/download the software now.

An inexperienced user with no hard curbs on the firmware may fly the drone into illegal areas, in violation of FAA regulations, or beyond the parameters of the airframe. Someone who does not understand the firmware may also "brick" the drone in the process. While usage of jailbreaking software or manually modifying the hardware or firmware should be on-hand *prior* to SHTF, actual removal of restrictions should be saved for when the rule of law is more flexible and the danger outweighs the legal repercussions.

## Misconceptions

A drone launch could alert your opponent of imminent offensive action, although I think this fear is overwrought. The phrase "when the balloon goes up" refers to anti-aircraft barrage balloons being launched prior to a WWI air attack or observation balloons being launched prior to a Civil War battle, depending on which etymology you choose to believe. This can be mitigated by skillful use of altitude and deceptive flying techniques.

Increased intelligence and awareness outweigh the disadvantages of the attention it might cause. The suppressive effects of a drone can be exploited as well, turning its overtness into an asset. Stealth can be used if a drone is kept high, used in a noisy environment, remains out of easy visual spotting distance of the enemy, and uses visual obstructions to hide behind. A wise user will not launch and recover the drone from the same place, if possible, and not from their immediate property, using terrain masking as much as possible.

I think the argument that "drones will advertise your presence" is stupid. Even if you have a really great hidden retreat in prepper paradise, eventually someone is going to stumble across you. Smart people aren't going to huddle inside their perimeter with no intelligence on what's going on in the outside world. Stupid people will do that and die.

There are a lot of things that can give you away. Someone with Google Earth can look on the map and note your location for post-SHTF exploitation. Smoke from your chimney or fire could give you

13

away. Bad guys might stumble across your patrol. Whether your drone advertises that you have "resources" or not, bad guys will try to steal from anyone they can, "rich" enough for a drone or not.

This whole debate reminds of me of caliber wars (9mm vs. .45) and open carry vs. concealed carry. It is stupid. Accuracy and bullet type, not size, determine lethality. Open carry and concealed carry each have their own advantages and disadvantages; sometimes you might want your gun visible and other times you'll want to be the gray man. In SHTF, you'll want to have the choice of every advantage possible tempered by the sense that launching a drone might be tactically inappropriate.

As for the EMP (electromagnetic pulse) argument, EMP hasn't been shown to affect devices that small, especially if they are powered down and indoors. An EMP is a very long shot anyhow. A more likely scenario is a cyber war or anti-satellite attack.

The GPS system relies on satellites and ground stations. In a major peer-to-peer war with Russia or China, GPS will be a target. The US military may also disable it or degrade accuracy of the signal. Without GPS, some features of the drone may not function and some models may not work at all. "Return to home" and pre-programmed flight paths may not function at all. Some models may refuse to fly without GPS input and all will have to be controlled manually by the pilot.

A loss of grid electricity or modern delivery systems does not have to be crippling. Anyone planning to use a drone seriously in SHTF needs to have multiple spare battery packs and alternative electricity sources. A generator or solar panel system and a way to store the electricity once generated (batteries or power packs) is a must. Spare parts can be ordered prior to SHTF and kept on-hand as one would stockpile things like high-wear automotive items that might be unavailable.

Drones are stealthy. They may not be heard or seen by people on the ground, often going totally unnoticed at high flight altitudes. Their stealth is an inherent capability due to their size. They may be operated at altitudes where the rotor noise is not heard or it easily blends in with the ambient noise. The airframes themselves are also relatively small and can be visually overlooked if flying at a high enough altitude or the model is quite small. Visual detection range is typically 100 yards and the sound can be detected at 40 yards.

Drones also don't replace tried and true methods. Just because you have a magic flying thingy doesn't relieve you from walking your perimeter, sending out patrols, or performing inspections in person. Technology is not a substitute for using your God-given senses to further investigate suspicious circumstances. Drones can't see everything and *will* change the behavior of those that they observe in ways actual humans may not.

The biggest obstacle to drone employment is cost, followed by owner piloting experience. Not all of us have the money to buy quality drones and all the peripheral accessories. Flight experience is also critical and some persons might just not have the technological proficiency and aeronautical ability to fly a drone.

## Drone operation tradecraft

Paint your drone in a neutral gray color as many military aircraft are painted. This color blends in with many different sky conditions and will help low observability against urban landscapes. Light sky blue is another color consideration. Disable any anti-collision or navigation lights for day or night flying.

When possible given the mission parameters, maintain visual contact with the drone. This is important as you may need to take evasive action if a "killer" drone is launched to intercept yours. The onboard cameras may not give you any warning of an airborne attack.

Treat launching your drone like a submarine raising its periscope. Periscopes pop up for just a brief span of time and are pulled back down as soon as possible. This is because the scope itself and its signature on the waves, the "feather," can be spotted by ships or aircraft. See what you need to see and land; constant observation isn't always going to be necessary.

When a shootdown is likely, a drone can be rapidly launched on a zoom climb out of range, the camera quickly spun in a pattern to get video of the area, then rapidly descended to safety. Video can be reviewed for intelligence once the drone is down. This minimizes the time the drone is in danger or that it is observable to the enemy. Submarine captains use a similar technique when making periscope observations.

Induce alert fatigue so your enemy doesn't associate drones with an imminent attack; repeatedly conduct reconnaissance only to lull them into complacency. When you attack, hopefully they assume the drone is just doing its usual flyby.

Don't be predictable.

- Always launch and land drones out of sight from potential adversarial observers.
- When possible, land and recover the drone in different locations away from your home or immediate area of operations to prevent adversaries from easily locating you.
- Flight paths for launch and recovery should utilize terrain masking to travel a distance away from the landing pad/operations area before ascending to altitude. Fly the drone between buildings, terrain, or trees. Ascend and descend well away from the operator.
- If possible, have the operator remain concealed a distance away from the landing pad and have someone else physically launch/recover the drone.
- Never fly a drone directly back to your area of operations or landing pad; fly in a different direction after reconning a target. Be sure to fly an indirect, deceptive course back.

Use visual obstructions to hide the drone when making low-level observations. Pop up and "peep" over structures, trees, etc. Don't just hover out in the open where an adversary can see your drone and shoot it down.

Note that low-level flights using terrain masking can increase the chance of a shootdown or collision with an obstruction. To avoid a shootdown, fly fast, frequently changing directions unpredictably, and never approaching from the same direction twice in a row.

When flown high, fly as high as possible to maintain a low visual and noise signature. Only approach as low or as close as necessary to make clear visual observations. Use camera zoom to your advantage.

Avoid giving away your target by slowly and casually overflying it in a straight line. Let the camera do the looking around while the drone passes by, seemingly to somewhere else. Deceive your adversary by taking lots of time to obviously survey random locations.

Instead of hovering, orbit the target to keep the drone constantly moving, although an unpredictable path is best. For reconnaissance of a fixed target, instead of orbiting or flying around the perimeter of the target, consider flying by each "side" at different times.

If possible, have multiple drones of different models, configurations, or paint schemes to deceive the enemy about how many you might have or into thinking two or more groups have UAVs.

Alert your neighbors and friendly forces when you launch a drone so they do not mistake it for an enemy craft. Monitor enemy communications for their reaction to the drone.

# UCAV: Armed Drones

The term "drone" has become synonymous with Unmanned Combat Aerial Vehicle, or UCAV, and small UCAVs have become common in modern warfare. Originally used for reconnaissance purposes in first rate militaries, the small, modern consumer drone has become a staple of irregular warfare. Cartels have mounted automatic weapons on drones and ISIS used them to drop bombs on their enemies. No longer a plaything or innovative camera platform, drones will be used in any domestic conflict in the United States.

Drone warfare, expressly at the domestic level, is a perfect example of disruptive technology. Drones add a vertical attack element and remote surveillance capability that until now was beyond the ability of most participants in a civil conflict. Expectations of civil war or unrest merely being street battles and fights to secure high points (drone operator's vantage points) need to be adjusted.

To date, irregular forces have used drones for:
- Video has been used for propaganda purposes including showing successful attacks.
- Battle damage assessment (BDA) and casualty confirmation.
- General surveillance and reconnaissance.
- Studying attacks, defenses, and responses.
- Delivery of explosives.

In the "Unarmed Drones" section we explored how drones can be used for your benefit. You must realize in a civil conflict your enemy will use them for *his* benefit. Additionally, warfare is not static and technology like this will be game changing. Armed drones will become more than the American insurgent's eye in the sky but his precision guided munition too.

Drones can perform suppression of enemy forces, in addition to direct attacks. By forcing you to take cover or hide from its camera, this degrades your ability to carry out your mission, the textbook definition of suppression. This can be intentional if the target is conditioned to react to drones or unintentional if the drone's presence or behavior causes the target to act. An armed drone can provide traditional fire suppression if someone attaches a weapon to it.

An example of suppression is a criminal being pursed by officers "going to ground" when a helicopter shows up. Suspects often attempt to take cover under anything that will hide them. This was easier to do before law enforcement aircraft were equipped with thermal tracking gear. I've even seen a helicopter locate a suspect hidden in elephant grass next to a golf course in daylight thanks to its FLIR camera.

While the helicopter is overhead, the suspect can't move. Assuming there is no FLIR, being unable to continue to evade capture, the suspect is stuck while ground units search the area for his location. A flying drone can provide the same effect and more against a neighborhood defensive unit. In war, instead of search and capture the ground units would be moving in for a kill.

Military forces have had the same aerial surveillance advantages since close air support was invented. Low flybys of helicopters and all manner of fixed wing aircraft can suppress ground forces. Nothing is new about drones being used for suppressive effect, except that the cheap, easy to use technology has democratized airborne reconnaissance and even attack.

## Weaponization

Drones can carry a surprising variety of weapons that are all up to the ingenuity of the user and their access to weaponry. A flamethrower was put on one. The Internet was put into a panic a few years ago when a drone owner posted video of a quadcopter with a pistol mounted below firing away. The contraption appeared to be a homemade model and the pistol's recoil noticeably pushed the drone backwards with each shot. This prompted a FAA investigation as putting weapons on drones is illegal.

Latin American drug cartels are using these to deliver IEDs, often using a second drone to provide surveillance and guidance. One drone bomb was C4 and ball bearings pressed into a Tupperware plastic container.[3] Some of these devices have been dropped like bombs while others have landed devices either as warnings or to emplace them for later detonation.

ISIS often dropped munitions out of a plastic tube when released remotely by a servo motor. 40mm grenades were popular with ISIS as they were light and could be lofted easily by consumer Quadcopters. Larger drones can drop 60mm and 81mm mortar bombs. Homemade bombs often using plastic explosive have been seen in Latin American cartel wars and in the Middle East. Weapons don't need to be dropped; a more accurate strike, at the cost of the drone, can be delivered in a kamikaze attack involving terminal guidance to the target and detonation.

Payloads depend on speed and range required. Maximum payload for a large quadcopter is about 4-5lbs. Optimal payloads are on average half a pound or less, up to 1.25lbs or half a kilo. About 1lb of C4 explosive is enough to destroy a truck. Bare explosives can be studded with ball bearings or other metal to create shrapnel; however, this may take the weight limit over what small drones can carry.

Thankfully, at least for now, it is nearly impossible to source explosives in the US without outright theft from military, construction, or demolition sources. Americans do not have the same access as insurgents in Iraq did. This may change in a civil war or if the military collapses. Domestic sources of explosives from commercial demolition companies or homebrewed plastic explosives are more possible in SHTF. Foreign actors may also supply explosives or munitions.

## Targets

---

[3] "Jalisco cartel adopts new tactic: drones armed with C-4 explosive," *Mexico News Daily*, 8/18/2020.

The issue with drones is not that they won't have enough targets but that there will not be enough airframes to attack targets. ISIS was able to use as many consumer drones as they could get delivered because they were well funded (until they weren't). Without both a reliable supply and the money to pay for drones, UCAVs being used as precision guided weapons is unlikely to be a ubiquitous part of domestic urban combat. This *may* be a concern if factions are being supported by foreign powers.

Even homebuilt drones will run out of parts eventually. A potential conflict with China only exacerbates potential supply problems as drones and the very components they are made of are manufactured over there or other Asian countries whose economies and supply chains would be disrupted by war. Tactical employment in battle requires a lot of drones. Thus, drone attacks will have to be prioritized.

Tactical targets are things like fortifications, barricades, or concentrations of fighters. Strategic targets are those that weaken or demoralize your enemy without directly killing them. Strategic targets can be broken down into two groups; local and regional. Local targets are those that affect your daily life while regional ones are larger sites and facilities. Here are some examples:

- Water: local, your neighborhood well or city pumping station; regional, state aqueduct pumping plant.
- Fuel: local, a gas station; regional, a refinery.
- Electricity: local, a neighborhood substation; regional, a powerplant or long-distance transmission lines.
- Transportation: local, drone-delivered IEDs on the road; regional, drones bombing semi-trucks on the Interstate.
- Persons: local, a militia leader; regional, a political or government figure.

Terrorists or insurgents are going to go after strategic targets in order to get the most impact. This would include bombing oil refineries, assassinating politicians or popular figures, destroying critical electrical or communication notes, or pumping stations for water, gas, and oil. They may also use drones in attacks against sports stadiums, large concentrations of people, or aircraft.

In an insurgency, the main goal will be to harass your enemy and degrade his ability to fight. It may also be to force relocation or withdrawal due to inadequate resources. It would be easy for bad guys to detonate a drone bomb on or near power lines or a local substation. The same for an Internet hub (usually inside stout buildings). The only water source, like a municipal well, might also be attacked. Not all of these locations can be guarded around the clock.

## Drone combat

In addition to the above discussed surveillance and reconnaissance roles, armed drones will be used in direct combat. Area fire that is ordinarily accomplished in militaries by mortars, artillery, and grenade launchers will be done by drone. Americans just won't have access to these weapons the same way that Afghans and Iraqis did. Explosive armed drones themselves may be flown directly into targets and detonated in the same manner as militaries employ missiles.

Drones may be used in the following manner to kill:

- Dual drone operations: Drone 1 overflies a target, performing reconnaissance. The same drone or another returns and delivers a hand grenade or explosive.
- Grenades or explosives may be dropped like an aerial bomb or the drone can be terminally guided into the target before detonation. Drone attacks should be considered precision attacks.
- Drones may perform pre-attack recon from high altitude and attacks from lower altitudes, utilizing buildings, trees, or other visual obstructions to conceal their approach.
- Some models are capable of crashing through weak windows in a kamikaze attack.
- ISIS used drones to guide vehicular suicide bombers to their target and then remotely detonated the bomb at the most opportune moment.
- A second explosive may be detonated to kill those responding to the chaos of the first attack.
- Unarmed drones may act in a suppression role by mimicking the attack pattern of an armed drone.[4]

- Dropping smoke grenades in the open to provide concealment to attacking or retreating fighters.

## Bombings

Let's talk about drones dropping bombs on suburban buildings. First off, I know nothing about demolitions and I was never on the bomb squad. Public information regarding the effectiveness of bare explosives detonated against civilian buildings is not easily accessible. Most of the demolitions data and video shows explosives inside homes, not falling on their roofs.

An explosive charge ≤5lb (versus a traditional mortar or aerial bomb with a metal shell) typically will not penetrate standard residential and commercial roofs *prior to detonation*. Military weapons have a metal outer case to enable some penetration before detonation and fragmentation after. A block of explosive with the consistency of modeling clay falling from a drone *shouldn't* break through the roof.

With the explosion occurring outside, at least half of the blast effects are going upwards. There will be no ground to focus more of the blast into walls, as if it were detonated next to the house. With the amount of explosive a drone can safely carry (probably 2lbs, 5lbs, at the most), a house shouldn't be totally destroyed. A wood roof in the area of the blast will be blown in and almost certainly the area below it. The shockwave will enter the home and cause additional damage.

Warheads detonated at window level outside will present a high-velocity flying glass hazard. For any detonation, residents in the home will face a danger of wood, metal, and masonry shrapnel. The shockwave itself will also be dangerous. Hearing loss, either temporary or permanent, is highly probable. The blast may weaken

---

[4] There are countless stories of military aircraft out of munitions making low passes over enemy troops to suppress them. C-130 cargo aircraft have flown high orbits as their armed AC-130 gunship counterparts to fool the enemy.

structural components of the house causing partial collapse. Gas or electrical lines may be severed. Fire may occur. Secondary explosives may be delivered after the first charge breaches the house.

Outdoors, unless a military weapon designed to produce shrapnel (grenade, mortar bomb) is exploded, blast effects and flying debris will be the main hazard. Explosions at a close distance are still quite hazardous and a drone could approach to mere feet before command detonation. Another hazard would be the airborne delivery of IEDs to be exploded at a later time.

### Shelters

Indoor shelters should be beneath a stout table or purpose-built reinforced structure nearest the center of the building on a ground floor. This structure should have a layer of sandbags on top to stop any shrapnel. The shelter frame should be strong enough to support a portion of the building structure in case of a collapse. As described in the next chapter regarding home redoubts, this shelter should have sandbag sidewalls to protect from lateral attacks or concurrent gunfire.

Outside shelters should be dug into the ground, where possible. This will also save sandbags or other containers. The spoil should be used to reinforce the roof or any gap between the roof and the ground used for firing. The roof needs to be stout enough to support several feet of earth or sandbags. Camouflage the shelter.

Outdoor shelters should have a camouflaged grid or screen to "catch" or detonate warheads above the shelter. Similar screens can be placed around the sides as well. The intent is that any explosion occurs several feet away from the actual sheltering surface instead of against it. Such screens can be made of dense metal grids, dense fencing, or failing that, metal frames reinforced with stout wire lattices. All screens must have openings smaller than 40mm.

# Actions to take

## Before attack

- Camouflaged positions from above are necessary.
- Weapons and tactical gear may need to be concealed or disguised to allow defenders to appear like average civilians.
- Uniforms or camouflage clothing may give away a tactical unit moving operationally.
- Fixed defenses or locations should have a shelter constructed with sufficient overhead cover.

## Immediate action drill

- Upon the approach of a drone, seek the nearest cover and freeze. Try to pick a place where you will be unseen by the drone and have adequate overhead and lateral cover from weapons fire.
- Civilians should take cover indoors under stout cover.
- Observe the drone. Determine its type and if it is carrying a payload (guns or bombs). Photograph it if possible.
- Wait until it leaves the area to resume normal operations, if possible.
- If it is within your capabilities and the drone is within range, you may attempt to shoot it down.
- Drone operators should be regarded as snipers and handled accordingly.

# Anti-drone countermeasures

Many prisons now have nets or cables to keep out drones that attempt to deliver contraband. Such an idea is possible for small spaces, but not feasible to protect a home. As described above, small screens can protect small defensive fortifications, but not large areas. Active measures will need to be employed.

## Shooting down drones

Shotgun drone shootdowns are not uncommon. To date, it has largely been on the range, by an annoyed neighbor, or by an angry man who caught the drone peeping. Based on the limited information provided, these drones were close and not attempting to evade. Drones engaged in combat operations will try to remain as distant as possible and *should* evade, making a shootdown more difficult.

Note that this is not a guide on how to take out an Amazon drone or your neighbor's toy. Shooting within city limits and built up areas is often illegal. Shooting down a drone is generally considered vandalism and you may owe the owner for the damage to his property. Rules vary and research is required. However, if this is a civil war or WROL type situation, that does not apply.

Drones are designed to be lightweight and thus quite fragile. They can be easily damaged by high velocity projectiles. Any impact may cause the drone to lose orientation and crash; the more violent the better. Shotgun shells may be the best chance at shooting down a drone at low level and a good skeet or trap shooter should be the one to make the attempt.

Range, altitude, and the drone's speed will all factor into the ability to hit it as much as the ability of the shooter, the gun, and the ammunition used. Wind, temperature, and altitude can affect range as well.

**Birdshot:** No. 8 shot is reported to be effective, but at an unknown altitude and range.[5] Typical birdshot loads will have a maximum flight distance (not effective range, but how far away the shot will return to Earth) of 300-400 yards. Generally shot fired upwards will not cause injury at this distance when it lands. Magnum shells and specialty loads may have additional capabilities.

An expert shooter can break clay pigeons at 100 yards, but ordinary range is 60-80 yards. Note that this is against a 4" target, so it may be easier to hit a larger drone target. Larger size shot will

---

[5] Cyrus Farivar, "Kentucky man shoots down drone hovering over his backyard," *Ars Technica*, 7/29/2015.

typically ballistically peak at 200 yards (horizontally from the shooter) fired at a 30° angle; this will result in an approximate maximum target altitude of 345 feet.

The longer the barrel of the shotgun, the greater the accuracy at further distance. Fowling barrels of 28-32" long would be ideal. The caveat is that at this length a choke may be needed to open up the pattern as longer barrels tend to tighten down the spread pattern.

**Buckshot:** Because buckshot has more mass, it has a horizontal range of up to around 75 yards. The greater mass would cause more damage to a drone. However, when fired vertically, due to the increased weight vs. birdshot, it will not fly as high, although I've been unable to find any data on buckshot used against aerial targets.

**Specialty shells:** 12 gauge Skynet Drone Defense ammunition, a three-pack retails for $20-25 as of this writing. The shell contains six weighted tethers in a star shape that is designed to entangle the rotors of the drone, causing it to crash via loss of control and lift. In the event of a miss, the expended projectile will fall safely to earth. Skynet shells in one test were fired at 70 feet (unknown if this is horizontal, diagonal, or vertical distance) and required 3-5 shots for a kill.[6]

**Other weapons:** A .177 air rifle pellet took down a drone.[7] A felon shot down a police drone with a .22 rifle.[8] There is nothing that would rule out using an AR-15 or other type of weapon or cartridge over a drone. 5.56mm rounds will fly further, to a higher altitude, and do more damage when they arrive. However, rifle rounds of any caliber will pose a further danger on the ground when they ballistically return. It may also be difficult to spot and track the drone

---

[6] https://www.youtube.com/watch?v=jlGdPrhRvBA
[7] Haye Kesteloo, "Drone captures shooter before being shot down itself," DroneDJ, 11/20/2017.
[8] US Attorney's Office press release, "Lake County Convicted Felon Indicted For Illegal Firearm Possession And Destruction Of Aircraft," October 13, 2021.

in the air. Also, aiming a rifle accurately at high angles to hit a target like a quadcopter will not be in the skillset of most shooters.

Multiple shots of any kind may be required and the drone may not be hovering, especially after the first hit. Test videos that are available show drones at relatively low altitude and close distances. The combination of the two make shotgun shootdowns a last-minute thing which can be further complicated by an enemy who is ready to counter shootdown attempts. Also, a successful hit at close distance against an explosive bearing drone may result in death or injury to the shooter.

Alternative anti-drone projectors will certainly be developed. Water cannons might be used if they have the range, but probably aren't feasible for the neighborhood defender. One suggestion is a modified "potato cannon" except that rapid, accurate aiming may be difficult.

## Best practices

- When shooting down the drone, attempt to distract the operator, who may see the shootdown attempt and take evasive action.
- Shootdown attempts should be undertaken at an angle and distance away from the distraction or the focus of its observation.
- Be prepared for follow-up shots/misses, multiple drones, evasion, and even returning drones.
- Anti-drone shooters should expect to be targeted by snipers, enemy forces, and even armed drones themselves.
- Ensure that fired bullets or shots are unlikely to impact friendly forces or innocent parties.

### Jamming

Drones can be jammed using radiofrequency "rifles" that send a directional radio beam at the drone. Radial antennas can provide area protection from drones as well. Jamming works by either overriding the control signal or depriving the drone from receiving GPS signals. Also in the same realm, but more complicated, is hacking the signals to take over the drone or spoof the command signals to crash the drone.

Jamming the control signal may cause the drone to hover, return to the launch point, or fall out of the air. A loss of GPS signal may also cause the drone to lose orientation and crash, however, if the control signal remains unjammed the operator may just fly it away.

Jammers may be difficult to purchase due to shipping restrictions and price. Some devices capable of drone or GPS jamming are available out of the box and do not require extensive technical expertise but may suffer from low signal strength and poor antennas. One such product is the Hack RF One with additional aftermarket antennas and software. Homemade models can be built if one has the technical expertise.

### Drone air-to-air combat

Shooting down a drone with a gun is not going to work against a pilot who is anticipating anti-drone fire, actively evades, flies smartly, and keeps the drone out of range. This means that the fight will need to be taken to the offending drone. Anti-drone air superiority will become a thing.

All combat is about what happens on the ground. Aircraft were first used in military applications for reconnaissance, then bombing. Naturally, the countermeasure was to develop fighter planes that specialized in shooting down aircraft. While fighter vs. fighter combat has captured the imagination and hearts of fighter pilots all over the world, the actual job of air superiority is to deny the airspace to the enemy. If fighter jets are waiting to shoot down his bombers and transport planes, he can't use his air force to support his ground troops or attack the enemy.

Though it would be expensive to have a lot of remote control planes and drones, it is possible to use drones against drones. Note however that one would have to fly their remote control aircraft physically into the drone to knock it out of the sky. For your small UCAV, this will be a suicide mission.

A light and cheap drone that can climb to a decent altitude and fly fast would probably be ideal. Practice can be done with easily repairable drones. An experienced drone pilot may be able to accomplish a mid-air collision without much rehearsal. The kinetic impact should be all that is required to crash most consumer quadcopter types. Once downed, the wrecked drone should be captured for intelligence exploit or an ambush can be setup to wait for the enemy's recovery attempt.

## Bottom line

Are you likely to be killed by a drone?[9] It is *highly* unlikely. In a future destabilized America immersed in urban combat, most deaths will be caused by famine and disease, followed by gunfire, as in most wars. Drone warfare will occur because it is a useful technology in warfare. In application, it is little different than modern militaries using attack aircraft, helicopters, precision guided munitions, or indirect fire weapons (mortar and artillery). It's just that drones make this kind of thing suddenly accessible to anyone which makes it scary.

Drones will be problematic mostly as a reconnaissance and command & control tool. I would be more worried about a looting gang launching a drone to see who is asleep before the 3 AM attack than I am someone flying a drone with C4 through my bedroom window.

---

[9] A civilian, consumer drone, not a government one, that is.

# Surviving Artillery, Drone, and Mortar Attacks

In the major modern conflicts of the last thirty years, lots of homes and residential areas have been reduced to rubble. Sarajevo was randomly shelled. Syria was shelled and bombed by forces on all sides. Villages in Afghanistan were turned into heaps of dried mud walls. Urban warfare affects the very homes that people live in.

To be fair, much of the residential areas that have been turned into ruins were in large cities. Many Americans do not live in the kind of cities that are found in Europe and the Middle East. Whereas centralized high rise apartment complexes are common elsewhere, they are not in the US. Dense urban cores of multistorey housing are mainly a northeastern thing. Most defenders reading this book will live in housing tracts.

The benefit to American housing patterns is more spacing between homes, apartment buildings, and complexes. This makes artillery and bombs less effective. A lot of modern housing is made of wood frame construction which has more "give" to it but is susceptible to burning and penetration of high velocity projectiles.

The thing about any kind of warfare in a city is that civilians will be at risk. General lawlessness that a collapse will bring is one thing. Random gunfire is the main threat. But what if that lawlessness turns into more traditional warfare or a civil war follows the patterns of 20th century wars? A drive-by shooting poses a much smaller risk to people in a house than does an artillery bombardment.

As horrible as the idea of this kind of warfare happening in a modern American (or Western) suburb is, life goes on. The people of Sarajevo during the siege went about their normal lives, as much as they could, while the shells boomed across the city.

**Note:** This section focuses mainly on air delivered weapons, not emplaced bombs (IEDs); see appendix.

# Types of explosives and explosive weaponry likely to be used

In a civil war, Americans may be faced with aerial bombardment from aircraft, artillery barrages, or mortar attacks. Artillery are guns that fire large shells, usually between four and six inches, over distances of 20 miles. Mortars are shorter range bombs fired usually at the infantry level in support of smaller units typically at 5 miles maximum. Grenade launchers fire a small explosive warhead from something like an oversized bullet.

If insurgents capture military weapons, they will likely have access to mortars for indirect fire, bazooka-like rocket launchers, and grenade launchers. Artillery will be least likely in a conflict that does not feature direct military involvement due to the large logistical tail required to fuel the transportation vehicles, supply the ammunition, and feed the artillerymen. A proper artillery barrage can devastate a city block easily.

Mortars require a small, trained team to operate them with reasonable effect. Without foreign or domestic military training, or operation by ex-servicemen, the usage of mortars becomes less likely, but not absent. With minimal knowledge they can be lobbed into a general area for harassment or lucky shots. The lethal radius is about 100 yards and they are capable of causing serious damage to small structures or vehicles.

Rocket launchers (AT-4, SMAW, Javelin, Carl Gustav, RPG) tend to be more accurate and more powerful than grenade launchers and in the third world, Russian RPGs are ubiquitous. Anti-tank rocket launchers like the TOW missile have proved devastating to tanks in Syria and are potent targets against structures or dug-in positions. These are very effective against small structures or fortified positions; however, they cannot engage in indirect fire.

Grenades fired from launchers can be used for indirect fire in an arcing trajectory. Their range is around 400 yards and have a kill radius of a few yards, although injuries can occur further away.

These can be fired from grenade machine guns or single launchers. They can be fired through point targets like windows.

Mortars and artillery shells can easily penetrate homes and most American commercial construction before exploding. Buildings can be reduced to rubble effortlessly depending on the type of shell and construction in cases of direct hits. Very strong, well built blast shelters will be required to survive a direct him. Near-hits can cause massive damage, including building collapse, or cause serious problems via shrapnel.

Without access to military hardware, any explosive attack in a future domestic conflict will be limited to homemade and demolition/construction sourced explosives. Usage will be most commonly in the form of Improvised Explosive Devices or IEDs. These can be hidden in places to attack crowds, inside buildings, or in the form of car bombs. The most notable attack in the US is the 2013 Boston Marathon bombing. I feel America will resemble Northern Ireland in many respects with random car and business bombings.

Note that IEDs can be remotely detonated to kill a specific person or at an optimal time. They can also be delivered by drones (which is covered in the previous chapter).

## Injuries and death from explosives

Explosives kill and injure in three ways: overpressure, fragmentation, and collapse. Explosions are the conversion of solid material into gas—really rapidly and with a lot of heat in a violent reaction. This release of energy creates a pressure wave that forces highly compressed air outward until the energy dissipates; a shockwave. The shockwave's strength depends on distance from the explosive and obviously the size of the explosion itself. Close enough in, hundreds to thousands of pounds per square inch of pressure can hit you.

The shockwave compresses the organs and tissues inside your body as they pass right through your body at supersonic speeds.

Gas filled organs suffer the most due to the incredible pressure differentials, including the ears, lungs, brain, and bowels. Deafness and Traumatic Brain Injuries (TBIs) are common injuries in survivors.

Besides internal organ damage and external tissue damage, the next major cause of death and injury from bombs is from fragmentation. Fragments include shrapnel and debris. Up to half the weight of a typical aerial bomb is in its metal case that is intended to fragment to destroy structures, equipment, and people. Pipe bombs generate shrapnel from the pipe itself. Pressure cooker bombs and other IEDs usually need to have metal added, like ball bearings, nuts and bolts, or other hard metal bits. These act like bullets when launched by an explosion. Debris can also act as unintentional fragments.

Finally, the effects of the explosion can cause collapse of a structure or debris to hit and kill people. In urban combat, structural collapse will be a real danger from the use of any kind of bomb or explosive. A collapse may not be total, but a beam falling at the wrong moment in the wrong place may kill someone. Flying debris, like wood splinters or glass, can also be lethal or highly injurious.

Fire and heat are less common causes of death and usually only very close in. Close enough to be killed by the heat generated by the explosive means your body is probably being blown apart before you know what happened. Secondary fires ignited in the damage the explosion causes are another source of injury or death. Firestorms have ignited from bombing raids.

## Sheltering

The average suburban American home is the worst type of home to shelter in. Wood frame construction is relatively resilient to impact but it is flammable and high velocity projectiles easily penetrate it. Beware that brick and stone houses in many cases only have a masonry veneer and wood frame construction beneath. The bullet resistance of suburban housing is covered in detail in

*Suburban Defense.*

Basements are the obvious place to shelter in during any type of event where exposure to firearms or indirect fire (artillery) is expected. Full basements are preferred but the ground side wall of a split-level home as far as possible from any exterior walls will also work. Basement shelters should adapt the below principles for above ground homes with particular attention paid to vertical protection. When sheltering in a basement, fire danger will be more acute so multiple exits should be available.

Storm shelters should also be utilized. Please note that above ground storm shelters probably cannot withstand a direct hit from artillery or mortars. Below ground ones might not either due to the penetration characteristic of the shelter and the lack of hardening. Garage models made of relatively thin sheet steel intended for tornado shelters may not withstand impacts from bullets or high-velocity shrapnel. Non-masonry above ground shelters reinforced make a good starting point.

For homes with no below-ground shelter, a hasty above ground indoor shelter can be built out of common materials. I would recommend having sandbags on hand as a general prep as they will probably be difficult to find after a crisis begins.

Your indoor shelter will need to be in the interior of the building and on the lowest floor. This gives the maximum protection that the construction of the building can offer. Let the roof and walls absorb and deflect what blast and shrapnel they can. A stout roof is necessary as are walls that can stop high velocity projectiles like bullets and shell fragments.

### Sandbags

An ideal shelter is taking a small room and placing sandbags to create a "redoubt" of sandbags in the middle of the room or against an interior wall. This will be a small bullet and shrapnel resistant hideout that utilizes the outer shell of the house to help redirect and slow down any shots that might injure or kill someone. Your family won't live here, but will take cover during any gun battles, aerial attacks, or drive-by shootings.

Standard 14" x 26" sandbags can be bought in bulk and used to construct a home interior redoubt. You may also want some for an outside fighting position. Their advantage is that they can be easily stored empty and filled when a crisis arises from local material. Keep in mind that large quantities of sand or earth is required and if you fill them from your yard, you will have giant holes outside your home. A cubic yard of earth is typically required for 100 standard sandbags.

Sandbags are commonly found in polypropylene (plastic) and burlap (cloth). Polypropylene is broken down by the UV radiation in sunlight and outdoors the bags will degrade in three to six months of heat and sun. Indoors at room temperature they will have an indefinite lifespan and are more likely to fail from accidental punctures than the material "rotting" away. If the bags are protected from sunlight, such as being indoors or covered, they can last indefinitely.

The bag is not filled up to the top. The top end needs to be left unfilled and loose because it will be cinched up and tied closed. The typical fill is one-half to 2/3rds full. A sandbag that is 2/3rds full will weigh about 30-40 pounds, depending on your exact fill, and the density and moisture content of the earth used. 30 bags will weight about a half ton.

Sandbags are slow to fill with a rate of 20 bags per hour by an average person using old-fashioned methods. This needs to be planned upon and a two-man team (one to shovel, one to hold the bag open) is best. Sandbags can always be pre-filled and staged somewhere until they are actually needed to stack up.

A quick fill idea involves a ladder and traffic cones. The ladder is supported horizontally on blocks a few feet from the ground. Traffic cones are then inserted upside down through the rungs of the ladder to form a funnel. Turn the base of the cone around to form a diagonal shape to be supported by the ladder. Place the empty sandbag around the cone-funnel and shovel sand into the cone, which will then neatly fall into the bag.

Sandbags do not need to be tied but can have the open end folded over. Keep in mind that tied bags are easier to handle because they are less likely to spill. You may need to make a time verses easy or tidiness decision when building sandbag shelters. A tied bag may be preferable if you are building indoors.

You will need approximately 60 standard sandbags for every 10 linear feet and one vertical foot. To build a box that is six feet long, six feet wide, and three feet high (say for a family of four lying side-by-side), you will need approximately 432 sandbags if the walls are 2-3 sandbags wide. Note that walls will taper as they climb and must be thicker at the base to support the weight. Stack them in an interlocking manner like bricks, overlapping as you go around corners and up levels, but always laid on their long ends.

Note that if sandbags are stacked vertically, they will need to have a triangular cross-section with a base that is wider than the top. The stack should be twice as wide as it is tall. This is to support the weight of the bags without them toppling over. Wooden frames or support from a building wall can be used if you need to cheat but ensure something prevents the bags from toppling onto anyone taking shelter. Temporary indoor shelters only need to have walls high enough to protect those who are lying, sitting, or crouching behind them—not full-height walls.

The preferred ratio per the Army Corps of Engineers is 1:3; for each vertical foot there is three feet of width. Three feet is the maximum preferred height with five being their absolute safety maximum. In this case, this is for flood defense and you will probably need to cheat on the exact dimensions, which is doable as long as the bags are braced and supported against collapse.

If relying on bare sandbags alone for ballistic protection, no intervening house, the bags should be 12-18" thick, depending on the expected caliber. This is about two to three layers, depending on your lapping, the fill, and the bag size. You will need to overlap the bags with parallel rows where they meet at the ends because of the gap that forms. Stagger the bags so there is no gap between them that a bullet could more easily pass through.

If aerial attacks are a concern (artillery, mortars, drone bombers) indoor shelters should be beneath a stout table or purpose-built reinforced structure nearest the center of the structure on a ground floor. Where possible construct this in the strongest part of the structure. The shelter table/frame should have a single layer of sandbags on top to stop any shrapnel. This should be strong enough to support a portion of the structure's weight in case of a collapse.

For better overhead protection, 18" of sandbags are recommended. This weight will need to be *well* supported against collapse. Sandbag walls that could fail after an impact won't do it. In any case, remember that for small arms fire, artillery fragments, and small IEDs the house itself is providing some protection. The material the house is made of will slow down any projectiles as they penetrate. Direct hits from aircraft bombs, missiles, mortars, or artillery shells will not be stopped by anything short of luck.

### No sandbags

Alternatives to sandbags are containers filled with earth, sand, and rocks. These are known as gabions. Gabions can be constructed out of anything that can make a box which is then filled in. Pre-modern militaries used large woven baskets. Today we use HESCO barriers which are large wire frame cages with a durable fabric liner.

Homemade gabions can be constructed using rock or bricks in a frame of strong wire mesh as is used in fencing or as concrete reinforcement. The sections of mesh can be wired or welded into an open topped box and then filled with rock or bricks that are larger than the mesh openings. This basically takes a pile of rocks or rubble and holds it in a useful shape.

Due to the size, this is only really practical outside. This may be a post-SHTF construction that you choose to put in place outside the front of your home or to create fighting positions. Keep in mind that any outdoor barrier you create may be used as a place for an enemy to hide behind and fire from.

Random repurposed containers will be more difficult to stack and overlap than sandbags. Cardboard boxes will have the least strength and not be able to be filled too high (if tall) or stacked. They may be reinforced somewhat. Wet materials will weaken the cardboard. Garbage cans or large barrels will be heavy and difficult to move.

Containers may split if shot or hit with fragments based on construction. Plastic cans have the potential to crack full length, depending on the state and quality of the material itself. Round woven baskets are ideal and are what was used in past times. Their construction makes them somewhat bullet resistant as damage in one area usually doesn't affect the whole basket.

*But what if the container breaks when hit?* Odds are in your favor. Unless someone is deliberately firing to penetrate, their bullets will likely be scattered in a random pattern. You may only have to deal with a stray shot or burst. One or two bullets fired at the same container in rapid succession will probably face the same odds of deflection even if the container fails. After the danger has passed, you can replace the container.

Being in the center of a structure, surrounded by as many walls as possible, is crucial. The more walls a bullet has to pass through, the greater the likelihood it will be deflected before it reaches you or your shelter.

If using bricks, be sure to use solid, dense bricks. Cinderblocks are hollow and will shatter easily, even if filled with sand or soil (but better than nothing). Remember that bricks and rocks can easily shed sharp chips when shot so eye and face protection may be a good idea. Shot bricks should be replaced and the damaged ones reused in less critical areas or as general rubble.

Thick pieces of metal plating (steel) can also be used. Examples are steel plates for road construction. However, steel is not bulletproof except when thick. At *least* a quarter inch of steel is required to have a chance at stopping rifle caliber bullets. Inside a home, where any bullets or shrapnel must pass through the stucco/siding and several layers of drywall, steel plates could be quite successful as shelter material.

The drawback is weight. Large plates weigh hundreds of pounds and are very difficult to move without machinery. They also are cumbersome. Sourcing may be difficult too. Steel plates also provide an ideal surface for ricochets if hit at an oblique angle.

## Other precautions

Strip any room you intend to shelter of any easily flammable materials; this includes drapes, carpet, upholstered furniture, beds/mattresses, lots of clothing, papers, etc. This should be done to any rooms fronting the house or any area where Molotov cocktails or other ignition sources may be present. The last thing you need in a gunfight is a fire because it can quickly overwhelm you and the fire fighting efforts can distract you from your defense.

Shut off the utilities, like gas and electricity. Water could also be shut off to prevent water damage, however, you may need it to fight fires. Remove any fuel stores to outside away from the house. This goes for propane canisters and fuel cans as well as large battery packs that may be damaged. Move cars outside of the garage, if attached.

Window glass and mirrors should be securely taped to keep fragments together if shattered. Security film laminates are even better. Windows liable to blast damage should be boarded up inside and out where possible.

Against grenades and explosive fragments (small shrapnel), furniture and common household or office items can be used. This includes mattresses, stout tables, or dense barriers made of other objects. This will only offer incidental protection against bullets. Do not attempt to toss grenades back or outside.

Smoke grenades and tear gas displace oxygen from enclosed spaces. Gas masks will protect you from the effects of tear gas, however, they cannot deliver oxygen as they only filter the available air.[10] Ventilation must be provided, to both evacuate the gas and draw in fresh air. Pepper spray (OC) does not have this effect, but a room contaminated with it can cause irritation. Any sort of smoke can create claustrophobia and panic.

Flashbangs and firecrackers will have their concussive effects amplified inside a room. This is more of a safety concern when it comes to more powerful military and law enforcement distraction devices and concussion grenades.

Be sure to lock, block, or barricade the windows and doors of unused rooms to prevent attackers from entering from them. Staircases may be barricaded as well.

### Outdoor shelters

Outdoors, simply dig a hole sufficient to shelter the number of people required comfortably. Cover the top with a reinforced roof. Sides may need to be shored up depending on the soil type. Refer to US Army field manual *FM 5-15 Field Fortifications* (1968) for how to construct an outdoor shelter and also fighting positions.

## How to survive explosive attacks

While some of these suggestions have applicability to IEDs and car bombs, they are centered on artillery, mortar, and drone bombings. There will be very little warning "left of bang" before the attack. An attack may begin with explosions occurring near or around you. Even something landing on top of you should spur you to action, not just freezing and waiting to die.

Suburban neighborhoods have poor cover opportunities,

---

[10] U.S. Marine Corps, *Military Operations on Urbanized Terrain (MOUT)*, MCWP 3-35.3, p. B-26

leaving digging foxholes in the front lawn as probably the only way a lot of people are going to get any cover. One idea is to put 55-gallon drums or large trash cans in the street and filling them with dirt or concrete. Concrete will need several men to move it and pains taken to ensure that it doesn't set to the street. Earth fills will need to be with dense soils and also well packed to provide maximum resistance.

Sand or soil alone won't be too protective and may spill out if the container is burst by gunfire, so I'd add any thick sheet steel or masonry I could. Soil and bricks or rock packed in tightly will provide increased resistance than just earthen fill by itself.

### Before attack

- Get indoors if you are outdoors.
- Move away from any windows, glass doors, or objects that may fall.
- Get to the most interior part of the building, which is usually the strongest.
- If you have body armor, wear it.
- Avoid crowds and crowded places. One market in Sarajevo was shelled twice; killing a total of 111 people total.

### During attack

- Duck and cover, just like with an earthquake. Get under stout furniture or in the corner of a room. Get low, curl your body up, and protect your head.
- If you are outside, hit the dirt. Seek cover below grade or behind solid cover. Cover your head. Before you get up, look around you, checking the near area first, then further out, for debris, secondary devices, or casualties.
- Cover your mouth and nose to avoid inhaling dust or toxic gases. Wet cloth can be used in-lieu of a mask. Eye protection is a good idea.
- Do not run blindly to get away. Be aware that panicked crowds could be headed into a trap or you may be running into the path of another weapon/attack.

### After attack

- If you are trapped in debris, make noise to alert rescuers by banging on things or using a noisemaking device. Yelling can use up air, cause you to inhale dust or dangerous gases, or weaken you.
- Get clear of the area as soon as possible and move the wounded. This applies to planted IEDs most of all. A second device known as a "secondary" may be set to detonate shortly after the first to kill first responders. A follow-up aerial attack may come for the same reasons.
- Normal routes out of a building may be destroyed. Be sure to use stairs instead of elevators.
- Be aware of falling debris or collapsing structures when evacuating to the outside.
- Armed defenders should be prepared for an assault as the explosive attack might have been the prelude.

## Repairs

Repair damage caused by shells and explosions as soon as possible. It may be undesirable to expend the effort but leaving your home or business open to the elements will only invite more damage. Weather will attack the interior of the structure. Water damage can lead to more extensive damage than just replacing broken pieces of wood and drywall. Animals can also more easily enter. If the building is attacked again, a solid roof or wall provides more protection than a tarp.

If permanent repair is not possible or feasible, do your best to close off the opening as well as possible. You may be forced to continue to live in the home or may have to return to it if alternative housing is not possible. Any war memoir can tell you that living as a refugee in your own home as rain drips through the ceiling and the wind whistles through the shell holes is depressing. Do what you can to maintain your home as habitable and comfortable.

# Urban Terrain Analysis and Combat Considerations

Urban terrain analysis is a mental exercise in wargaming and playing the devil's advocate. You can't just study the terrain around you and memorize maps. You have to actively evaluate how you or an adversary will be affected by the landscape around you. To use a sports metaphor, analysis is more than walking up to the tee box and reading the placard with the description of the hole. You have to get down on one knee like a golf pro and inspect the green to estimate what the ball is going to do when you putt.

There are some terms that help us with this analysis, but I don't want you to get caught up in too many terms. Field manuals and classroom education gets too caught up in terms rather than abstract thought. Think like a general with a sand table or a chess player plotting his moves.

## KOCOA

KOCOA, the USMC term, and OCOKA the Army usage, describe military terrain analysis. The acronym means: Key terrain, Observation and fields of fire, Cover and concealment, Obstacles, and Avenues of approach. Each of them tends to play off one another and have to be considered as part of a whole.

It's a good start for our own urban terrain analysis, but not perfect. We can't just say that the police station and freeway is important and leave it there. What these acronyms are intended to do is spur you to begin thinking about how terrain can be used for *and* against you.

**Key terrain** should be better described as "decisive terrain;" that which gives and advantage to the possessor. This can be a structure, artificial terrain feature like a roadway, or natural geography like an open space or high point. Control of certain places can be make or break, such as losing control over a water source that a gang now taxes usage of. Thus, possession or at least denial to the enemy of that terrain has to be maintained or you will be in danger.

**Observation** is about maintaining situation awareness; what's going on around you and what's coming. This begins to dovetail into fields of fire when you are looking at kill zones/engagement areas within rifle range. Observation considers vantage points (high ground or buildings), trees or structures that might block views, down to nighttime or adverse weather conditions affecting visibility.

**Fields of fire**: Where is the enemy going to be most exposed? What access does he have to cover and concealment? Can you realistically hit the enemy at a given distance? Humanitarian or political concerns in an urban environment have to be factored in, such as occupied homes being the "backstop" for bullets.

**Cover and concealment:** For a defense, ideally you want the enemy to be in the open, but with yourself protected by cover or concealment both during a fight and approach/withdrawal. Remember it works both ways: what are your blind spots and how can you take advantage of the enemy's blind spots?

Movement to an attack might be done through an avenue of approach that is hidden from view. Such approaches don't have to be behind physical things but done in darkness or favorable weather conditions. For instance, in my novel *Hard Favored Rage* I set the climax in a camp surrounded by wide open strawberry fields. The protagonists have to wait for a zero visibility ground fog before attacking.

It is not just tactical in nature, hiding from the enemy or blocking bullets in a gunfight. Demographic concealment can describe enemy combatants blending in with the local population, such as gang members do in ethnic enclaves. A pursued enemy may ditch his weapons and try to look like everyone else. Or he may be totally out of place in your neighborhood when on the prowl or attack.

How is offensive or criminal activity, or the identity of the perpetrators, hidden? An ideal tactic is to strike distant communities so retaliation is more difficult because of distance and the inability to locate/recognize the suspects. Guerillas mix in to their populations and hide amongst them because they *are* the local population.

**Obstacles** impede movement. Small picture this is barbed wire and K-rail in the road.[11] Larger picture can be the infeasibility of crossing a freeway which has become a sniper's alley. Traffic jams are obstacles. Remoteness itself can be an obstacle through sheer inconvenience if nothing else. Something like logistics can become a kind of obstacle if you do not have the means to overcome remoteness and distance.

Note that an obstacle used in defense isn't effective unless it is covered by fire. Someone has to be there to physically stop people from negotiating a barrier or at least be able to shoot them when they are stopped. Otherwise obstacles are just speed bumps.

**Avenues of approach** boil down to "How can they get to me and kill me (or I them)?" and "How can this be exploited?" Not only are these travel routes, but these may be dividers like a freeway that separates neighborhoods. The chokepoints on this road can be used to ambush an enemy, slow him down, or used by a gang to extort travelers. Concealment is also another major factor (see above) for avenues.

It is important to examine who do these avenues serve or "point" at? For instance, the arterial street serving your

---

[11] Obstacles are only effective when they are enforced. This means you have to be watching it to detect intrusion attempts and able to fire on or interdict intruders. If you can't do this, it's just a speed bump.

Now you don't necessarily have to guard an obstacle, but you do have to cover the choke point it creates. Let's say you have a nice spot outside your immediate perimeter that is easily and well covered by shooters. In this spot, why not block the road by turning a car sideways, flattening the tire, and stringing up barbed wire. Any obstacle you plant in the roadway or in the path of an attacker forces them to slow down or go around. This gives you an opportunity to kill them at this point.

neighborhood may lead back to the freeway which leads to a city with low-income persons of a different cultural heritage who may regard your community as a source of gain for criminal enterprise.

How do they facilitate travel? Freeways link disjointed communities and wide urban areas together. This allows distant strangers to travel long distances quickly with fewer navigational challenges. Thus, traffic can be "foreign" and fast. Rural road networks will be less efficient, slower to traverse, and be more difficult to navigate. Rural roads require local knowledge, maps, or directions to not get lost.

## Tactical vs. strategic range

Terrain analysis can be divided up into **tactical range** and **strategic range**. Tactical short range includes any defensive or battleground considerations. In other words, what you can see where you're going to be fighting or the area around your neighborhood. If you have a guy on top of a tall building or hill, everything within range of his rifle. Strategic range includes the larger strategic picture of your neighborhood, your community, and the region at large.

Tactical range terrain analysis will be more concerned with things like observation, fields of fire, and cover/concealment. Strategic range will focus on things like key terrain and avenues of approach. On the strategic level, I focus on three main areas:

- Facilitation of travel (avenues of approach),
- Concentration of people, and
- Terrain divisions.

What allows people to move, where are people going to be and who are those people, and what divides, or can, divide people?

### Facilitation of travel

**Freeways/Interstates**; they are high-speed avenues of

approach that allow long distance travel semi-anonymously. The closer you are to an off-ramp, the greater the chances of being victimized by groups traveling on them to plunder other communities.

**Arterial roads and highways**; these permit the movement of large groups of people, like riot mobs, and also have the same disadvantages of freeways.

**Intersections and major road junctions:** it may be important to control this area because of the reasons above. Is it practical to control them and who is likely to take control? Will the public, both local and commuter, resist local traffic restrictions?

Concentration of people

**Large park or school facilities**; can these be used to house refugees (domestic and foreign), internees, or outright concentration camps? Will they be used to distribute aid which may invite attacks or large crowds? Could these facilities support military forces?

**Commercial buildings;** where will commerce and human traffic be? What will attract people to your community? Where will concentrations of good people be ripe for exploitation by bad guys?

**Housing density:** Apartments will make austere survival more difficult, which may lead to them being abandoned or residents more desperate. Larger or more rural lots may be more self-reliant. Low-income, high density housing projects may be a source of theft and violence.

**Housing demographics:** People of like ethnic or ideological backgrounds tend to live near one another, leading to concentrations in some areas. Certain cultures, political identities and ethnicities may have different values, making them more or less susceptible to desperate behavior or control by authoritarian bad actors.

Terrain divisions

**Division or obstacles** can be natural topographies, like a river, or artificially like a freeway. Freeways, even with crossings, can make very powerful psychological divisions in a city. Connections being severed are a consideration as well. In a time without vehicles, a seemingly trivial trip like Hoboken to Long Island or the San Fernando Valley to LAX might as well be something out of *Lord of the Rings*.

# Urban terrain is unique

Urban terrain is unique in that it affords lots of visual obstructions, concealment, hiding places, and even cover. It can be as exposed as a pool table and as confusing as a maze. High vantage points, natural and artificial, can put observers snipers above you. You will frequently find yourself boxed in by walls and fences. Large cities and suburbs are no place to fight as the siege of Sarajevo showed.

Cities are contradictions when it comes to battlefield terrain. Each advantage is often countered by a disadvantage. Uniformity on a map doesn't translate to reality on the street. The considerations are not just physical geography as inside every city there is a population that can be with you, neutral, or against you and how you fight can change that dynamic. Analysis of urban terrain is a social and spatial exercise.

While we can discuss the physical elements of fighting and maneuvering, a deep understanding of your community at the human level is necessary. We have to think beyond simple geography and consider the human terrain, demographics, as the population itself is an adjunct to the lay of the land. Demographics and interpersonal politics may dictate the outcome of confrontations or events. This is discussed in *Suburban Defense*.

In terms of observation and fields of fire, walls, structures, and landscaping block views and reduce distances. Long streets, open plazas, and grid designs can open up very long sightlines. These same sightlines might be great on top of a house but lousy at street level where a retaining wall limits cuts the view at a man's standing height. High buildings or elevated terrain can be a great vantage point for an observer but also increase the conspicuousness of that observer and draw fire.

At the same time as there are plenty of cover and concealment in modern cities, there can be very little. Conscientious defenders may not be able to hide behind or inside a building because civilians are inside. A block wall may protect the people behind it from view while those on the other side are caught naked in the open like a rat in a bucket.

The best way to understand a city is to walk around it and imagine oneself having to fight and defend an area. Where would snipers be? IEDs? Ambushes? Identify concealed routes of movement. Who are the likely enemy and what would they control? When you wargame things, you might realize that the barricade in the middle of a narrow street bounded by high walls puts you into a shooting gallery so you change that plan. The following is just a basic overview of the advantages and challenges that defenders may face.

## Long range observation

Sightlines will be long, usually along streets and in open spaces. For non-arterial streets, this means up to 300m within tracts, usually 200m or less. A quarter to half a mile is not unusual especially on main roads or where elevation is involved. Sightlines will be interrupted by terrain and objects. You might be seen at half a mile down an arterial street, but parked cars, trees, shadows, etc. might make effective shooting at that distance difficult. Other visual obstructions may be:

- Natural terrain such as inclines and dips.
- Hillsides or natural contours forcing the road to curve.

- Artificial terrain changes such as designed curves or roads built around existing property.

There are gentle undulations in every road that we seldom notice. From a driver's perspective a rise of three or six feet in the roadway might as well be flat. At eyeball level, or lower in a gunfight, that height is significant. Like any elevation change, it can either work in your favor or against you.

If you have the elevation and are looking down, generally it is in your favor because you can see targets over the crest of the road with less exposure to yourself. With steep slopes, the area just beneath the crest may be obstructed without a lot of exposure. Freeway overpass bridges have a very long danger zone.

## Open areas

Take time to observe large open areas before moving. Don't just step out expecting that everything will be fine. Carefully watch for movement and use binoculars to inspect high points that a sniper could be in. If you can't move under cover or concealment, move through the periphery of the area.

## Roads

Roadway travel will be noticed in a post-SHTF situation. Traffic is likely to be dramatically reduced for a variety of factors so cars will draw attention. Even without enemies watching you, seeing armed strangers walking around will be something that people will pay attention to.

## Intersections

At intersections, stick to buildings as much as possible. If you can move through alleys, parking lots, or hop fences to cross a ways down from the actual intersection, that's better than just walking right through the middle of it. Avoid intersections with little cover where you have to cross them directly or those with walls or terrain that tend to create funnels. Generally, if the intersection has a traffic signal, be cautious because that means it is/was busier.

Sightlines at intersections suck until you are exposed and you will be exposed at nearly every angle at an intersection. You can use the surrounding urban landscape to conceal you basically in an angle from a single direction. If your intersection is bounded by masonry walls and the enemy far away (and in one direction), you stand a better chance of being able to pull back around the corner safely. This is only because the enemy's view is as bad as yours is.

Pre-approach: clear the area leading to the intersection first. That means houses, yards, businesses, parking lots, open areas, etc. Recon intersections and the road in all directions before attempting to cross them. Use backyards to peep over walls. Go inside two story houses. Launch a drone. Look through concealment (landscaping) on the corners. Watch windows in buildings that overlook the intersection.

Approach and clear intersections by slicing the pie, one angle at a time. Look behind landscaping or large signage that may be hiding armed persons. Use the pie slices as the basis for sectors of fire when clearing and crossing. As the pre-approach is made, a patrol leader should begin assigning sectors for watch and fire.

Cross intersections in bounds, with part of your element providing cover. If necessary, lay down a smoke screen, although due to the size of the intersection this will require intensive use of smoke grenades.

On the other side, take cover and wait for a few minutes to see if anyone saw you and followed. Understand that if forced to retreat, your avenue of retreat may be back down another "funnel" you spent time traversing. Pre-plan and brief your escape plans.

Use whatever cover is available, including curbs. Be careful around electrical boxes. Large above ground transformer boxes, if energized and shot, could explode under the right circumstances.

## Arterial streets

Arterial streets will have danger zones of around a half mile to a mile, however, accurate fire is not to be expected beyond one quarter mile. Cross exposed roads at their narrowest points preferably where curves obscure you from one or both directions. Don't use pedestrian overpasses and be cautious when using underpasses.

Moving along any natural terrain feature, like a watercourse, a road, trail, etc. is easier and human nature. This is called "handrailing" and is what the unskilled do. Don't navigate your patrol right down the main drag; parallel it through the "littoral" spaces of yards, parking lots, alleys, and all the semi-concealed spaces that run near main roadways.

Newer cities and developments will have less in the way of mature trees and landscapes, whereas the older ones will. Avoid streets that are wide with little landscaping and cover, more so if they are surrounded by multi-story buildings close to the road. Brushy, thickly planted (think hedges), or overgrown areas near roads could be concealing attackers. Imagine where homeless people might hide near a roadway.

Streets with landscaped medians or roadway edges can provide concealment to bad guys. Terrain and plant life may conspire so that an observer may see you approach while you don't see them. For example, someone half a mile away and slightly downhill can see your legs while all you see are tree branches above the pavement.

Arterial streets can turn into small canyons with little cover if both sides are bounded by obstacles. The streets in my hometown mainly have walls abutting the sidewalks because homes abut both sides of the road. In master planned suburban areas tracts built in the last half century will probably be like this. In these funnels, you cannot run far enough away fast enough to survive. If half of the street is open (front yards, open space, business, etc.) stick to that side. Avoid the walled side or double-walled in streets. If you must traverse them, each man should be able to jump a wall on his own with full kit on. Consider carrying a small, rope or compact ladder.

Many modern American suburbs have commercial and shopping districts along wide arterial streets to handle the high volume of traffic that the businesses generate. This is different from older towns and cities (and European ones) where the main or "high" street shops are right along the street. The advantage to this is you're not right underneath a bunch of windows and roofs or in front of the storefronts. The American shopping area is like open ground perhaps dappled with more concealment.

Large streets with commercial areas on one or either side should not be approached straight down the middle of the street. Walk behind the buildings in the alleys and parking lots. If you must, go along the front of the building, using whatever concealment and cover is available.

Don't run back and forth across the street to vary which side you're on to confuse enemy observers. Only switch sides when necessary or the other side provides better cover/concealment. Each time you run back and forth you're exposing yourself in an open space.

Some streets and their adjoining properties or spaces may be so open and wide that they are practically uncrossable safely. You may need to regard this open space as an artificial terrain feature that is technically traversable, but not without great risk of snipers, etc. Freeways are the easiest example. They, and major thoroughfares, often form the boundaries of different gang territories, although this is mostly for expedience than necessity.

If you can't get across the highway without being shot, the highway might as well be a giant wall. Only the suicidal, brave, or desperate are going to risk it. Crossing it safely might only be done at great risk on a dark night under optimal conditions and with the best of luck.

Rivers that couldn't be safely crossed were forded at shallow points or ferries operated at calm, narrow spots. Your equivalent is where arterial roads narrow, curve, or diverge. Natural crossing points such as drainage channels may provide concealment. These ideal crossings will be easy to identify and can be targeted or exploited as chokepoints.

## Freeways

Freeways allow high volumes of traffic to travel long distances in relative anonymity at high speed. In my experience, this makes it great for organized burglary (or shoplifting) gangs to come up from LA into the suburban communities, make their hits, and disappear.

Don't use freeways to travel on and avoid crossing at ground level whenever you can. They are horribly exposed and called "freeways" because access is controlled. If you must cross them at-grade, do so only when traffic is essentially non-existent for obvious reasons and only directly across. Pick the narrowest crossing you can with the most foliage or other concealment on either "bank" of the road. Cut through the fencing with as little exposure as possible.

Monitor traffic before moving if there is *some* infrequent traffic, no greater than one car every minute. Get a good estimate of how often cars come by, from what direction, if they are potentially hostile, and if the drivers are paying attention. Your dash should take less than one minute, although it may take longer if the sides are banked and/or consist of ankle-grabbing ice plant or rip-rap. Cross in two elements so that the other can provide fire support as necessary and the other can cut the other side of the fence, etc.

If you have to cross an overpass, keep in mind that you are going to be visible for a long way off. The worst exposure is to anyone perpendicular to the route being crossed. Usually, the slope of freeway overpasses tends to obscure the far side approach until anyone crossing is well exposed above the crest of the road. Making these areas more hazardous are the fences often found along freeways and all the open ground for highway exits or intersecting streets.

Keep in the middle of overpasses or bridges to obscure the patrol from any observers below. Run across the bridge, using one element to cover the other. Try and avoid long bridges or overpasses.

Going under a freeway is the preferred way to cross, preferably in drainage culverts or channels. Underpasses present less of a visual giveaway to people going under, except they are probably channelized worse than overpasses without even the option of jumping. Scouting the other side of an underpass before the rest of the group passes is important. Road tunnels should probably be bypassed as they are long shooting galleries.

## Residential

Most suburban areas have homes with fenced yards making traveling through backyards very difficult. Don't go yard-to-yard hopping walls and fences. Any cop or suspect who took foot bail will tell you that this sucks. It is energy intensive, there are lots of hazards you could land on, and if this is SHTF, homeowners will *not* be happy to have armed men hopping the wall. This kind of movement should only be done when in danger, trying to escape, or when engaged in some sort of nefarious business that requires an unconventional, but risky, approach.

People will be suspicious of you moving or stopping behind their rear walls. If they live against a major street, a wary and capable homeowner may take your presence very seriously. If you have to hop a wall in a hurry, check walls for the equivalent of broken glass set in the top. Try your best not to land on something like cactus.

If you aren't being shot at or imminently in danger of incoming fire, walking along the sidewalk or just in the street is viable in residential areas. Walking through yards is difficult due to fences, landscaping, and homeowners who might take offense. Remaining close to the houses gives you the ability to quickly dash to cover or escape over the back fence if necessary, while making good progress in the public right of way.

Be wary of apartment complexes. There will be more people and a higher likelihood of meeting people who are going out and about. Some complexes may have higher numbers of unsavory characters living there. All of this increases your chances of a confrontation. On the other hand, because the residents have little interest in the property, other than living there, it will be harder for them to form a cohesive bond to defend the place.

## Shopping centers

American retail has moved into the big box, big parking lot phase. Older communities tend to have big box stores in stand-alone lots, whereas newer communities (or new built commercial developments) tend to centralize the stores into one large sea of parking lots. This may or may not include elements from strip malls. Smaller stores tend to be clustered into strip malls. A huge portion of suburbanites do their shopping in a land of comparatively widely spaced buildings, parking lots, and decorative trees.

Shopping centers and big parking lots, any commercial area really, has a lot of concealment and little cover. If you are fighting in most shopping centers, you are fighting in a lightly forested plain that has really hard ground. It's like being caught in the open on the savannah except you are a lot less likely to want to flop down on the asphalt when being shot at. You will be shooting through concealment, which may be cars, landscaping, or more natural vegetation. Figure on effective ranges of approximately 100 yards but shots up to and beyond 300 yards are not improbable.

Landscaping along the street may have a slight incline or decline to it for aesthetic purposes that can be used for screening. For instance, you might move inside or outside the landscaping depending on where you want the concealment. Or an enemy force could be flanking you from behind it, taking cover against the low side to fire over the top of the mound.

Try and walk in a way so that distant landscaping, like trees along the perimeter of the parking lot across the arterial road, conceal you. For a basic rule of thumb, if you can't see them then they can't see you.

Assume that parking lots will be empty. Why? Because having minimal to no cars means less "cover" and less concealment offered by the parked cars. Your shots may be easier, but there is a lot of dead ground out there in an empty lot. If a rifle fight is breaking out I can't reasonably foresee the circumstances being such that the parking lots will be full (not that it won't happen). A full parking lot with cars and people will be a very difficult situation and it is best to just withdraw.

Be sure to look up and check the rooflines and keep checking them. People always forget to look up and pretty much any commercial building with a flat roof has ladder access somewhere. The parapets around the top are a great place for a sniper or assault team to wait in ambush. Once we had homeless people living up in an attic-type area inside the parapet of a warehouse. Be aware of doors in the rear of businesses. Someone could be hiding behind them to ambush you.

Be very wary about building fronts, especially if you must traverse open areas. Look for open doors, broken windows, or sudden activity at your appearance in the open. Shooters inside the business will, if they are smart, fire from inside the room or entrance so that they are not visible from the outside (and no muzzles protrude from the door/window). If you must go past the front of commercial buildings, hug the front. In an emergency, you can break in and escape through the rear of the building or fight from inside.

Shopping centers that are out of business (abandoned, looted, burned) may be popular with looters, rioters, refugees, and the homeless. Retail and commercial areas should be treated with special caution as this is where people have learned to associate these places with the acquisition of things. Any businesses that are open will generate traffic and attention, positive or negative.

## Vehicles

Always be prepared for vehicles to make a surprise appearance. Assume it is in concert with an attack or vise versa. However, don't automatically light up a car because it coincidentally appears when you see someone or come under fire. Before shooting at a vehicle, attempt to ascertain its intentions.

Potentially hostile signs:

- Vehicle travel is very unusual anymore (fuel shortage);
- Unusual pattern of travel for this location and time;
- Vehicle description is known to be associated with hostile forces;
- Accelerating towards you or other people;
- Gunfire/guns coming from the vehicle; and,
- Occupants flashing gang signs or yelling.

Don't assume that a vehicle is hostile because they are behaving irrationally. One would think that a driver in the wrong place at the wrong time would stop and back up as fast as possible. My faith in the intelligence of American drivers has been destroyed by years of traffic control at emergencies.

Experiences in Iraq would correlate. You can't assume that because someone is speeding up and driving towards the gunfire that they are part of it. A lot of drivers are so stupid that they can only think about driving forward and fast to get away from danger, even if it takes them through the middle of a gunfight.

Defender patrol deployment by vehicle is something else that might happen. You may live in an area with a lot of wide open spaces, like the Midwest where it seems new construction has highways and parking lots as big as the prairie. Movement between points may be done better by vehicle so that you aren't walking around exposed as much.

Mounting/dismounting should be done behind cover, like

behind a building out of sight of observers. False pickups and insertions should be made so that anyone tracking the vehicles isn't sure where the patrol got out. Vehicles should park nearby in a concealed hiding place, ready to move in an instant, guarded at all times.

## Storm drains (above ground)

A storm drain is a great way for low profile movements, but absolutely sucks in a gunfight. There is no cover or concealment. Shots taken down the channel are as close to a shooting range environment anyone will ever get in combat. The only way out is probably up the side and into the surrounding yards or terrain. The sides may be steep or vertical. Ladders or other access can be easily controlled.

Due to limited access points, the direction of travel and potential divergence points for someone using the drain are easy to predict.

- Access is controlled usually at select road crossings;
- The courses are almost always fenced, gated, and locked;
- Side channels or culverts may be closed with debris bars; and,
- They may go underground unpredictably for long distance.

Pay special attention to storm drain inlets along the street. A bad guy could be lurking inside just like Pennywise, the evil clown from Stephen King's *It*.

## Underground

Shooting a gun, even a suppressed one, will be very loud underground as the hard concrete walls just reflect and channelize the sound. A couple of reporters who wrote a book about their explorations of the tunnels beneath Las Vegas carried bludgeon-type objects with them in the event they were assaulted.

Movement through them is very dangerous if detected by an enemy. You could be burned alive; the Nazis pumped gas into the sewers of the Warsaw ghetto for one.

- All access/egress points are known and easily controlled.
- Redundant sources of lighting are required.
- Difficult to navigate.
- Exits could be blocked by debris, water, or secured by utility workers.
- Flash flooding or noxious gases could kill.

## Tall buildings

The tall buildings in most American suburbs will be multi-story apartment buildings and offices. Typical height is three to six stories. The maximum reasonable height for an elevated shooter should be less than one hundred feet above street level. Taller buildings may be encountered in suburbs and almost surely in the downtown cores of large cities.

The proximity of a tall building will increase the range at which you are in danger of rifle fire. Once you get about thirty feet up, you're over the tops of most trees used for landscaping and parking lot decoration. Lower buildings put shooters at treetop height, limiting how far one can see and shoot. Ground level can improve the distance by moving out of the way of obstacles, but then the height advantage isn't present.

Be prepared for long-range rifle fire from tall buildings; long range being over 300 yards. Beyond 300 yards, the average person with an AR-15 and unmagnified sights will begin to have difficulty in hitting a target. Trained and better equipped shooters will be effective with an AR out to 800 yards or so, larger caliber rifles probably up to a quarter-mile. This would be your untrained sniper or someone in perhaps a fourth-story apartment building taking potshots.

Multi-story buildings that are not high-rises will be a favorite for troublemakers, psychopaths, gangs, and defenders. Expect to have certain places covered by snipers or elevated shooters who watch these areas to take a shot. Such places include intersections, open space, common pathways, or cover that is exposed to a distant building one side.

Tall buildings should always be bypassed when possible, using buildings or terrain to shield patrols from observation. Use the full extent of cover and concealment. Try not to get in the open within 300-800 yards of such vantage points when possible to maximize the chances of a miss from a poor shooter and/or one who is under equipped.

## Ruins

The US military MOUT field manuals are full of great advice on how to navigate through ruined buildings in a city. Unfortunately, this manual has its origins in planning for WWIII, so the buildings are typically European ones. American construction is not the same and has only been diverging from the kind of European Theater urban combat the manual writers had in mind.

It would be great to go through the side of buildings using mouseholes and navigating a strip mall this way, but it is unlikely to happen. Most American construction is wood frame, meaning that buildings that are knocked down will either become match sticks or burn. Suburban construction is low on masonry and high on materials that play well with a hammer and nails.

Buildings built out of masonry and steel are loaded down with flammable materials. We've already seen large buildings burned in riots. SHTF will not be an exception. Sure, the Walmart complex might have cinderblock walls, but if everything except the cinderblock is burnt out, just how useful is that hollow shell going to be to you?

Be aware of the hazards around you, such as broken gas lines and fallen power lines in the aftermath of a battle. If "mouseholes" in the walls of a building are available, use those instead of doors.

## Obstacles

Be wary of obstructions in your way that may be tempting to move as they could be booby trapped. One tactic that was a favorite of Russians in Afghanistan was to leave items of desire like food or ammunition behind so that the finder would trip a detonator recovering the item. It could also be to lure you into an exposed area so a sniper can shoot you.

If you must go over a wall or fence, roll over the top as low as possible to minimize the exposure of your body. Use ladders or objects to more smoothly and quietly climb them. This isn't the academy or boot camp; you can get a boost off a trash can. Try not to cut fences or knock out slats if you can avoid it. Don't alienate people just to get through an easy way.

Manned roadblocks should be treated as potentially hostile contact. You do not know if the persons manning the roadblock are citizen defenders like you or if they are an extortionist gang. Try and avoid being seen by a roadblock because the presence of an armed patrol will pique their interest. Take a defensive posture behind cover and plan to be hit by a frontal or flank assault in the worst case.

If you must make contact, send one person forward under a white flag or by making other arrangements for peaceful contact. Cover that person while he approaches. If part of the patrol is going to go forward, have the other portion stay behind as cover until you are totally assured the roadblock is *not* a threat.

In the event you are refused passage, leave. Do not argue or negotiate. Would you allow the same thing at your own barricade? Arguments may lead to a use of force or degrade any future relations. Also, regardless of the relations, do not reveal any sensitive or critical information about who you are, where you come from, or what you have.

When evading, don't go one block over and attempt to cross. That area may be blocked too and/or under the observation or control of the roadblock people. Detour widely through the area. Backtrack for a short distance unseen and then turn to go around. Assume that you have been spotted by a concealed observer, a drone, etc. and someone will try to flank you.

Be aware of tall buildings or other elevated vantage points where you could be watched from while moving in the open. Consider where this roadblock is located. If at the entrance to a neighborhood, it's likely defensive in nature. On a main street it could be a gang operation or the immediate area could be under the territorial control of a large local group. A roadblock or checkpoint set up around a curve or in a place that's hard to see or escape from could be a trap.

# Patrolling for the Suburban Defender

Patrolling outside your defensive perimeter will be necessary. This might be checking your perimeter and talking to people on other streets or it may be hunting for bad guys to kill them. Patrols allow you to leave your perimeter in relative safety to get a feel for what's going on outside your sightline and interact with people. In law enforcement, as it is applicable to the citizen defender, patrols serve to prevent and deter crime through early detection and an officer's presence, apprehending criminals, and providing a sense of security for the public.

Patrolling at its heart is about awareness and maintaining dominance of your territory. You cannot expect to know what's going on beyond visual range of your perimeter if you never leave your defensive area. You can certainly not expect to control the area outside if you do not challenge bad guys who are operating around you. Failure to assert yourself will allow bad guys to have the benefit of initiative and surprise.

**Note:** this entire chapter is oriented towards people with no military experience and very little tactical experience. Basically taking random American suburbanites who maybe have played first-person shooters or a little airsoft/paintball and putting them in the field. I am *not* writing this from an infantry perspective.[12]

### Why patrol?

"Gee Don, you just spent the last book telling me I should stay inside and not get mixed up in trouble, so why are you telling me I should go on patrol outside my lines?" That, my friend, is an excellent question. The short answer is, if you sit around and wait for things to happen you will be reacting at the mercy of the

---

12 For the basics of a military style patrol, please see Joe Dolio's *Tactical Wisdom* series, particularly *TW-4*.

circumstances outside. Survival is going to depend on things like early warnings, intelligence, deterrence, and relationships with your neighbors.

If you spend day after day at home you might just be surprised by the changes that take place in a short period of time. Usually this is something benign like road construction or night shift folks switching to days and having to sit in traffic jams again. In a SHTF or WROL situation, you might spend months inside your barricaded perimeter until something arrives at your gate.

Maybe had you gotten out and talked to the people living on the other side of the big avenue you might have learned that raiders were making incursions into your suburb before they raided *you*. Perhaps you could have gotten together a group of guys with guns and run off the scouts for the gang. Or maybe your experienced defenders could have had conversations with the other housing tract and gotten them into a defensive posture as well.

A real life example I talked about in *Suburban Defense* is during the George Floyd riots of 2020. I drove by my local Walmart and Target and saw that they were using carts to barricade the entrance and were closing early. There were armed security guards parked out front. That told me that someone expected looting at those stores, so I should be prepared myself in case riots/looting came here.

You will have to remember that if we have a functional collapse of our country, we will probably lose cell and Internet service. That means technological substitutes for first-hand intelligence will be gone. You will have to talk to your neighbors instead of using the NextDoor app and if you want to see what all the sirens and smoke is about, you will be taking a walk or drive. There will also be no police who are going to run off troublemakers or can get out in the middle of the night to see why a man dressed in all black is prowling around your back fence.

And finally, who is going to defend your city and town? If there are no police, it will be up to the citizens to protect themselves from looters, bandits, and gangs. Fight them in the field or fight them on the doorstep; the choice is yours. Humans banded together and went in search of bad guys from time immemorial. They didn't need official sanction, just some trustworthy men.

## What are you trying to accomplish with a patrol?

Going on patrol is not just leaving your secure zone and walking around with guns looking tough, nor is it a field trip. It is not to intimidate or bully other non-threatening people into doing what you want—that's gang behavior. Patrols are intentional things done to accomplish tasks. As the US Army says[13], patrolling has several purposes applicable to the suburban defender:

- Reassuring or gaining the trust of your neighbors.
- Preventing public disorder.
- Deterring and disrupting criminal activity.
- Providing security.
- Protecting infrastructure and bases.

Broken down a bit more, I characterize these as:

- Providing cooperative support and reassurance to friendly citizens in the area (community relations).
- Establishing and maintaining dominance (security control) of the area.
- Challenging troublemakers operating in your area of influence.
- Detecting infiltration attempts, hostile surveillance, or impending attacks.
- Gathering intelligence on events, activities, and life outside your perimeter.

All of this may seem confusing. Too many field manuals, policy booklets, and general orders I've seen are long on theory and less on what the actual actions needed are. We'll discuss details further on. In short, much of what this actually looks like is going outside, talking and doing stuff, or just making observations (intelligence

---

[13] US Army, *The Infantry Rifle Platoon and Squad*, FM 3-21.8, pp. 9-1 & 9-2

gathering), but while heavily armed and with other guys.

## Establishing and maintaining dominance (control) of the area

Control of the area immediately surrounding your defensive perimeter (street, neighborhood, etc.) is impossible if you do not physically patrol the area. You need to be seen outside to establish to both the residents of that area and outsiders that you are part of that community. Put another way, if you are trying to win the cooperation and trust of the people who live around you, they are going to say, "Who are you?" if all you do is stay behind your barricades.

We all have territorial interests by virtue of living in a given area. Our neighborhood and community are larger than just the street, complex, or the tract. It involves a nebulous area around you that you live in. What happens several streets over is just as important as what is happening on your street. All of us who live in close geographical proximity are invested in the health and safety of our little part of the world, even owe a civic duty to it.

Gang members hang out on the street partially to maintain their territorial claim. Being visible allows them to intimidate enemies or those they wish to subjugate. Yes, it exposes them to a drive-by or walk-up shooting. That is the trade off for being visible in their community and asserting dominance through simple presence. One of the bottom rungs of the use of force escalation for peace officers is presence; that you are there and have a meaningful capacity to respond is a deterrent in and of itself.

What good is trying to control an area if you are purely reactive? Physical possession and control of an area requires that you are out and about in it. A group that lays claim to territory but never makes use of the area, doesn't go into it, and doesn't contest challenges to its authority doesn't have control or possession. It looks weak and invites confrontation.

As the saying goes, a good defense is a good offense. Armed

and alert men walking around an area is a deterrent because predators who see you patrolling in the community may choose a softer target. To regular citizens, it shows that your group is harmless to them and is willing and capable of offering security in the area.

Territorial dominance is maintaining the integrity and security of your area through visible presence. In short, you're walking around with your guns out so that people know that armed people are there and move around in this neighborhood. Even if you don't directly act on other's behalf, your presence can have a preventative effect.

Patrols can detect and intercept incursions as well as deter them by simply being out there. Unpredictable patrols and an adversary who is *willing* to defend his perimeter by being in the margins outside of it complicates hostilities for an enemy who seeks an easy conquest. In gang terms, rival gangs (usually) stay out of enemy turf because the locals will defend it against outsiders. Let enemies see that you are alert, tough, and proactive so they leave you alone.

### Challenging troublemakers operating in your area of influence

A partner of mine once complained that too many of our fellow deputies on patrol didn't actually patrol. Sure, they drove around and did stuff, but too many of them stuck to busy areas and main streets looking for pretext traffic stops or obvious crime. He and I had a philosophy of cruising through neighborhoods, taking the long, winding way across town and checking out places that were "slow." You don't catch burglars in the act of carrying a TV to a car or cutting the locks on a warehouse roll-up door unless you drive through those sleepy residential streets and back alleys.

A pure defense of waiting for trouble to come to you is not the best policy. If there is no rule of law, its downright stupid (unless you don't have the capability). You cannot provide safety and security to your neighbors or have some sort of meaningful security cooperative agreement if you never leave your own perimeter. Hearts and minds in third-world villages are eroded when the Americans do nothing to stop the insurgents' retaliatory raids to chop off the arms of all the vaccinated children.

Failure to police your own surroundings will allow any interlopers or challengers to depredate the area unmolested. Being able to operate without interference right under your nose only emboldens those that would victimize you. This is why police "harass" gang members and ne'er-do-wells loitering around town. Popping a couple guys for open containers might mean that there will be no fight that escalates to murder that night. Terry Stops and probation searches on gang members catcalling women just might send the guys home for the day to get away from the cops.

You aren't going to find bad guys doing bad things in your surroundings if you don't get out to where you might find them. With no police, it will be up to you to provide the prophylactic presence against crime. You want word to spread that the Maple Street defenders challenges anyone within a six-block radius who seems suspicious and will fight robbers, rapists, looters, and burglars. If an area has an active security operation going on in it, it makes it very difficult for bad guys to operate unhindered.

Remember, you will have to be the police when there are no police.

### Detecting infiltration attempts, hostile surveillance, or impending attacks

The most basic and necessary task of a patrol is to check your perimeter for hostile activity (intrusion attempts mainly). How are you going to know if someone is trying to sneak in if you never check the places they might sneak in? Enemies prowling around the outside of your neighborhood can do so without interference if you sit at home waiting to react. The Marine Corps says that "patrolling keeps the enemy off balance, […], allows us to retain the initiative, and guards against surprise."[14]

First off, you can't have a ground level perspective of the outside of your defenses without physically walking them. There are many blind spots in a neighborhood that you can't properly examine from "behind the wire." You need to see the enemy's perspective and to test your own perimeter. This will also make infiltration attempts easier to detect because you'll be much closer to the "spoor" a bad guy will leave behind.

Hostile surveillance can easily be done if you aren't checking for it. All a bad guy needs is a position where no one goes and/or some good camouflaging. Homeless people hide in brush right outside housing tracts all the time. You would never even notice they were there if you didn't wade into the brush or weeds. Now imagine that's a sniper watching and waiting for the right moment.

Unoccupied homes and businesses are also good places for enemies to hide. An observation team gathering information on your defenses could be hiding on the roof of an abandoned warehouse. Maybe the raid team for tomorrow night is already in place, staked out in some dead person's house one block away. If you don't check these places out for suspicious activity, there is nothing to stop anyone from using them for nefarious activity.

Finally, your being out and about might coincidentally put you in the right place at the right time. To see an attacking force come together. Depending on your strength and capabilities, you might choose to engage the enemy right then and there. Or you can sound the alarm and be ready with greater warning than the first gunshot at the end of your street.

## Provide support and reassurance to friendly citizens ( community relations)

Persons you expect to work with have to believe that you care about them or provide some benefit to them for them to willingly cooperate. Why should more distant neighbors trust you if they

---

[14] United States Marine Corps, *Patrolling Operations B2H3317*, p. 2

don't know who you are or that you are not a threat? Persons you expect to work with have to see that you have some competency, that you care about them or provide some benefit to them, and that you are not a rival or predator. If you don't interact with them, no opportunity for this cross-pollination will happen.

Trust is why the US military, chiefly special forces, engage in so many "hearts and minds" operations. On a basic level, things like small construction projects and medical care to villagers is a bribe. Through it we also demonstrate that we mean the civilians no harm and care about their wellbeing. By these tokens we can show we are not an enemy and can (hopefully) provide safety, stability, and an improved lifestyle; something the bad guys cannot offer.

We win favor and our benevolent acts deny bad guys legitimacy. Physical protection enhances that further. In a counter-insurgency as the occupying force, this is a large carrot approach to the native population. Cooperation with them means intelligence, the decrease or elimination of aiding bad guys, and even fighting the enemy. In suburban defense, we get these counter-insurgency benefits and more by being good neighbors.

It's not just about security but being a part of your community. In a basic sense, we're trading a willingness to defend others slightly more removed from us in exchange for their aid, whether that is in fighting, skills, or goods. You might have a doctor on your street who can treat the kid of a guy who is growing much needed fruit.

Isolation will also breed resentment. Relationships are built and maintained by interaction. That your patrol ran off some troublemakers means that Ash Street will send some guys over to help defend Maple Street when looters arrive. A willingness to embrace danger on behalf of another is cooperation in action.

The alternative is that no one takes you seriously because you are unwilling to help anyone else out. They never see you leave your fortified cul-de-sac, never come to help, and have nothing to offer. Or if you try and pressure people into something that may not be in their primary interest, they see it as coercion rather than compromise because you've never reciprocated.

People who stay inside, travel by car, and don't interact with their neighbors don't have friends in their neighborhood. Easy travel, telephones, and distractions inside our homes made it easy to disconnect from those who live around us. Many of us have very little to no interaction with our neighbors or even know their names. In decades past, virtually everyone on a street would be known to each other and would have some sort of community engagement because entertainment and human interaction took effort to get to.

In SHTF, distant friends across town aren't going to be visiting each other. Technological distractions like Netflix and informative apps like NextDoor may not exist. You will need to rely on the humans around you for skills, trade, information, and simple companionship. The quid-pro-quo of information and companionship is not all.

Neighbors will still need to help each other. There will be less reliance on government services, charities, and businesses that make house calls. Your patrol might be flagged down by a single woman who needs help with something that she can't get elsewhere. You may be escorting a midwife to a delivery or a church group that has food.

### Gather intelligence on events, activities, and life outside your perimeter

Intelligence gathering cannot be done entirely remotely. For instance, how much information about what happens in a community is not covered by local news? In years past, what wasn't picked up by the newspaper had to come from local gossiping and swapping stories. Today we have the NextDoor app and Facebook as social media has supplanted face-to-face relationships. In a world without the Internet, we have to go back to talking to each other. Not everyone is going to have a radio.

The best way to learn what is going on with other humans is by conversing with them. A foot patrol is visible and easy to approach for both average folks and other defenders. I've found that walking around is a superior way to encourage public interaction than being in a car, although people could easily flag me down or call Dispatch. Spontaneous public contact is only going to happen if you get out there.

Being on foot also gives you a better understanding of the environment. You hear more and see more owing to not having a vehicle cabin around you. Walking also gives you more time to be out and around, to see and hear things that you would miss otherwise. Your perspective also changes looking in instead of out. People will react differently to you in a car. A drone might just spook people into hiding or attacking.

Human intelligence is also impossible if you aren't talking to strangers. Not everyone is going to come see you or have a radio to pass on information. Meaningful conversations won't happen if you do not leave your perimeter to interact with the people around you, which leads us to intelligence.

Spending time in the urban environment is the only way to learn certain things. It gives you a very close up view of how people behave. Maybe people are defiant, heads held high, then one day they are very shy, afraid, and refuse to look you in the eye. From a distance people might look well fed, but malnourished and dirty up close, telling you something without a word.

## Types of patrols

There will be two types of patrols that you will go on; **overt armed patrols** and lightly armed **stealth patrols**. These will form the basis of your patrols' objectives because what you are trying to accomplish will fall into one of these two categories. That is, you're either going out heavy and looking tough or you're going out light and sneaking around.

For armed patrols; you either plan to engage the enemy or there exists a high probability of a combat engagement. Stealth patrols do not plan to or intent to engage the enemy but are prepared for combat.

A third variety is a combat patrol: seek the bad guys out and kill them, including ambushes. This offense, beyond this scope of this work. Frankly, if things get bad you probably will need to go out and kill bad guys proactively, but I am not the authority for that kind of thing.

Heavily armed overt patrols are either going out looking for trouble, expecting trouble, or ready for it. The arms and gear are to deter trouble through visible evidence of strength and firepower. Contrary to what you might think, camouflage, uniforms, plate carriers/load bearing equipment, and openly carried rifles are to the patrol what bearing fangs is to a tiger.

You have the ability to respond decisively and are openly sending that message to would-be challengers. Since there is very little in the way of concealing terrain in a non-ruined suburban environment, there will be no hiding and sneaking around like in the woods. If you are seen armed openly by a hostile force, you must be prepared to fight and win, or at least effectively cover your withdrawal to safety.

A patrol may serve multiple purposes. For instance, it goes out to check the perimeter and in the process scout certain locations where enemies might be, such as looking to see if there is a looting mob in the parking lot of Walmart. Here are some examples of what you will actually be doing on a patrol:

- Perimeter inspections for intrusion attempts, booby traps, or other enemy activity, such as surveillance or sniper hides.
- Detecting and deterring criminality and violence or interrupt it if it is in progress by scaring off perpetrators.
- Escorting vulnerable persons to market, medical help, etc.
- Guarding and monitoring critical infrastructure.
- Catch or kill those that are committing acts of theft or violence.
- Being a visible reminder to the public and your neighbors that someone is looking out for them.
- Talking to your fellow citizens, exchange information, and provide what help you can to each other.

- Tracking changes to the human and urban environment.

## Stealth patrol

A stealth reconnaissance patrol (in our context) is one that involves stealth, disguise, and deception. In other words, the "gray man" approach. You don't want it to be obvious that you are an armed and capable defender out doing defensive stuff. A hard approach might alter the behavior of those you want to observe or open arms might cause a defensive reaction that prevents you from achieving your goal.

The observer effect states that subjects being observed change their behavior when they know they are being studied. People being watched by an armed group or seeing them march past will behave differently than when someone who seems to be just part of the normal street scene goes by.

A thuggish neighborhood may be harassing travelers but you never could confirm this because they always ignored your armed patrol and tried to look innocent. Maybe you want to gather intelligence by talking to people in a market or aid distribution line as you don't seem any different than them. FBI Surveillance Specialists often disguise themselves as street people because no one pays attention to them.

An excellent example of using the invisible man approach to do reconnaissance and more is in Tom Clancy's novel *Without Remorse* (pass on the movie). Former Navy SEAL John Clark, after tragically losing his girlfriend to a gang of drug dealing pimps, takes revenge on them. In the gritty streets of Baltimore of the 1970s, he goes to great lengths to hide among the homeless population of the city. Not only does he successfully conduct close quarters reconnaissance, but he is able to effect many offensive operations.

While you certainly are not Mr. Clark, you can use his techniques to your advantage. We rarely give any thought to homeless people as long as they leave us alone. Beyond this, we don't think much about joggers, people waiting at bus stops, bicycle commuters, or men with hard hats and high-viz vests scribbling on clipboards. Take a look at the street environment around you and adopt a persona that fits what's going on.

Instead of plate carriers, camo BDUs, and rifles, you're wearing a concealable soft vest, are carrying a concealed pistol, and wearing worn-out clothes. The backpack that has your broken down AR-15 in it looks a lot like the kind that you see weekly at the swap meet that shoppers use to tote home their produce. Your behavior appears unthreatening, like scavenging garbage for food or useful items while you observe the area and people around you.

### Reconnaissance
- See what's going on;
- Monitoring specific events or activities (such as a protest);
- What do things look like? and,
- Gathering intelligence on events, activities, and life outside your perimeter.
- Talk to people.

A reconnaissance patrol, stealthy or overt, does not seek to engage any enemies and may use considerable stealth to avoid any contact. A combat or dominance patrol actively seeks an engagement. Recon patrols can be **point**: obtaining information on a specific location or group; or, **zone**: obtaining detailed information on activity within an area.

## Overtly Armed Patrols

### Security patrol
- Warning and chasing off troublemakers operating in your area of influence;
- Catch or kill those that are committing acts of theft or violence; and,
- Interrupting imminent or in progress criminal or violent acts.

### Perimeter inspection
- Detect enemy surveillance;

- Detect any enemies moving to the attack or setting ambushes; and,
- Detecting infiltration attempts, hostile surveillance, or impending attacks.

Perimeter inspection patrols are to detect any potential hostile activity or intrusion along your perimeter or within your area of operations. Basically, you want to know if there is someone out there or signs that someone has been out there to prevent them from infiltrating or ambushing you. You want to catch the bad guy in the act. A security patrol may encounter hostile forces and engage them if they are present.

### Deterrence patrol:
- Intimidate weak enemies;
- Signal to strong enemies you are armed, organized, and prepared; and,
- Reassure locals that defenders are out.

A deterrence patrol may proceed down certain high visibility streets and through "troubled" areas, or in front of troublemaker's homes, to send a message to all who see you. This route is maximized to cover as much distance, be in front of as many eyes, and either scare or bolster the morale of the maximum number of people as possible.

### Escort patrols
- Escorting vulnerable persons;
- Walking refugees and other outsides through or past your perimeter/area of operations; and,
- Protecting transportation of goods.

**Community engagement** or performing general tasks with/for neighbors but armed and in numbers. Certain things that need to be accomplished by neighbors or community groups may have to be done by armed individuals as the workers might be attacked. Think of the Seabees, who are prepared to fight infantry-style while doing construction.

## Presence patrol

- Establishing and maintaining dominance (security control) of the area,
- Guarding and monitoring critical infrastructure, and,
- Walks through vulnerable areas; standing at strategic locations.

### Presence

Whether or not it is a primary goal of your patrol, unless you are sneaking around trying not to be seen for a reason, the very act of being seen is an ancillary benefit to patrolling. Your presence has a preventative effect on crime and violence. Presence means that someone who can interfere with violence or crime is present in the area. Actually seeing someone on patrol is worth far more than simple word of mouth or hoping that bad guys assume that potential interference is around.

A presence patrol operates in the highest visibility manner possible as tangible representation of force projecting an air of strength about the defenders. It needs to be a *positive* representation that shows competency through bearing, actions, and personal interactions. Patrol members are well discipline, well equipped, polite, but also determined and not easily intimidated. It can also gather information/intelligence.

Walking around in your gear, carrying guns, while things remain uneventful may sound dangerous and a waste of energy. Yet one never can know how much being seen on the streets by someone who is inside peering through the blinds or hiding in the bushes can make a difference. Bad guys who are thinking about operating in your area should be discouraged from doing so because your patrols compound the risks of being confronted. This is the rattlesnake shaking his tail warning people not to come too close unless they want to get bit.

Sometimes you might decide taking cover and monitoring a

certain area, such as a crossroads where a lot of foot traffic comes through, is the best way to go. Imagine you are a cop or a sentry stationed somewhere to scare off bad guys or prepared to run them off if things get hostile. This also includes guarding critical infrastructure, like taking turns making sure that no one seizes control of a municipal water source to extort citizens who just want to fill up their jugs for the day. Protecting critical infrastructure will is discussed in its own chapter.

# The Patrol Itself

## Composition

Patrolling isn't to be taken lightly. SHTF patrols, even though in your own neighborhood and even if things seem "safe" need to be considered as combat. After all, the core reason you are out there is to stop bad guys who you might just encounter. Everyone who goes on a patrol must be able to fight effectively as a team. Having a rifle and kit is not a qualifier for who can patrol; physical fitness, marksmanship, and courage all have to be considered. Those going out must be able *and* willing to fight.

Patrolling will be among the most dangerous and difficult things you will do. Unless the men going with you are combat arms veterans or have played airsoft/paintball, they will likely have poor tactical instincts in a fight. Playing wargames, even if you haven't been in a firefight, tends to instill a sense of awareness and fighting skills that can't really be learned any other way.

Note that this chapter is written with the average American suburbanite in mind; they probably will not have military experience, and if they do, it will not be infantry experience. I have eschewed a military or even law enforcement approach and instead tried to think about what average people will be able to do. It may seem unorthodox to those readers who have combat experience.

### Selection

I'm assuming that a good portion of the audience of this book or those whom the reader is grouped up with will be suburbanites who might have no military or paramilitary training. That will leave men with varying levels of physical fitness and experience with weapons. The leader (who should be a military vet) needs to pick the best he can get.

Men need to be selected primarily on physical and

psychological toughness, not just gear. Having the right tools for the job and proficiency with firearms is great, but potentially becoming engaged in battle with bad guys will be physically and mentally stressful. Can the men going with you sustain walking or running for several miles without rest? Can they hop obstacles and climb walls?

Mental toughness is as important as physical fitness. The men on patrol can't simply hide or break and run because things might turn violent or give up when they do. You don't need violent men but you need men who aren't going to turn into cowards when dudes with guns challenge you or start shooting.

Basic requirements (example):

- Can jump/climb a six foot fence without aids, can run a mile in ten minutes, can sprint a city block without becoming exhausted, and can walk four miles in about an hour with gear.
- Any military or police training; priority to infantry types.
- A good shooter who practices regularly, preferably with dynamic training or matches (ex. IDPA); even paintball or airsoft.
- Can carry a pistol and rifle (or other long gun) safely with regard to muzzle and trigger discipline.
- Can restrain themselves emotionally and verbally in tough situations as well as follow orders.
- Is capable of thinking and navigating independently.
- Preferably has been tested in combat/dangerous situations and does not panic "under fire."

Some of these requirements may not be realistic for who you have work with, so consider them as fitness goals. Otherwise, you will have to use who you have available and work within the parameters of what they can do.

## Women

You should avoid taking women with you if at all possible. Women should only be brought on patrols that have a mission where a woman, or that woman's particular skill, is necessary, such as bringing a nurse to some ill neighbors. Societies that don't protect their women will quickly find that they can't reproduce.

Ruthless enemies may specifically target women or patrols with women for two main factors; the perception that women are physically and psychologically weaker or to capture the women. Women may be deliberately targeted for capture or incidentally taken prisoner. Time and time again, when things are really bad, bad guys rape women. Having a woman from your neighborhood captured, raped, and killed will be devastating for morale. It will be a victory for the enemy who will see you as weak and target you for further depredations.

There are several biological reasons against women in combat roles. Men are typically bigger, faster, and stronger than the average woman at comparable fitness levels. In hand-to-hand combat, a fit man will typically dominate a woman. Men compete for women's attention; trying to compete while on patrol could make for stupid decisions that put the patrol at risk. Men have a natural instinct to protect women; in a decent society that's what men do. Part of the whole reason you are running a defensive operation is to protect your wives, daughters, and mothers. The mission may be compromised if members of the patrol attempt to do the woman's job or shield her from her share of danger.

If you have no other option than to have a woman go on patrol or engage in some other combat, take only the most fit woman you can find and she had better be both brave and proficient with weapons. In this case, avoid using mothers and look for childless, athletic young ladies. You may still lose someone valuable to your society but if she doesn't have kids, at least there is not a child growing up without a mother.

## Patrol member roles

Four to eight men will be enough to provide security for themselves and fight effectively against similarly experienced/sized enemies. This number is also realistic for small groups of neighborhood defenders. Even numbers are best though so each man has a buddy to fight with.

A larger group has more resources where a smaller group is less noticeable and takes fewer men away from defenses. Four men is the absolute minimum to mount a patrol except in utter desperation. For patrols that are intended to demonstrate strength, the more men the better, as long as it doesn't weaken the defense at home.

The most important man in this group is the patrol commander or leader. The patrol commander needs to be a tactically oriented person (preferably a combat arms veteran) who is alert, intelligent, has natural leadership tendencies, is brave, and is familiar with the area. He will have to make quick decisions that could affect both the patrol and the neighborhood or folks back at home.

A scout should go ahead of the patrol and direct, as necessary. His job is to navigate and scout ahead of the main patrol to see what lies ahead around corners and down streets. By necessity he will leave the patrol at times to check the area out for advance warning of contact with other citizens, hostile groups, or ambushes.

Your scout should be a fast, nimble person who can move stealthily. The scout will trade off "point" duties with the point man. Preferably this person will have military experience.

I suggest this role because with a team of people who may have no military experience and little tactical awareness, having someone who does have that experience and skillset going out ahead first can potentially keep the patrol from stumbling in to trouble. A horrible analogy is putting an adult in charge of a group of kindergartners who would otherwise just wander out into traffic.

Up front with the scout is the point man, who should also have military experience. The two roles may be one and the same, but I like to imagine that the scout will be moving around at a short distance from the patrol itself. The point man is responsible for looking for ambushes, booby traps, and potential threats that the scout doesn't alert to. He is on alert. He cannot be on autopilot blundering blindly down the street as if he was out for his evening constitutional thinking about whatever.

The others in the body of the patrol need to pay attention to their surroundings, divided up into sectors. Since most people are right handed, long guns will naturally be carried to the left, so two people should be carrying left handed to cover the right side of the patrol. Each man should have a sector; forward right, rear left, etc. that he is responsible for paying attention to. This makes an ideal patrol "body" four men minimum.

Rear security is as important as the front. The "six" man at the tail end of the patrol is responsible for physically turning around every so often and making sure that no one is following. He may want to stop behind cover and concealment to watch what happens as the patrol moves away or disappears from sight. He should communicate with the patrol leader as he returns to the group so no one is spooked.

Have someone on your team that has the gift of gab. One of my partners and best friends is a very witty, friendly guy. When the two of us are together, he's the good cop and I'm the bad cop. I shove my foot in my mouth and he's the one to rescue the situation and get the subject laughing. Another friend, who is your typical pugnacious guy from Philly, is a natural interrogator. He can get almost anyone talking and keep them talking, steering them right where he wants them. Find the guy in your group that could chat up a mute person and make him your human intelligence gatherer.

# Patrol planning

## Intent of the patrol

In law enforcement, patrol is always rather self-directed. One sort of wanders around looking for people or events. From an energy and security standpoint, you can't afford to be aimlessly wandering around. A SHTF patrol isn't an evening constitutional. Set out what your purpose for the patrol is, what you wish to accomplish by it, and where you plan to go.

I like the task/purpose binary for planning. What will you be doing (task) and what do you want that thing to accomplish (purpose)? Really it's purpose that the dictates the task, but you get the idea. If you cannot clearly define why you are doing a thing or what that thing *should* achieve for you, then it's back to the drawing board. Patrols are not an excuse to go out and parade around in your kit.

- Decide what overarching thing it is you hope that this patrol will accomplish for you (**purpose**).
- Create a specific set of goals for your patrol to further outline your purpose.
- Determine what actions you will need to undertake in order to complete your goals (**task**).

**Task:** Walk down Palm Street.

**Purpose:** Remind defenders of Palm St. that you Maple St. defenders are on the same team and Palm is a public right of way.

**Goals:** 1. Get down Palm St. amicably; 2. Exchange intelligence with Palm St.; 3. Go past the gang house on Palm and Main so that they see you and know they aren't alone; 4. Check storm drain gate for a cut lock.

**Roles:** Carl is patrol leader, David is the radio operator (RTO), Nimble Jack is the scout. The other five guys make up the rest of the patrol.

In other words, **what** you're going to do, **why** you are doing it, **how** you're going to do it, and everyone's **roles**.

## Planning and briefing

Pick your team. Designate the members of your team with their role for the mission, i.e. RTO, interrogator, and the guy that no one likes who gets to poke potential bombs with a stick.

Determine when you are going out. Daytime patrols are for visibility and night time patrols are for when you want to do things unseen or can't do X in daylight without being spotted. Night patrolling can be suspicious; anyone would be suspicious of armed dudes sneaking around in the dark. Notify all participants and those staying behind of the time and plan.

Review the terrain, both geographical and human, and plan your route. This will include the actual patrol routes, obstacles, hazards, waypoints, check-in points, objectives, and expected deviations. Plan for rally points if separated. Never double back on a patrol or return the same way in order to avoid any potential ambushes. Be sure to record this so that your base knows where you are, what you are doing, where they can find you, and how they can reach you by radio.

Brief all participants and principals who will remain at base. Go over the intent, goals, etc. of the patrol. Show everyone the route and identified points along the way. Prep everyone for their roles. The leader gives out general orders. Discuss and hash out what you plan to do, how you want to do it, and what might go wrong. Spitball the whole thing and rehearse it.

## Tools and equipment

Group equipment that can be divided up among members of the patrol can include:

- Large bolt cutters.
- Prybar/crowbar.
- Sledgehammer.
- Axe or hatchet.
- Rope ladder (6-8ft).
- Local maps.
- Binoculars or monocular (because raising your rifle to look down the magnified scope to see things better is not the appropriate use of a firearm).
- Periscope or hand mirror.

Adequate water and snacks should be carried if the patrol is extended or forced to belly up for an unknown extended period of time. I've had days on patrol where I suddenly found myself going from a half-hour to lunch (Code 7) to being stuck on a crime/accident scene for a 16 hour day. Clothing should be appropriate to the weather for the same reasons and layered.

Uniforms are great if you can all standardize on colors or camouflage, but this is unlikely to happen. Much of this is discussed in *Suburban Defense*, but in short groups will likely come together at the last minute in ad hoc form without the ability to standardize or buy gear. The best idea is to try and pick a common color and use colored arm bands to denote members of the team.

## Communications

There should be one UHF/VHF radio per person, with ear piece and remote mic. Taking your radio out of its pouch to hold it in front of your face is a distraction, a waste of time, and might cause you to lose it. Use shoulder or lavalier style microphones for ease of communication and an earpiece to avoid broadcasting everything the radio receives into the surrounding environment.

Personal radios can be turned off on patrol as long as the patrol is in close formation. The RTO and leader should always have theirs on. Any separation or loss of sight with the others requires turning the radio on to the patrol frequency. At a minimum, the leader and RTO have radios.

The RTO should have as a baseline:

- Two UHF/VHF radios. Depending on the radio plan, one radio could be the intra-team radio and the other could be the patrol-base radio.
- One scanner for monitoring other frequencies or COMINT in the field.
- All radios and scanners should be equipped with high gain antennas of at least one-quarter wavelength.
- Full ear headphones, preferably noise cancelling shooting style with a mic and the ability to switch between 1-3 audio inputs.

- A "ham in a can" style VHF/UHF or HF backpack radio can also be used in lieu of one of the smaller units.
- The RTO or patrol leader should always have a spare radio in case a team member's HT is disabled or there is an emergency where the main radios get lost.

Keep your radio transmissions short and concise. You may want to use easy to remember code names for locations while on the move in case your radio traffic is being monitored.

Ideally, your patrol will have a separate radio channel from the base neighborhood defense channel. Monitoring this channel is a "dispatcher" back at home. This channel should only be used for patrol/base communications or among the members of the patrol. Like a police dispatcher, your base station commo person monitoring the radio can hear what the patrol is up to and plan accordingly.

This way, if a firefight erupts, the dispatcher can hear the patrol's radio calls to each other and send help without waiting for the patrol to switch to a separate frequency and call for help. The one frequency model eliminates the need for a specialist RTO; anyone can call the base (although one person will probably be the designated communicator). Fewer frequencies means fewer radios and faster transmissions.

There are two schools of thought about patrol radios. My school of thought is straight out of police thinking; you want your base to hear what's going on in case you need help. However, this requires that radios broadcast a lot of power, high wattage that is, giving you a greater radio signature to anyone listening. This is a liability if the bad guys are conducting electronic surveillance on you.

Military thinking is as low transmission power as possible to limit how far away your transmission can be intercepted. The trade off is that you will need a separate, higher powered radio to reach your base. Now radios can be easily programmed to transmit at low power on one channel and high power on another, but by having two channels, you now need an RTO to monitor the base frequency.

Using standard 400 MHz UHF radios transmitting at 1 watt, in ordinary urban terrain the radio will have decent reception for 1-2 miles, depending on hills. Those with sensitive antennas and those in elevated positions will hear you better. Based on computer models and again depending on terrain, someone in ideal conditions could hear you up to 4-5 miles away. So low frequency UHF isn't exactly silent at a distance.

If very short range radio communications with low probability of intercept is what you need, 900 MHz radios are probably the way to go. These frequencies are intended for hams and businesses, so operation for defensive purposes may not be strictly legal. At very low power, effective range will be about a mile, with the above caveats about opportune interception. However, this means another radio to purchase and a lot of these radios may be stolen units from businesses in the hands of bad guys being used for *their* communications.

Defensive operations should be on a separate channel so that defenders and the patrol aren't talking all over each other. You could probably get by with a "main" channel for basic neighborhood defense and a "tactical" channel for patrols or side conversations.

Check in with the base periodically so that they know you aren't dead. Check-ins should be done a specific periodic points, say either time-based at once an hour or whatever or based on geographical progress.

Radio transmissions shouldn't be made unless radio communication is necessary to transmit information. Unless the patrol is gone for a while or there is actual apprehension of danger, status checks to make sure that everyone is alright shouldn't be made. A status check once every two or four hours should be sufficient, otherwise, no news is good news.

Ensure that patrol members do not use the radio to chit-chat with each other or make calls back to base. The only persons who should be calling the base or other units not on the patrol should be the leader and RTO, barring an emergency. If the guys can't keep their fingers off the PTT button, they aren't mature enough to have a radio or probably be on the patrol. Let your stupid enemies be the ones blabbing away narrating their evil deeds.

## Patrol procedures

Humans tend to fall into routine and patterns, which is deadly in a combat situation. Do not patrol at set times, in the same places, using the same routes. Be unpredictable and vary not only where you go, but how you get there and the time you go. Mixing things up to confuse an enemy is obvious, but events may occur or things may be visible only at certain times. If you only go out at a set time, you'll never know what is happening during the other hours.

Keep a patrol log and write a report of what you saw and what happened when you get back. Take a camera along to document things visually. Even after an EMP, someone is going to have a working cellphone that could end up being a photo device.

No talking on patrol unless it is related to the patrol and necessary. Don't whisper but talk in as a low a voice as possible or use hand signals. If you need to speak, talk so the two of you can keep watch in opposite directions and try to look around instead of at each other as you would in normal conversation.

Test your gear to eliminate any noise before leaving. Hard, flat surfaces like concrete walls will amplify sounds. Normally urban areas are loud, and thus quiet sounds don't usually carry very far, but an SHTF city will have a lot less traffic and ordinary background noise.

Scan the area around you. Your head needs to be on a swivel. You are most responsible for your sector. Do not sling weapons over your shoulder. Carry them in your hands, such as at the low ready (butt high, muzzle low), pointed in a safe direction.

Studies have shown that persons carrying at the low ready are much less likely to have a "mistake of fact" shooting. These are shootings where the (almost always officers) believe that a furtive movement, object, or something else is a threat, when it isn't. The simple answer is the additional time to raise the weapon and aim it allows officers to observe, orient, and decide than one on target that just needs to pull the trigger.[15, 16]

At night, use red light filters or infrared. Let your eyes adjust to dark at least half an hour before going out. Put small patches of luminous tape ("cat's eyes") on the back of your clothing/headgear. If you have only one person with night vision, put him in front. If he shoots all tracers, he can designate targets for the others to shoot at.

### Listening halts

You will need to make listening halts. Every so often, stop, listen and look around. This isn't a break to eat a snack, take a drink, or adjust your gear. You are stopping for a five minute period to listen and look around in silence. You aren't making observations if you don't stop for an appreciable length of time; you're just passing through. The length of this stop is essentially increasing your sample size versus stopping for thirty seconds. It also allows you to detect noise/motion if someone else happened to stop when you did.

For a short halt, everyone stays in formation as much as possible while using cover and concealment the best they can. The patrol should preferably crouch or get low without sitting down. Everyone needs to remain on alert and continue to maintain security.

For longer halts, such as long observation duties or breaks, everyone should move into a formation that allows them to provide security for 360°. If a break, half of the patrol can relax a bit, put down some of their gear (while it remains at hand), and do their break stuff. The other half maintains an alert posture and security. Everyone should be ready to fight or resume movement at a

[15] Paul L. Taylor, "Engineering Resilience" Into Split-Second Shoot/No Shoot Decisions: The Effect of Muzzle-Position, September 30, 2020.
[16] OODA Loop: Observe–Orient–Decide–Act.

moment's notice.

## Movement

The patrol should travel at least five yards apart from each other. Unless you're having a necessary conference, buddies should not be traveling together. This way, one shot, a burst, or a hand grenade can't easily take out two of you at once. This is important when taking cover as well, although if you are already under fire it is better to get behind something solid than to worry about splitting up.

The scout should go ahead of the patrol to check out the area before moving across the danger area. When it is time to move, half of the patrol should be taking cover, conducting 360° security, and ready to provide fire support for the crossing half. The crossing half should have engagement responsibility for threats in the area in front of it as they move. Once they are across, the crossing half swaps roles with the other half as the rest make their crossing.

Whenever possible, move behind cover or concealment. Use low areas like ditches. Pick areas with poor visibility, such as in the shadows. Any time you can, get off the roads. Use alleys, parks, railroad rights of way, golf courses, bike paths, along waterways, or empty land. In modern cities with strip malls and parking lots everywhere, stick to those to avoid traveling down roads which could easily be a sniper's alley.

Use caution when traversing unfenced yards, storm drains, golf courses, or any space that is close to homes. A group of armed individuals unknown to the area could be seen as a dangerous force skulking through rather than the defensive neighborhood group on the other side of the big arterial street. In residential areas going through front yards where there is landscaping to conceal you and hopefully some cover is temping but hazardous. Be wary of residents who don't know your intentions and may attack you for traversing their yard.

In a combat situation, or where you expect to be fired upon, utilize the protection of buildings. Military doctrine dictates that a platoon (approximately 40-50 men) move down both sides of the street to support each other. I think the average group of citizen defenders will be lucky to have half a dozen men who can patrol, so I'm recommending they all stick together.

Move from one position of cover to the next with your buddy or element providing covering fire. Trade off as each person moves. Fire from *around* cover, which is to the side of it, rather than doing the movie thing and going over the top, which will expose more of your head and body.

Don't just pop over or around walls or solid fences. Look first, preferably with a periscope, or by exposing as little of your head as possible. Peep from around the *side* of the wall as close to the ground as possible if you can. If you have to hop a wall or fence, make sure the other side is free of stuff like cactus or a vicious dog. Roll over walls instead of vaulting them.

Take corners, doors, and windows by angles. If you've taken a home defense or CQB course you know about "slicing the pie." Avoid letting a weapon muzzle protrude out past the corner which will give you away. Stand back from the opening and move slowly, clearing the exposed area bit by bit without exposing yourself all at once all while looking over the sights of your weapon (high ready).

## Field interrogations

A lot of time in law enforcement people want to talk to you because for some reason a lot of people like talking to or (positive) attention from people in positions of authority. Being a bunch of armed dudes, who have maybe saved the locals from bad guys at time or two, you may experience this phenomenon. Or you might find that people are scared of you. Some may hate you and might make things as awkward as a vindictive ex yelling and throwing your clothes over a balcony.

When encountering people, if they are peaceable, make it clear that you mean no harm. Next, ask them something to the effect "Is there anything we should be concerned about?" Not only are you asking about immediate danger, this phrasing implies that you are willing to care about what the person might be concerned about. This invites them to share their thoughts with you.

Your gifted friend can then chat away and gradually steer the conversation to topics of importance. Don't just directly interrogate them with a list of questions like some sort of interview, get them talking naturally. I've found that once I ask all my direct questions, more information tends to freely flow. Let them paint a picture of how they are living, what things are like in their area, and what they and their neighbors are worried about. Rumors are just as important as facts and when rumors start correlating with each other or with facts, there is some truth to them.

If you develop a regular source of information, this person is an informant. Never bring an informant "home." Meet them in a secluded, neutral location. Meeting on their territory may put you in danger of an ambush.

Be cagey about what you reveal about yourself. Mutual information exchange can be a good thing and even necessary, but don't give away the farm. Do not reveal information about your strength, defenses, or operations. Talk about outside observations and warnings. Generally, don't trust anyone and always carefully vet other groups and informants in case they are spies.

### Your perimeter

Check your perimeter while you are on patrol. You may be unable to check the whole thing, as the purpose of your patrol was not for perimeter security, but closely examine what you can as you go in and out. What you're looking for is anything that seems out of place that could indicate intrusion, booby traps, or surveillance. Open gates and broken padlocks are obvious signs of intrusion, but here are some more subtle ones:

- Disturbed or discolored earth or sod, indicating digging;

- Unusual footprints or mud/dirt well above ground level;
- Cuts or repairs to wire or chain link fences;
- Missing fence slats, bricks missing from walls, or hollow bricks broken in to create steps;
- Broken branches, bent or broken plant stalks, trampled grass or brush;
- Objects that are out of place and could be used to hide something or as climbing aids;
- Strange chalk, dirt, or paint marks;
- Ropes or cords (may be a sign of a boobytrap);
- A padlock that has been removed and replaced with a different one;
- Gate chains that have been wrapped, but not locked;
- Foliage that has an unusual color and/or texture or looks out of place (may be a camouflaged hide);
- Garbage or debris that shouldn't be there;
- Game or other hidden cameras; and,
- Graffiti (tagging).

These are just some indicators of suspicious activity.

Pay attention to structures or ideal vantage points that overlook your position or perimeter. If there is an abandoned house that looks at a vulnerable spot, routinely check out the house. Consider installing motion or trip alarms. Don't be afraid to cut down vegetation in spots that abut your perimeter or could be used to conceal a sniper or observer.


## Deployment and returning

When you are re-entering your perimeter, radio ahead if possible to both notify the defenders and get clearance to enter. It may be unsafe or sentries may not be aware of your arrival.

Entry and exit will be the most dangerous time for your patrol. If you cannot utilize a stealthy sortie or return through a hidden sally port, leave in the most protective manner possible. Have your defenders take up defensive positions in full combat gear. The patrol should then quickly move out of any danger area to whatever cover they can, moving as fast as possible and ready to fight. Once they are safely away from likely ambush areas outside the "gate," the normal patrol pace can resume. Cover must be used well and movements have to be smart.

Should someone be watching and waiting to ambush, everyone is there to return fire in force. Hopefully seeing everyone turned out in battle rattle will be enough dissuade ambushers into not taking the field that day. Otherwise you've put on your best effort to fight back.

Suburban housing tracts are lousy for secret entrances and exits. Where I grew up, the homes were built in the 1960s-1980s for the most part. Yards are large and so are the tracts themselves, which tend to follow the terrain. New housing tracts seem to be dense blocks dumped into whatever land is leftover with one or two exits. No patrol should be entering and leaving from the same point, nor should it be habit to use proper street and pedestrian path entrances.

Get used to using unconventional entrances and exits. Use creek banks, storm drains, and utility rights of way. Talk to friendly neighbors whose homes back up to roads and open spaces to get them to allow you to leave from their yards. Climb a ladder over their back fence or wall to get in and out. Designate and discreetly mark the yard. Just make sure to warn the homeowner when you plan a patrol so they aren't alarmed when armed dudes suddenly hop over a fence.

## Types of contact on patrol

Avoid chance encounters, especially with potentially hostile forces. Make contact on your terms. Even if you didn't anticipate someone coming, at least observe them before they see you.

**Casual encounter:** approach by or contact with an apparently unarmed or non-threatening person.
- An aggressive posture is probably counter-productive. Remain on the defensive and wary, but not

standoffish or hostile. The person you are interacting with may be helpful, friendly, or grateful.

- Children, women, and the elderly will be naturally treated with a more relaxed attitude.
- Keep some of the men on watch and ready in case the encounter is exploited by hostiles or is a trap.
- Avoid giving out supplies (food, candy) or sensitive information.
- Attempt to obtain information from the person about the general situation or specifics you may have an interest in.

**Hard encounter:** interaction with an unknown or unfriendly armed force *without* indications that fighting will occur *or* contact with hostile forces without actual/imminent initiation of combat.

- Example: coming upon another patrol or a roadblock conducted by antagonistic defenders.
- Immediately halt and move to cover upon contact. If you are making contact with a "hard" group, split the patrol and have the non-contact persons take cover and to provide fire support if needed.
- If no one is shooting, determine if shooting is the best course of action. This decision may need to be a snap spot decision, based on intelligence and well-thought out strategy, by the patrol commander. A command to fire can be given simply by the patrol commander opening fire.
- Should some accommodation or rapprochement be impossible, withdraw from the area and leave or go around.
- Do not taunt or insult, nor should you be goaded by the same. Don't let verbal games escalate to violence. Fight on your terms, not because you are hotheaded.

**Hostile encounter:** actual or imminent combat.

- Example: an ambush or seeing enemy gunmen taking up firing positions.
- If hostile intent is ascertained and violence is imminent, take the initiative to begin the fight. This is known as a "hasty ambush" in military parlance.
- If fired upon first, take cover. Return fire while moving to cover and support your team members as they move.
- If you do not need to have a decisive fight then and there, break contact. Withdraw to safety and survive to fight

another day. You are *defenders* and probably lack the skills and weaponry to assault through an ambush and decisively destroy the enemy.

## Being ambushed

Avoid chance encounters with hostile forces. Make contact on your terms. Send a scout out ahead or take your time to observe before moving. If you see the enemy before he sees you: freeze and signal the patrol to freeze as well. Quickly and quietly move to cover or at least concealment. The patrol leader should rapidly make a determination if the patrol is able to win the engagement or if they should attempt to withdraw unseen.

If ambushed or seen immediately return a high volume of fire, as accurately as possible, while moving to cover. Break contact. Since you are not in the military and the men you are with not conditioned to combat operations, I advise *against* assaulting into the ambush and instead withdrawing.

Those caught in the kill zone have to get off the "X" and to cover immediately, preferably while returning fire. That is, movements like the Australian peel and taking turns to provide fire while the other runs. If not in the kill zone, use cover and return fire to cover and relieve pressure on those who are in the kill zone.

Utilize smoke, covering fire, and cover and concealment as you withdraw. Ensure that the enemy doesn't follow, and if he does, ambush him in return. Do not stay in the open. Get into a nearby building, preferably one that is suitable to defend. If fired upon from a building, do not attempt to assault the building and clear it without the skills, training, and experience to do so. Return fire as best as possible, withdraw to cover, and go another way.

If you suspect you are being followed, try to avoid going right home. Evade and find a place to hide until your pursuer gives up or clears from your area. Ambush them if need be. Don't lead them back to your neighborhood.

# Guns, Shooting, and Urban Gunfights

This chapter contains some general musings on the topic of firearms and shooting in urban areas. It does not cover basic tactical principles nor does it teach Close Quarters Battle (CQB) tactics. There are other sources out there that can do all that much better than I can, so these are my thoughts that I don't see covered much elsewhere. I'd refer everyone to reading the *US Army Ranger Handbook* for a practical and comprehensive explanation of many tactical concepts.

## High angle shooting

The importance of urban high angle shooting, from ground level into a high floor of a multistory building, became evident after the October 1, 2017, Route 91 Harvest Festival massacre. The killer opened fire with multiple AR-15s from the 32nd floor of the Mandalay Bay casino, firing out and down on the concert from approximately 350 feet above ground level.

In a future domestic conflict, snipers firing from high ground will be a factor. It was very much so in Sarajevo. While many suburban defenders will not be faced with buildings quite so tall, multistory buildings are not unknown in suburban areas. Defenders in downtown areas or that have to go down there for some reason might have very tall buildings. The same challenges that Las Vegas Metro police had that night will be in the laps of citizen defenders.

Typically, bullets tend to hit high when shooting either up or down, contrary to the folk notion that bullets hit high when shooting up and low when shooting down. The more accurate yet generic advice is to "aim low because the shot will hit high" is true.

Bullets hit high in either case because the effect of gravity on the projectile is greatest when a bullet is fired level. Gravity acts as a downward force on bullets, so bullets fired perpendicular to that force will be pulled towards the ground, creating the characteristic down sloping ballistic arc.

When fired vertically, that same downward force of gravity is pulling the bullet backwards, reducing its velocity. This the same reason a truck slows when climbing a hill; both are fighting gravity. Scopes and sights are calibrated for shots that are roughly horizontal to the horizon which factors in the droop caused by gravity.

Remember that a bullet exiting the barrel of a gun flies in a straight line until acted upon by other forces (gravity and drag). Again, the initial path of the bullet is straight, even if it is up or down when compared against a fixed reference point; it doesn't actually climb upward as a ballistic chart shows. So shots taken at extreme angles fly straighter and hit higher because the sights are calibrated to compensate for gravity's drop on level shots, not angled ones.

Most citizen defenders are not going to be measuring the distance and angle to the target then doing math. The easy answer is to get a laser rangefinder that will measure both distance and angle to calculate and spit out the dope for the shot. Lacking one of these, the good news is that within 300 yards (typical maximum urban engagement range, historically) there is not much appreciable change in impact point except at very extreme angles.

For an officer at street level on Las Vegas Boulevard that night, had they returned fire, this would have been a 200-300 yard shot at roughly a 45° angle. This would be a very difficult shot for the average AR-trained officer whose skills with an AR would approximate that of an average civilian. The best realistic outcome would have been suppressing fire; however, any misses would have put guests in the rooms at risk from the stray bullets. Personal accuracy is probably going to be the largest consideration, not high angle deviation, so a citizen defender must consider collateral damage when shooting up at buildings.

## Shooting into houses

**Note:** See the section "Bullet penetration of suburban homes" in the Fighting and Combat in a Suburb chapter of *Suburban Defense* for more information about the ballistic resistance of a home.

If you need to shoot into houses, shoot through the windows. They are going to be the weakest point in any home or business, even if reinforced. A steel plate or six feet of stacked sandbags behind the drapes are unlikely, so shoot through any plywood covers if you have to. Any respectable rifle bullet will penetrate and cause damage inside.

It will be hard to know if you are hitting anyone and you will need to use a large volume of fire shot randomly into the room, but you can at least get a suppressing effect and maybe a lucky shot.

Doors are similarly weak points. Also aim for the walls just to the side of the doors where someone is probably taking cover. If you can fire downwards from a height through the door or window, even better, as anyone inside is lying on the floor if they are smart.

Please note that indiscriminate shooting into a building may injure or kill innocent civilians that you may not even know are present in the building.

## Shooting across the street

So you've fallen back to your home and now have to defend the perimeter. If you have multiple defenders doing the same thing at each home, crossfire will be problematic. This is on top of the already existing hazards of penetrating homes' exterior walls and hitting innocent neighbors taking shelter inside. This will be most dangerous when shooting at external targets from your home.

Looking across the street from my front window, I can see that the street is about two feet below the level of my front door. In most suburbs, it is common for the houses to be graded a few feet above the street. This is for drainage purposes. That means that someone standing in the street will be a few feet lower than you will be. From a prone position, which puts my torso shots right at about the ground level, one to two feet, where someone in a house may be hiding.

So if you're taking cover inside a house, do it at the back of the house, not in the front street-side rooms. Get behind actual interior cover and sandbags or other bullet resistant material low at the front of the house is a good idea.

For me as a shooter, I need to consider that the chest or head shot at 100 feet across the street, if someone were standing on my neighbor's stoop, would go over any sheltering peoples' heads (in theory). In reality, the bad guy is likely to be slightly lower than me, meaning the angle of my shots into someone in the street that miss or over-penetrate will go into a house at that danger level.

I don't have any suggestions to avoiding crossfire. There is no sure-fire (pardon the pun) solution to avoiding blue-on-blue. A sergeant I knew died in a very chaotic situation due to friendly fire and he and the other officer were probably two of the best patrol cops on duty that night for that situation. When SHTF, any plans will go out the window. In a neighborhood, there is no 180 degree rule and there really can't be without sacrificing the need to shoot a bad guy.

My one suggestion is to really be sure of your shot before pulling the trigger. Being "sure" is a multi-factor consideration:

- Aim well. Make that shot count and be sure it really will hit your target.
- No spray and pray. Deliberate shots only.
- Ensure that at the moment you take the shot, the background and a few feet to either side (in case of a miss) are free of any friendlies.
- Do not take shots that are likely to penetrate a home and hit someone inside; i.e. don't shoot someone in front of

a window or shoot the guy in front of the garage instead of in front of the bedrooms.

- Accept the fact you may do everything right but good people still get hurt.

Best practices aren't always going to be the most life-saving things and you might not remember them during a fight. At least you are mitigating risk by *trying* rather than becoming fixated on your target and wasting them without thinking.

In an apartment complex, especially if you are shooting upwards or level with upper floors, be mindful that you have a greater chance of hitting someone. Upper floors may have less structural strength on the walls, more windows, and it is more likely someone will be looking out a window or within your line of fire. Bullets traveling down at an angle will penetrate the floor/ceiling into the below apartment instead of into the ground. Elevated shots that miss will travel a further distance the further above the ground they are due to most obstructions that could deflect a bullet being low.

## Quiet carbine: oil filter AR-15 suppressor

If combat suddenly develops, you may not have time to put on ear protection. Suppressors help keep your ears from bleeding in these situations. Firearm suppressors, or silencers,[17] muffle the report of a gun as it fires. At their core, they are the same technology in your automobile muffler and both were literally invented by the same guy, Hiram P. Maxim, the son of the man who invented the machine gun.

These will not make your gun entirely silent but lower the sound level of the shot. Well-designed models can make full power weapons nearly ear-safe without hearing protection on. Even less

---

[17] Either term is correct. "Suppressor" describes what the device does and is considered the more technically correct term, while "Silencer" was the original trade name and is what the US Government calls them legally.

efficient designs can make the gunshot less painful to the shooter and make locating the shooter more difficult.

Suppressors are regulated (as "silencers") under federal law by the 1934 National Firearms Act. They require an extensive background check, a special ATF application, fingerprinting, and a $200 tax. Background checks can take months to a year, depending on the backlog. Some states, like California, ban them entirely.

Suppressors again don't make guns into super silent assassins' weapons that make that weird beep noise used by cheap Hollywood productions. Used indoors with regular ammo, suppressed gunshots can be very loud and painful. Ideally, they will lower the sound of a gunshot by up to 30 dB. Using subsonic ammunition makes them quieter as there is no longer the "crack" sonic boom component of the gunshot. With the right ammunition and suppressor, gun shots can cause a lot less hearing disruption and damage.

You would want to use this in a situation where you don't have time to put on your "ears." In a gunfight, you usually don't have time to put on ear protection. Inside a home or if you are ambushed it might be nice to fight without going deaf immediately or suffering from tinnitus for weeks afterwards. The other main use is that if you are concealed from your enemy, they may hear the gunshots, but since the sound is muffled, they can't easily use their hearing to identify where the shots are coming from.

A lot of people who might want suppressors won't be able to get them due to politics or supply issues. Once SHTF happens, buying a suppressor and hoping the ATF approves your tax stamp might go out the window. Even if no one cares about the ATF anymore, expect supplies of suppressors to dry up overnight. If the big factories are out of business, the only people making them will be skilled machinists in local shops that you may never learn about.

There is one solution that dog-killing ATF agents all over the country frown upon. Using a common thread adaptor and automotive oil filters, one can make a relatively effective improvised suppressor. Please note, this is a federal felony and could get you in a lot of trouble. Even possessing the thread adaptor, a firearm that it could fit, and an oil filter could be construed as a crime. Having all these things in one's possession and the "intent" to assemble them into a regulated device is considered "constructive possession" by the ATF.

If you are going to do this, don't do it until the end of the world when there is no law or ATF anymore. If you choose to purchase all the parts now, store them separately and make no modifications to the items or any weapons. Purchase the parts for cash anonymously and hide them.

What you need are: **1/2"-28 to 5/8"-24 thread adaptor** (or converter). Other threading can be used; however, it is very crucial that you obtain one that adapts 1/2"-28 to whatever as ½"-28 are the threading specs for an AR-15 muzzle. Know that the first number in the pitch threading is the outside diameter and the second number is how many threads per inch. Firearms pitches are fairly standard, but check the manufacturer's specs, and be sure to check the threading on the filter mouth.

If using this on non-AR style weapons, be sure to check what the pitch of the barrel threading is to buy the right adaptor. And yes, you need a threaded barrel. AR-15s with muzzle devices that are not pinned or welded are already threaded and usable with just a wrench. You will need a **crush washer** as is used for AR-15 muzzle devices. You can reuse the existing one if need be.

An **oil filter** that fits the threading for the adaptor you have is required. I'm not aware of any filters that will screw on without an adaptor. A smaller diameter filter is better as it is less likely to obstruct your optics. The oil filter may obstruct your optics, depending on the diameter of the filter and how low your optics are mounted.

A hole will need to be drilled concentric with the threaded hole on the closed end of the filter. This is a delicate operation and is necessary to allow the bullet and gasses to escape. Do not try and shoot a second hole out as the pressure may damage the filter, your firearm, or you. Be sure to paint the filter in black or other dull colors.

Filters will not last long being used this way. Full-power rifle and pistol ammunition may last you for a few magazines, at best. Expect perhaps a 20 dB reduction in sound with performance that degrades over time. The filtration material inside will likely be torn up and expelled by the gun gases. Material may enter your rifle over time. Filters could overheat and catch fire with extensive use.

Best performance will be with subsonic rounds and in .22 LR caliber. Very quiet subsonic ammunition can be had, especially in .22, that will make the sound of the gun's action louder than the suppressed gunshot. Another method is a "wet" suppressor where oil or water is added to the suppressor's interior to absorb more sound. The improvised filter suppressor will likely be ineffective after 100 shots, less with larger calibers and more powerful rounds.

## But I don't know...subsonic .22LR rimfire ammo

Okay, so you don't want to do the above but you want to shoot quietly. Get a .22 LR rifle with a minimum 16" barrel length or a revolver with a 6-8" barrel. Shoot subsonic .22. These rounds travel below the speed of sound, hence "subsonic," and do not create the characteristic *crack* of a supersonic bullet as it breaks the sound barrier. There will still be the *boom* of the gunshot, but it will be less loud without the mini sonic boom, because the cartridge is small, and because subsonic .22 rounds often have less powder.

Various brands of .22 subsonic have different loadings. This varies from manufacturer to manufacturer and product to product. Some have a lower power load than standard rounds, others even less, to ones that only fire from the primer itself (the quietest). With very quiet ammo and a long barrel, .22 subsonic can be very quiet without a suppressor and even less than a 9mm or 5.56mm supersonic *suppressed* gunshot.

As with a suppressed rifle, the sound reduction will make the report of the gunshot harder to identify and locate. .22 subsonic bullets will have less effect on target and fly for a shorter distance than will ones from full power cartridges. Practical effective range will be about .50 yards and best fired from a rifle.

## The Civilian Light Support Weapon

The Marine Corps' new infantry rifle the M27 IAR or Infantry Automatic Rifle. Scuttlebutt is the Corps wanted a new rifle, specifically the HK 416 which the M27 is derived from, and the IAR concept was how they sold it. Basically, the concept is a rifle that is better suited to careful marksmanship and sustained fire than the M4 carbine. More guys with more accurate rifles that can put out a higher volume of fire, supposedly revolutionary like introducing semi-auto rifles were.

This role is known as "support by fire." I am personally against trying to combine roles. The M14 was one such attempt and it failed miserably. The Marine and professional jury is out on that concept; I guess we'll know how the rifles perform soon, if we haven't gone to war with Russia or China by the time this hits the printers. Give me a good rifle and support from an M249. Nothing like a belt fed when you need one.

Citizen defenders can make use of a dual role rifle/shooter with such a rifle, as is possible. This Light Support Weapon or LSW can provide a lot of shots really fast when required or switch to more accurate shots at longer rangers than unmagnified iron sights or red dots can provide. This is done with use of the bipod and scope for prone shooting and fast-firing triggers to approximate full-auto fire. With one of these faster firing devices installed, even if the trigger still has to be pulled for each shot, mag dumping into a crowd or rapidly suppressing a point target is easier.

However, citizen defenders are going to have a hard time acquiring a belt fed machine gun even if you can afford it. Belt-fed upper receivers for AR-15s with or without full auto lowers or bumpfire things are also kind of iffy. Binary triggers, where legal, and fast-reset triggers, if still available as the ATF is pursuing them, and bumpfire stocks if you haven't turn them in or the ATF rule is thrown out, are the closest questionably legal compromises. Making a drop-in auto sear is also possible, but highly illegal, and then the rifle is full-auto only.

Should you make one of these rifles? Well if you are a prolific AR builder looking for a new project and you've got the money and the other preps squared away, why not? Use will be niche but could make the difference in certain circumstances. Like any weapon, it will not turn a bad shooter into a good one or compensate for poor accuracy, etc.

Important features:

- Heavy profile barrel, 16-20" (the longer the better).
- Bipod.
- Binary or fast reset trigger (optional).
- 4x or variable magnification scope.
- Magpul D-60 sixty round magazine (or like type) loaded as the first magazine.
- IR laser and illuminator (ideal platform for NV use).

## Fingerprints, a short story

**Note:** The following factual information is presented as a fictional exchange.

"Hey, wear gloves while you're doing that."

"Huh?"

"Look at what you're doing. You're shoving that cartridge into the magazine with your thumb. Gonna be a big, fat thumbprint on each one of those cases. It's like rear-ending someone and then doing a hit-and-run, leaving a perfect imprint of your license plate on the other guy's bumper."

"I'll just pick up the empties."

"No, no, no. That's not going to work. They're gonna be ejected out, remember? Ever notice how hard it is to find all the brass you shot at the range? Now imagine you're doing a job in sand or gravel. You shoot five, six times—you're not sure. It's night and it's dark out there. How are you going to find those empty cases, some buried, when you don't even know for sure how many times you fired? That's why you wear gloves when you touch your ammo."

"Oh, okay."

"In fact, whenever you touch your ammo, wear gloves. You never know if they'll start dusting prints off cases they find way out in the boondocks from target shooters to see who has guns still and who doesn't."

"You're being paranoid."

"Trust me, you don't get old doing this kind of thing without being paranoid. Paranoia is what keeps them from locking your ass up. You take all precautions. If you start being cavalier, then you need to find another way to spend your time."

"What about the gun?"

"That's another thing. Obviously, you can wipe it down and remove the serial numbers. Serial numbers are kinda iffy. Since guns are outright illegal now, you stand to lose nothing by removing the serial. An extra charge on top of firearm possession won't mean much. Cartridges are the real key to identifying the shooter though."

He went on to explain that serial numbers couldn't just be ground off. When the serial number was physically imprinted on the gun, it altered the metal below it. This meant that even if the top layers were gone, certain processes could reveal the number below. Vertical deformation had to happen to change the metal beneath where the number was stamped. One way of doing this was very careful and strong hits all over the digits with a punch. It was best if a machine did it. Then the top could be ground off.

"Can they get fingerprints off a gun?" the other asked, switching back to prints.

"Not very well. Firearms are designed in ways, for totally unrelated reasons, which end up with them being poor retainers of fingerprints. Guns are checkered for non-slip grips. Your Glock there has that high friction stippling on it. Even ordinary polymer surfaces hold prints poorly. The only places on guns that tend to hold prints well enough are flat surfaces, especially the slide. You know how it seems like every time you handle your gun, you get oil on your hands? Well that lubricant leaves nice prints on those smooth surfaces. Even then, prints are recovered off guns only about five percent of the time.

"Remember that even if your hands are clean, if you are nervous or it's hot, your hands will sweat. The salt from the sweat, mixed in with bits of dead skin, dirt, and skin oils will remain behind as fingerprints. You don't get fingerprints with clean hands in cold weather. Yet a smooth, almost perfectly round cylinder like a brass cartridge case will leave great prints. Once they find one of those with an undisturbed print, they can pull it off and run it for matches. Even if they don't find a match, once they find you, they'll tie you to the crime. Ten percent of crime scene fingerprints being usable might not seem like much, but if you had a ten percent chance to win the lottery, wouldn't you take it?"

"So wear gloves when loading, but not when shooting?"

"I didn't say that. Don't take the chance that you leave prints behind on a gun. Also all those ridges and checkering could catch a bit of skin underneath. Then they have your DNA. Also if they catch you before you can thoroughly wash your hands, they can test for gunshot residue on them."

To emphasize the point, his mentor tossed a pair of rubber gloves across the table. The message was understood loud and clear.

# Less-Lethal Generally

It's 3 AM on a freezing cold morning. For the second time this week, a skinny teenager is trying to cut through the fence that closes off the end of your residential street. You could kill him, but that might upset the refugees he lives among in the regional park. You raise a shotgun and fire a rubber slug. He falls and rolls to his side before jumping up and running away, clutching his belly. Back in a tent next to the playground, his mother says, "You're lucky they only used a rubber bullet."

This scenario illustrates a conundrum that the SHTF survivor will have to face; balance of force. Under the circumstances, an intruder might well be justifiably shot trying to penetrate a perimeter. Yet in this case, there is a risk of a riot from his fellow refugees who might find it overkill. Neighbors might disagree with the harshness of lethal force. Having a less-lethal option to discourage and deter bad guys is prudent. "Shoot 'em all and let God sort 'em out is not proper strategy."

In *Suburban Defense*, we looked at crowd control and how paintballs and pepper spray (OC) can be used against a mob. This section will touch more on kinetic less-lethal projectiles or (mainly) shotgun bean bags or rubber rounds. The discussion here is more than riots.

Less-lethal weapons are called that because they are *less* likely to kill. Sure, non-lethal weapons exist (unless really misused) but we're talking about weapons that *can* easily kill if a mishap occurs. That understanding is vital to your decision to employ these weapons and cartridges especially if a death *does* result.

Before using force, consider that using force may not be the proper thing to do at that moment given the circumstances. One type of force may be better to use than another, such as using a bean bag to warn and dissuade someone sneaking into a garden versus outright killing them. This is not a decision to make reflexively or take lightly. Do you really want to be justifying yourself for the next

20 years for killing a teenager digging up your potatoes?

Less-lethal impact munitions (kinetic projectiles) are discussed here as a half-measure before killing someone, not as a replacement for lethal projectiles. None of these items should replace pepper spray, Tasers, or old-fashioned punches and kicks in situations that don't warrant someone being killed. Nor is it a way out of shooting people with bullets when that is called for. Less-lethal ammunition usage is about giving yourself options when resorting to lethal force may carry undesired ramifications that you'd like to try to avoid.

These projectiles are designed to transfer their kinetic energy generated in the barrel into a human body without significant penetration of skin. Even so, breakage of the skin does happen.

Usage of these weapons will typically require medical attention. Wounds may vary from bad bruising to serious penetration injuries.

Impacts against the lungs, heart, or other organs can cause major internal injuries. Eyes have been put out and headshots have killed instantly. Death is uncommon but not unheard of. Of those killed, a majority of deaths were due to penetrative injuries, followed by blunt injury to the head/neck and chest/abdominal areas. 15% of survivors have permanent disabilities. The study did not provide clear data on what types caused what injuries and appears to have included traditional "plastic bullets" in the data.[18]

If there is a rule of law, I highly advise *against* using these items against people. These guns are still firearms and they are still potentially deadly. Killing someone, although you intended not to, can still be construed as murder or manslaughter as these are real firearms and capable of causing death with lethal or less-lethal ammo.

Do not attempt to use less-lethal projectiles in non-SHTF scenarios or at the risk of your life. Because of the potential legal

---

[18] Haar RJ, Iacopino V, Ranadive N, et al Death, injury and disability from kinetic impact projectiles in crowd-control settings: a systematic review. *BMJ Open* 2017;7:e018154. doi: 10.1136/bmjopen-2017-018154

ramifications of using real firearms that could potentially kill someone, we recommend against non-WROL use of less-lethal projectiles. Let's be real here: these are for contingency uses and the perfect scenario is probably that of fiction. However, life has a way of showing us that the one-off situations tend to happen more than we expect.

## Arguments against less-lethal use

Using a firearm designed to fire lethal ammunition, but repurposed for less-lethal rounds, is still using a firearm against someone, the same as if you fired a lethal shot. If the person isn't killed or seriously hurt, great, but if they are, you've potentially committed from manslaughter to murder. Courts may not differentiate a lethal gun firing less-lethal shot from a lethal gun, even though they might give police the benefit of the doubt.

Police get the benefit of the doubt because they are empowered to keep the peace. The law gives officers the legal ability to compel people to do things, prevent them from doing other things, and allows officers to use force to do so. Typically, civilians do not have that power. You can only arrest someone, use force sufficient to prevent the offense, or use lethal force against threatened death or serious injury.

As with the previous reason, using potentially lethal force against someone to stop behavior that might be technically legal (such as walking down your street, even as part of an unruly protest), is not within the average citizen's right. This argument goes out the window when there is no police and it's kill or be killed, however, it's still worth considering for the non-WROL world.

The prior paragraphs are legal and moral in nature. More practically speaking, do you have lethal cover able to protect you if your less-lethal round is not effective? Less-lethal rounds do not necessarily incapacitate even if you get a solid hit; heck even lethal rounds don't always immediately do that. You are relying on creating enough pain and fear that the target gives up. Only lethal ammunition can ensure that the target cannot continue his attack or use a weapon against you.

Again, if you want to use less-lethal ammo to be "nice" or to serve as a warning because you don't have the wherewithal to kill someone when justified (either legally or WROL morally), you have no business being a defender. Less-lethal ammo is a way to try and avoid complications that might come from killing someone, not as a substitute for shooting those who need to be shot.

## Arguments for less-lethal use

### Where are you going to stack all the bodies?

If you shoot indiscriminately into a large crowd, there is a high probability that multiple people will be shot, even killed. The potential body count only increases if you mag dump into the mass or if more than one shooter is firing. In a panic situation, it's not improbable to have half a dozen guys fire off thirty rounds each. The amount of dead could be staggering and that number will only get higher with no medical care as the wounded lie incapacitated and bleed out.

With no functioning police, the coroner is not responding to take away the body of a bad guy you shot. Calling a funeral home probably isn't going to be an option. This is not a prepper/survivalist fiction book where the bodies magically go away after the turn of a page. Disposing of one body is bad enough, now how about a few of them or even a dozen?

You will need to physically lift the body into a truck bed, wheelbarrow, or something, then move them to a proper disposal location. A place where you can bury a body or at least leave it is not going to be close or convenient. Chances are, you will need to go some place so remote that no one is going to notice a body rotting in the sun or care about the smell. If you bury it, that will involve a lot of digging.

All of this will need to be done considering your own security. Your home perimeter will need to be manned. Your disposal detail will have to provide its own security. All of this has to be considered in the context that you were just attacked by hostile forces, killed some of them, and you are now sending some of your armed men outside the wire. The friends and family of the people you just killed may want revenge. During a heightened period of risk, your security forces will be distracted and diminished with handling the burial.

The friends/relatives of the dead may come to collect the bodies from you, but again this presents risk. Now people with a motivation to inflict vengeance on you are just outside the gates witnessing the carnage first hand. Things will be emotional and could get out of hand. America is not guaranteed to be like Iraq where Iraqi women came out to dutifully collect the dead, taking their jihadi loved one's death with the fatalism we saw there.

So before you assume that every violent situation post-SHTF will involve just shooting the bad guys, think about what you are going to do with the bodies. A less-lethal option may put a crowd on the run instead of giving you a dead body problem.

### Scenarios

Scenario 1: An aggressive, starving man is outside your house demanding food. He is unarmed and pretty helpless, but he refuses to leave. If anyone goes outside, he gets in their face and grabs at them.

Option 1: wait until he gives up and hope he doesn't come back.

Option 2: kill him. Figure out how to dispose of the body and hope no friends or family come back to avenge him.

Option 3: use a less-lethal or non-lethal weapon to incentivize him to leave.

Scenario 2: An angry mob of hundreds of people are outside the gate to your complex demanding food. They are trying to climb over and tear down the gates.

Option 1: shoot into the crowd indiscriminately until they are all dead or fleeing.

Option 2: shoot the climbers or people working on breaking the gate, hoping you don't kill the less-active participants or that an armed person in the crowd doesn't shoot at you.

Option 3: wait until the gate is broken down and they are swarming to exercise option 1.

In this case, you may want to try to use less-lethal force to disperse the crowd because of the ramifications outright gunfire might cause.

Problem 1: you have multiple or dozens of dead bodies rotting outside your gate to dispose of.

Problem 2: the crowd also decides to use indiscriminate lethal force or they come back later to kill you this time.

Problem 3: killing members of the crowd would alienate you badly within your complex and neighborhood, potentially at the risk of being able to safely survive.

Scenario 3: A mentally disturbed man is harassing, threatening, and shoving children. He pulls a gun out.

Option 1: You hit him with a less-lethal and he drops the gun. Then what do you do?

Option 2: The less-lethal round misses or is ineffective and he shoots you or someone else.

Option 3: The less-lethal round is effective, he drops his gun, and runs away but comes back the next day delusional that he is invincible now.

In each case, you are taking a chance that things don't escalate. In the first option, he might get violent or return the next day with friends who could overwhelm you. If you kill him, that might turn your friends, family, or neighbors against you. His loved ones might come for you as a result. Or you could want to avoid killing him because it is immoral without him becoming an immediate threat.

Less-lethal *can* preserve your other options. Handcuffing a bad guy and transporting him to a lockup isn't going to happen and dumping him off in the middle of nowhere is impractical. A face full of pepper spray or a bean bag in the stomach is the equivalent to kicking someone's butt to deliver a message. Of course, in this case you imply that if he comes around again being aggressive or causing you problems, next time you will kill him.

The use of lethal cover *cannot* be ignored as Example 3 illustrates. Less-lethal rounds don't work and are a heck of a lot more psychologically effective if the subject thinks he is being fatally shot or that the next thing that hits him will be lead. A lethal threat needs to be met with lethal force; if for some reason you are going to use less-lethal force against lethal force, have someone with a real gun ready to shoot.

# Post-SHTF 12ga Less-Lethal Shotgun Usage

## Less-lethal impact munitions

Impact munitions (less-lethal ones) can be thought of remotely delivering a staggering blow to a person using a firearm or launcher. These projectiles are intended to cause pain through blunt force trauma to elicit compliance. Injuries typically include bruises, welts, and lacerations. Of these, the most common injuries are bruising and abrasions, though they may be severe, followed by lacerations. Penetration is uncommon.

Less-lethal is the preferred term (over "non-lethal" and "less-than-lethal") because these weapons can cause death in extreme cases.[19] Some rounds may penetrate the skin, hit vital areas, and can cause serious injuries. They can penetrate clothing and damage commonly carried objects. Headshots that don't penetrate can still cause concussions and traumatic brain injuries (TBIs).

One legal note; usage of less-lethal impact munitions in ordinary times is *not* recommended for civilian use. Using a firearm, even if it has an orange stock and is pumping out bean bags, is still a firearm. The projectile is less-lethal, not non-lethal, and firearms are still firearms capable of inflicting death and firing lethal ammunition.

Usage these days could be construed as assault with a deadly weapon to murder in the off-chance someone is killed. The items discussed here are generally only for post-SHTF employment. All the factors used when firing a lethal shot are involved when firing a less-lethal one, from trigger discipline to legal justification.

---

[19] I personally saw a man, high on meth, shot with a bean bag round die from excited delirium. He was already in an excited state as he refused commands while attempting to hack through a windshield with a metal traffic barricade. This kind of death is not uncommon among drug addicts and is not limited to any one particular less-lethal weapon.

A variety of less-lethal impact munitions are available for use. This includes:

- Rubber or plastic bullets loaded into standard firearm cartridges (usually with low powder charges);
- 37/40mm foam and rubber baton rounds;
- Specialty rounds for "Can Cannon" launchers (not intended for defensive use); and,
- 12 gauge bean bags, rubber slugs, and other plastic projectiles including rubber or plastic shot.

## 37/40mm

37mm flare launchers resemble the slightly larger 40mm M203 grenade launcher (which is why California and other states ban them; they look scary). These launchers are not capable of firing grenades. Instead, they fire large marine flares or other ammunition. Two common types of cartridge are pyrotechnic rounds under various names that are essentially a firework or a flashbang. Smoke rockets are also available. None of these are intended to hit people.

37/40mm impact rounds and projectiles are not illegal, however, manufacturers and retailers typically only sell such products to law enforcement. Empty shells are often sold freely to civilian launcher owners to build or reload their own cartridges. Attempting to create one's own less-lethal projectile for these (or any) weapons should be left to owners who are experienced reloaders in dire end-of-the-world emergencies only. Anti-personnel usage requires a formally NFA registered Destructive Device.

37/40mm launchers should only be used in defensive roles by trained and experienced owners. Training rounds (chalk rounds) should not be employed against persons. True NFA regulated 40mm grenade launcher owners may be able to more easily purchase controlled specialty ammo. Such owners should take additional training or seek a qualified law enforcement/military user to employ these rounds in a tactical situation.

I do not recommend 37/40mm launchers to average citizens without extensive firearms knowledge and experience. Common 37mm launcher rounds that would be useful *and* easily available are distraction pyrotechnic rounds that can deliver flashbang effects into a crowd from a safe standoff distance.

Usage of surplus plastic bullet ammunition is not recommended. "Rubber bullets" have a negative connotation and these cartridges are intended for usage in training, not as anti-personnel weapons. The velocity of these bullets can cause serious injury or death. Usage of a regular, unmodified firearm firing at people, even with plastic bullets, may cause confusion as to what is going on, potentially creating a more dangerous situation than before.

## 12 gauge less-lethal shotguns and shells

For the average citizen defender, 12 gauge shotguns and less-lethal shells will be the most common impact munitions available. Construction is usually of a durable, yet sturdy material such as rubber, plastics (Zytel or Nylon), or Kevlar and lead bean bags.

There is a wide variety of shells available, including non-impact distraction type shells, as well as the legion of individual shotgun models that can be adapted for a less-lethal mission. Shotguns are near the top end of the less-lethal distance spectrum (versus Tasers and OC/pepper spray) with a maximum range of about 40 yards, depending on ammunition type.

Weapons specially designated for less-lethal employment should be equipped with bright orange furniture to provide a visual signal to both user and potential targets that the weapon is not being employed as a lethal weapon. Note that less-lethal shotguns have no permanent modifications to prevent loading of lethal ammo, so color and ammo segregation is important.

LAPD uses unique green (almost teal) stocks for its less-lethal shotguns; however, orange shotgun furniture is more common. Orange is also universally recognized as a warning color and more easily understood as a less-lethal platform than other colors. Green in particular can be confused for "zombie green" that was a fad in years past, a custom paintjob, or even a toy gun. Note the barrels remain unpainted in black as they are still potentially lethal and legally firearms.

## Weapon choice

Note that most less-lethal 12 gauge rounds do not create enough velocity to reliably cycle semi-automatic shotguns. Less-lethal shells should not be used in semi-autos and preferably only in pump action shotguns.

I am familiar with 14" smoothbore barrel Remington 870s equipped with a sidesaddle. The length was adequate from what I could tell and handy in tight quarters. Ultimately, I think the decision to go with this length had more to do with the fact it fit easily in the Crown Victoria trunk rack more than anything else.

LAPD uses Remington 870s with rifled barrels (18 ½" long & 1-35" twist) firing CTS Model LAPD 2588, also known as the "Super-Sock" bean bag. This is a cloth tail stabilized bean bag round. These are firearms dedicated to a single ammunition type; do not attempt to use other ammunition types (shot or slugs) in rifled barrels unless the ammo manufacturer specifically approves rifled barrels. It is worth noting that bean bags can be used in smoothbore barrels or even with paradox rifling.

Longer barrels are most optimal for proper projectile and shell separation as well as accuracy. Effective deployment on-target may be dependent on velocity and rifling-imparted spin depending on the exact product used. Barrel length does seem to dramatically affect accuracy at ranges of 10-50 feet. Even 10" barrels will perform adequately at under 50 feet, but 18" have been shown to be the most accurate at all ranges and up to 80 feet. 14" may be an optimal compromise up to 50 feet, after which its performance falls off substantially.[20]

18" seems to be fairly standard but short-barreled shotguns (SBS) are also common within law enforcement. The National Firearms Act (NFA) complicates citizen procurement of SBSs. Mossberg Shockwave type weapons (essentially a 14" shoulder stock-less shotgun) can be used and equipped with standard Mossberg accessories (legality may change depending on what you put on). As of this writing, Shockwave type weapons *are not* NFA regulated and legal in many states.

Ordinary shotguns can be repurposed to less-lethal duties. This would typically involve replacing the furniture with orange furniture or using labels, stenciling, and orange tape to indicate the weapon is to be employed as a less-lethal weapon. Smoothbore single and double barrel break-open shotguns can also be cheaply repurposed to less-lethal. If at all possible, lethal and non-lethal ammunition should not be mixed or used in the same weapon. Less-lethal shells should only be used in less-lethal only shotguns and vise versa.

## Ammunition characteristics

Less-lethal shotgun ammunition comes in three main forms: rubber or plastic slugs, bean bags, or rubber/plastic shot (or pellets). Some variations exist, such as single or double balls or plastic "stars" that resemble a child's squishy Koosh ball. Accuracy in decreasing order is rubber/plastic slugs > bean bags > rubber/plastic shot.

Some manufacturers make shells that are intended specifically for use against animals (bears) that are not suitable for use on humans. Civilian marketed ammo is typically intended for wildlife control and not for anti-personnel use. Ammunition for this purpose

---

[20] Charlie Mesloh et al., "Modular 12 Gauge Shotgun Beanbag Accuracy Study," *Journal of Testing and Evaluation*, Vol. 36, No. 5, 2008.

may have higher velocities to give extra engagement distance and provide more terminal force on thick hides. No one wants to get close to a bear. These differences in "formulation" may prove lethal or extra injurious to a human.

**Note:** if employing less-lethal ammunition in a shotgun, do *not* attempt to mix less-lethal and lethal rounds in the same weapon. Keep the two separate and not even on the same person. Shotgun proponents tout their versatility but mixing less-lethal shells with buckshot or slugs is a recipe for a tragic, fatal mistake.

Minimum recommended engagement range is 10 feet, though they can be fired at 5 feet to 45 yards (or more, if the particular shell has the range). Optimal ranges for a balance of safety and terminal effectiveness is 7-25 yards. There is no minimum distance, though very close distances may produce more serious injuries or risk a greater chance of death.

A majority of less-lethal engagements take place at vary close range, often within 7 yards (during police engagements). Multiple rounds may need to be fired to be effective, as the projectiles may not impact properly or the target may be pain tolerant. Most engagements are resolved with less than three shots fired and a little less than half require just one shot.[21]

Effectiveness of the munition will depend on more than just the type of projectile used. If the target is wearing thick clothing, padding, or body armor the impact will be absorbed by those items. Fit, muscular persons and fat, flabby people will react differently than an average person. Someone who is under the influence may not react as desired. On the other hand, the psychological effect of being "shot" may do wonders to someone who isn't prepared for a less-lethal hit.

### Bean bags

---

[21] Chris Sciba, San Jose Police Department, "Projectile Impact Weapons," (undated).

Bean bags are so named because they are a ballistic fiber pouch filled with pellets of (usually) lead. This is the most common 12 gauge less-lethal round used by American law enforcement. Bean bags generally won't break vehicle windows that have been tinted or windshields, although they may break standard building glass without special laminating films.

Bean bags come in square "pads" or "sock" versions. Most projectiles now are in "sock" configuration and will appear as a round, bulbous tear-drop shape. They may or may not be drag stabilized with a tail of material behind them. Modern "sock" designs do not require a minimum distance to unfold or stabilize.

With traditional bean bags (square or rectangular "flat" profiles) or "pads," these are coiled into cylinders to fit the shotgun shell. They then are supposed to expand to a bag shape in flight. Yaw in flight is responsible for their profile on impacting the target, meaning that they can fail to hit with the proper square profile for optimal affect. A narrower profile can also increase the chance of penetration, serious injury, and death.

Studies have shown that rifled barrels provided nearly 100% proper deployment of the bag. Smoothbore barrels only had about 20% effectiveness. The centrifugal force spin imparted by the rifling is responsible for the bag opening properly. Accuracy at 40 feet was approximately 7" inch groups.[22] Another test found 3.8" drop and a spread of 5.5" inches.[23]

Manufacturer instructions and warnings should be closely adhered to. Note that many manufacturers of civilian marketed less-lethal shells are often smaller shops that *may* not have the reliability of large ammo makers or law enforcement oriented manufacturers. Do not mix various types of less-lethal ammunition in

---

[22] LAPD study data from: Doreen Hudson, "A Flexible and Effective Beanbag Platform," LAPD, undated PowerPoint presentation, https://aele.org/lapd-beanbag.pdf.
[23] Ibid. Mesloh.

a shotgun (or lethal shells either).

## Slugs and single hard projectiles

Rubber or plastic slugs are typically in an exaggerated rocket ship shape with a fat front end and a molded tailfin section. Some of these projectiles can have a cavity containing a chemical irritant but civilian rounds most commonly are solid, intended for pain compliance. Cavity rounds are typically not sold to the general public.

Rubber or plastic rounds (slugs or shot) are often made from rubber, PVC, or other plastics. Hardness may vary. Low temperatures can cause the rubber or plastic material to harden. Fiocchi hourglass shaped rubber baton rounds have been reported to work well at below freezing temperatures without causing significant injuries to bears.[24]

Rubber slugs tend to deliver the most terminal energy to targets due to their weight and construction. Such solid rubber or plastic rounds are typically designed not to deform on impact. These stand a greater chance of penetration than other projectile types but will give the most range. Large rubber balls, often singly or doubly loaded into shells, have a more aerodynamic shape than slugs and retain velocity better than other types of projectiles.

Star shaped rounds are low mass and impact at high velocity. Upon impact, the material compresses and transfers its energy into the target. One manufacturer advertises that it imparts its available energy across a larger surface area than other projectile types. They claim that the star causes less injury that other types.[25]

Anti-personnel use depends greatly on the design of the projectile and the manufacturers recommendations. Some rounds intended for animal usage may be too powerful for use against

---

[24] Polar Bear Deterrent - Training Manual, Instructor Guidelines, Module 4, US Fish and Wildlife Service, undated.
[25] Lightfield Ammunition product advertisements.

humans. Rubber slugs are more likely than bean bags to cause serious injuries or death.

### Rubber/plastic shot

Rubber shot can be employed as lead buckshot would be (preferably aimed away from the face and other vital areas) or fired at the pavement or another surface to skip the pellets into the target's legs. Skipping pellets at the lower body off the ground is generally the way to use it. Shot can be also used against groups as the individual projectiles will disperse in flight. Due to its dispersal characteristics, use against crowds or closely clustered individuals is an ideal usage.

When used against a human, the spread of the projectiles is used to provide more pain over a wider area than a bean bag or slug. However, the impact area size is dependent on the spread of the shot in flight, which is less at close distance and larger at long distance. And while the area that hurts may be larger in size, the overall pain and any associated "stunning" effect may be less due to lesser terminal velocity delivered as a function of the shot's lower mass.

Anecdotal reports show that less-lethal shot exhibits extreme spread, perhaps up to several feet. At close range, the spread seems to be enough to cause many hits to a torso sized target. Rubber shot should be patterned on a paper target from the intended shotgun prior to contingency usage.

### Rock salt and bird shot

Rock salt has a very low mass, so the muzzle velocity will be high, but it will also loose velocity quickly and have little to impart to the target. Videos of firing shows that it often creates a large white cloud. Effective range is believed to be 20-50 feet. Firing at closer ranges may cause serious injury.

Rock salt at close distance will typically penetrate ordinary clothing. Penetration into flesh is likely to occur. Tests have found ¼ inch penetration into ballistic gel of large crystals *after* going through clothing and up to 1 and ½ inches in bare gelatin.[26] Anecdotal reports indicate that skin typically stops any deep penetration of crystals into subcutaneous tissue.

Close employment (room distance) will cause more serious injuries. Rock salt also comes with more risk that chunks will hit the eyes or other sensitive body part, causing serious injury.

Birdshot should never be used as less-lethal ammunition because it can be quite lethal at near ranges. Should it be employed without an intent to kill, it must only be done as a last resort when there is no rule of law *and* circumstances dictate that if death were to occur, it would be morally and tactically justifiable. Employment of birdshot in such a role will not be discussed here.

### Skip shooting

Skip shooting is also known as the ricochet effect where a projectile strikes a flat surface at an angle and then is redirected to travel parallel to that surface. This technique is used to shoot around or under cover; for instance, around a corner (without fully exposing oneself) or under cover (such as beneath a car) at a partially concealed target.

This is most often taught in the context of being able to see a suspect's legs and feet beneath a vehicle but being unable to shoot them in the torso as they've taken cover behind the wheels and/or engine block. Buckshot (or even bullets) are skipped off the pavement into the exposed body part. This is why trainers teach students not to hug cover.

---

[26] "Seasonings Greeting: Testing Rock Salt Shotgun Shells," https://www.ammoman.com/blog/rock-salt-shotgun-shells/

Bullets and lead shot, when shot at a shallow angle to a hard surface such as asphalt and concrete, will ricochet and fly parallel to that surface at about 6-12" inches. This is because they are not elastic and their original inertia that was perpendicular to the surface is lost and translated into a parallel direction.

Rubber and plastic projectiles will not behave the same way. They are malleable and have much more potential to rebound at odd angles. Skip shooting is notoriously inaccurate and has resulted in some notable adverse media coverage regarding injuries sustained during riots and demonstrations. Even with adequate professional training and practice, these rounds are not a sure shot against individuals and best employed by amateurs on area targets.

Typically designed "skip" rounds are for 37mm and 40mm launchers.[27] 12 gauge ammunition, in this case Defense Technology 12 gauge rounds, can be employed in direct or skip fire.[28] Specifically, it "is intended to be direct or skip-fired at the discretion of the operator, but it is necessary to keep the trajectory low so the projectile spread will not engage the subject above the breast line." Note both methods of targeting are permitted by the manufacturer.

Bouncing rubber buckshot off the pavement, lest you are guaranteed to kill someone, seems to be fuddlore. Idiots on YouTube shooting each other with rubber buckshot is hardly scientific, but direct shots do not seem to produce much more than large contusions that produce a round divot that does not penetrate subcutaneously. Fatal and serious injuries using modern shotgun rubber buckshot are not certain and would be outlier events.

Rubber/plastic slugs have more energy, and thus are more likely to cause more serious injuries, but they come in a wide variety, some of which also do not create serious wounds. Please note that

---

[27] Such as the Defense Technologies 40mm Stinger™ 60-caliber rubber ball round.
[28] Defense Technologies 12-gauge stinger® 32 caliber rubber ball round data sheet.

law enforcement, and official trainers, want to avoid serious or chance fatal injuries (and liability) so they will teach or require the most conservative use. This is not to disparage those who recommend skipping rounds, but in a post-SHTF situation you are not going to have the liability concerns that a trainer or agency has.

### Warning shots

Fire less-lethal rounds as warning shots to avoid the danger of a live, high-power bullet potentially injuring someone. If you want to warn them, the sound of a less-lethal shot and the thumping punch of the round's impact on their body is a great deterrent.

Actual bullets can travel for a mile or two and kill people you can't even see. Rounds fired at the ground could also be deflected into an innocent person. And it's kinda paradoxical to say, "I didn't want to kill him so I fired a lethal round in his general direction."

Less-lethal rounds can also be used to dissuade people who may be testing you. Shooting a person breaching your perimeter with a less-lethal round gives you the opportunity to see how determined he is. If he persists or escalates and draws a weapon yourself, you know you can shoot him without remorse, or he turns and runs, knowing you are serious enough to use force.

# Deployment of Less-Lethal

## When to use less-lethal and when to use lethal force

Only use less-lethal methods before or in lieu of lethal methods when there are:
- Adequate defenders to provide lethal cover and defeat the threat;
- The benefit of less-lethal usage is greater than lethal usage;
- The risk of ineffective deployment is not immediately life threatening;

- There is time to use the less-lethal option; and,
- You are able and willing to use lethal force if less-lethal force fails.

Less-lethal munitions will not stop a threat quickly and surely enough as lethal rounds will. So when it counts, use lead. Bad guys might also mistake using less-lethal rounds as a weakness; that you are unwilling or hesitant to use lethal force.

### Violent crowd control

- Single projectiles (slugs, bean bags) against individual point targets, i.e. a specific person who poses a threat, like an instigator.
- Rubber/plastic shot against the crowd itself or multiple individuals closely clustered together.
- Any projectile can be used indiscriminately in final protective fire (or FPF—shoot everything) to prevent being overrun or in an extreme contingency.

### Non-immediate threats

- A deranged person or someone who is holding a weapon at the ready (slung/holstered gun, a sharp object far away) that needs to be disarmed and kinetically dissuaded but shooting them is not preferable.
- An unarmed (or possibly armed) trespasser who refuses to leave.
- An aggressor who continues to approach.
- Someone who is trying to get through/around defenses.
- As a humane warning shot to a desperate person before lethal force is used.

## Procedures

The less-lethal bearer should not have a lethal firearm at the ready; lethal weapons need to be holstered or slung out of the way. He should not be trying to juggle an AR-15 and a less-lethal shotgun. If at all possible, the less-lethal bearer should *not* also be armed with a lethal shotgun, nor should he have any lethal shotgun shells on his person, to avoid mix-ups.

"Less-lethal ready/up!" is the announcement the less-lethal

bearer is in position and ready to fire.

"Less-lethal, standby!" is the incident commander or primary team member delegating the authority to fire. It also serves as a warning to those around that a less-lethal weapon will be fired.

"Less-lethal out," should be yelled and/or radioed after the shot or string of shots so distant team members know what happened.

Other variations can be used as long as they are clear and unambiguous. Additionally, the type of less-lethal ammunition can be substituted for specificity, i.e. "bean bag." Note that circumstances may necessitate immediate deployment based on the less-lethal bearer's observations of the situation. Good communication should be maintained with the details for the need of the weapon going out so that upon hearing a gunshot, distant team members don't mistake it for an incoming shot.

- Ensure lethal cover is present and ready in case lethal force is needed.
- Take into consideration the clothing, equipment, and build of the target, as well as their position, their actions, and any persons in close proximity to them.
- Utilize cover and concealment as you would engaging with a lethal weapon.
- Maintain a minimum stand-off distance from the target and any other hostiles to prevent the barrel from being grabbed. Minimum recommended engagement range is 10 feet.
- Each shot should be assessed individually as to its effectiveness. This may be a split second judgement based on what is observed through the sight picture.
- Psychological effectiveness of the projectile may be heightened by simultaneous use of pyrotechnics or distraction devices.
- Expended projectiles and empty shells should be collected.
- As these are low power rounds, there is a non-zero chance of projectiles becoming lodged in the barrel after multiple shots. Barrels should be inspected and cleaned as part of the after-action process.
- Do not attempt to reload and reuse expended projectiles.

**Aimpoint:** lower center of torso (belly) or more specifically the belt line to the navel.

Aim for large muscle groups, abdomen and below. Arms and legs should be avoided when in proximity to vital areas. The preferred dorsal target area is the legs (away from the lower spine).

**Avoid:** head, neck, sternum (upper chest), spine, kidneys, and genitals. When firing at the target from behind, do not aim for the center of the back due to the risk of spinal cord damage. Firing at bare skin should be avoided when possible.

**Do not** fire at pregnant women, young women, or the elderly if at all possible.

**Do not** fire at a target who may fall from height or into dangerous areas.

Minimum safe range: 5 feet
Minimum recommended range: 10 feet
Optimal minimum range: 21 feet
Maximum recommended range: 50 feet
Optimal engagement distances: 7-25 yards
Average maximum range: 40 yards

- Self-defense and justifiable homicide laws should be obeyed as much as possible.
- Force should be proportionate to the threat and used sparingly as a last resort.
- Aimed weapons should be used directly against specific persons who are engaged in actions that pose an immediate threat of death or serious injury.
  - In WROL, this could be expanded to agitators and serious property damage. In this case, the danger posed may be more theoretical than immediate.
- Less-lethal rounds can be used judiciously to discourage certain individuals from crossing barricades or engaging in actions that may escalate the risk of death or injury.

- Firearms used indiscriminately should only be used against crowds as a last resort to disperse mobs, stop rushes, or against concentrations of rioters who are presenting the greatest threat.
- Do not put yourself or other "good guys" at undue risk trying to employ less-lethal rounds.

## Conclusion

Now in ordinary life you're probably never going to use less-lethal ammunition against a human. I would recommend against it, actually. If you're going to shoot them, make sure you can legally use lethal force and preferably use lead to make sure the threat is stopped. If you aren't going to shoot them, it's easier and less legally risky to punch them, shoot them with a Taser, or give them a face full of OC spray. But then again, the Second Amendment was written for those outside contingencies.

**Disclaimer:** I am not an attorney nor an expert. This should not be taken as legal or expert advice. Get specialized training before using less-lethal ammunition and any action taken is at your own risk. You probably shouldn't be using this kind of ammo against humans unless the world has really ended.

# Vehicular Gunfighting

So you were unable to evade in the vehicle or use it as a weapon against the bad guy. You're caught in the kill zone and it's time to fight from the car. This is the least advantageous situation to be in but also a highly probable scenario considering how much time we spend in our cars. I can't overemphasize how beneficial it would be to watch videos of vehicle-related shootings and training videos. Without being able to shoot up a car in practice, this is a great way to start visualizing responses.

Some preliminaries: if you're being physically attacked in your vehicle by someone outside, before resorting to shooting, try driving away. Or roll up the window or smack them with the door. One time someone who shall remain unidentified once knocked a suspect on a bike off by slamming him with an open door.

Fighting in and around a car is a bad idea. Situational awareness should be primary so that things never progress to the gun stage on either side. Never put yourself in a position where the fight begins when a criminal or carjacker raises a gun at your side window. **Your best defense in a gunfight once things have gone sideways in or near a vehicle is to drive away or use the vehicle itself as a weapon.** From there you can assess and fight from a more advantageous position or flee.

Failing that, Option 2 is to duck and get low. For an attack from the side where the shooter is at a distance, make yourself as small as possible behind the B pillar. From there you can assess and fight or flee. This isn't such a good idea if the shooter is much closer, like outside the window, or shooting from another position. Ducking and not fighting allows the attacker to have the advantage of suppressing you while he can adjust his aim or advance on the vehicle for a kill shot.

## Before the danger
Always keep your the pistol in a holster. In the infamous 1986

Miami FBI shootout, FBI Special Agent John Hanlon lost his primary weapon after a collision. He sat it on the seat and the sudden change in velocity caused the gun to slide off the seat and out of reach. Sadly, he and Special Agent Grogan lost their lives. Having your gun on your body so you have it in the same place you would expect it if you fight on foot. This helps you with muscle memory and allows you to retain the gun after a crash or if you have to get out.

Do not stick the gun between the seats or in a cupholder; it is not secure. Open carry holsters (outside the waistband) are best for in-vehicle use. Vehicle mounted holsters are not preferred because if for some reason you must fight outside the vehicle or bailout, you will have to remember to grab the gun, rather than just go and have the holstered gun already attached to you.

Rifles and long guns should be wedged between the seat and the center console on the inner side of the vehicle. This provides security for the weapon (it's not gonna slide around like a pistol will) and doesn't hinder your egress out the door. Pistol racks in the back window are a bad idea because they advertise presence of weapons and may lead to guns being stolen from an unattended vehicle. Any firearms left in a vehicle need to be in a locked bracket or case secured to the vehicle itself.

Take your seatbelt off, preferably before trouble starts if crashing is not a major risk. A common cop tactic is to remove one's seat belt 30 seconds before arriving on scene. Always use your non-dominant hand to release the buckle and then sweep the belt back and away. When removing your seatbelt, grab it high over your shoulder with your non-firing (or driving) hand and slide the hand down the belt to the release. This way, you can always find the release no matter what orientation the buckle ends up in or what kind of crap you have on your belt.

However, wear your seatbelt! You're only taking it off when you think you're gonna have to bail out or move around. Seatbelts save lives and help keep chunks of your scalp (and hair) from being stuck in the windshield cracks. If you are wounded and have to drive away, a tight seatbelt will help keep your body vertical. A seatbelt extender is a great addition especially for open carry because you are not having to reach down between your butt, gun, and the console to find the release.

Starting with the fact that most people are right handed, the driver will need to practice shooting one-handed, especially with his left hand (to engage left-side targets while driving). A driver will probably be steering with his left hand on the wheel and right hand shooting at any targets in front of the vehicle. Off-hand and single hand shooting is more common in the real world than people believe. A passenger can shoot with both hands.

If gunfights are a real danger, try not to travel with your family. If you must, train them to get down (duck) without question. Equip them with body armor. Make sure your spouse or another able-bodied person can shoot back. Plan your trips to avoid times, places, and circumstances where you may be victimized.

## Drawing, presentation, and aiming inside the car

Draw your firearm from your holster, being sure to keep your finger off the trigger and the trigger guard free of obstructions. Keep the muzzle pointed forward until the gun is raised. Imagine a solid wall between you and the passenger seat. As you raise your firearm up and straighten your arm, do not break this imaginary wall so as to ensure your muzzle does not sweep a passenger. Use the same procedures in reverse to holster the gun. Take your time. Speedy re-holstering causes careless accidents.

When as the driver shooting out the driver's side window, be sure not to turn your body as you are turning the gun so that the muzzle sweeps your body. Sweep over the steering wheel in an arc to aid you in this and avoid having the pistol hang up on the wheel. If shooting to the front, do not sweep the passenger, who may be thrashing around in the front seat or trying to fight as well.

One thing police will do when in a vehicle and they are concerned about sudden violence is draw their weapon and hold it in their lap. *End of Watch* features an excellent example of this (It also features a great scene of dealing with an ambush at the end of a vehicle pursuit). While LAPD can get away with this a lot more easily than you and I can, technically speaking there is nothing illegal or provocative about this. The extra seconds may save your life. If you see a weapon in evidence and surmise hostile intent, do not wait for the bad guy to raise the weapon or fire. Kill them before they have a chance to kill you.

## Crashes and disabled drivers

If you stop hard and fast, the seatbelts will usually automatically tension; the same for impacts. In a crash, which is highly likely in a gunfight where you may be injured, distracted, or ducking, the airbag could deploy. The bags themselves do not remain inflated after they deploy but instantly deflate before you even know it. Deflated side-curtain airbags will interfere with side visibility and egress.

Airbags can produce friction and chemical burns, often to the forearms. The bags are packed in a dry chemical substance (sodium azide, potassium nitrate, and silica) that can cause irritation to your lungs and eyes. The "dust" itself could obstruct your vision. The violence of the impact itself and the airbag deploying will probably stun and disorient you.

Fuel pump shutoff sensors may also activate, killing the engine, and requiring a manual reset or replacement before you can start the car again. Be conscious of the fact that a collision may jam doors shut as the body panels crumple. Modern unibody designs are wonderful at transmitting the energy around the people inside the tin can while trashing parts of the car that weren't even directly impacted. Be prepared to exit through windows or other doors.

If the driver is shot and unable to drive, the passenger should attempt to drive the vehicle to safety. This may involve climbing over and sitting in the driver's lap or leaning over to work the pedals and steering wheel. Get to a safe location, move the driver, and get into the driver's seat or ditch the vehicle.

Drive the vehicle out of the target area. In traffic, always stop your vehicle so that you can see the tires of the car in front of you; this will give you enough room to turn out. If you are surrounded by a protest, drive through the crowd. Use unpredictable escape routes that may include driving on sidewalks, lawns, or sideswiping other cars.

## Exterior vehicular fighting

Odds are a gunfight around the vehicle will begin with you still in the vehicle. Preferably, you can just drive off and return suppressing fire from inside the car until you are safely away. Should it be necessary to fight outside, consider engaging the target before getting out of the vehicle. By this, I mean firing a few shots at a very close attacker. That puts him on the defensive, you might kill or wound him, and is a heck of a lot better than remaining a target yourself while you get out of the car. You should not overly delay your egress just to shoot back, however.

If you're gonna get out, put the vehicle in park and take off your seatbelt. I've had to chase down my moving unit before and it's a hilarious story about a parking violation, not a story about me being shot and/or run over. You also don't want to bailout with your seatbelt still on or partially wrapped around your arm. Take your rifle with you and a bail-out bag if you have one.

Keep fighting as you exit the vehicle. Move to actual cover if you can. Otherwise, move towards the rear of the vehicle to put the maximum amount of automobile between you and the bad guy. Take a knee and get low; shoot through the windows if you have to but don't stand up and expose yourself through the glass like a naked person in a hotel window who thinks they're invisible.

We've all seen the cop movies and news footage of officers taking cover behind their unit's open door. This creates an area called the "V" for its obvious shape. The door and vehicle body (if the car is angled properly) provides concealment and minimal cover. If you do this, attempt to angle any vehicle towards the threat when stopping to put most of the engine block between you and the threat. Your car is like an early 2000s Crown Victoria; no Kevlar panels in the doors.

Stay low, crouch, and do not fully stand up when fighting around a vehicle. Use the cover of the door and body as much as you can. The cover isn't great but bullets being stopped or deflected after striking random components give you a better chance. Don't crowd the door or hug body panels, but crouch back a foot or two to avoid fragments or redirected bullets.

Crouch down outside the vehicle. The best cover is going to be behind the engine block and the wheels. Keep in mind that these are smaller than they seem and your body will be exposed. The engine doesn't take up the whole compartment and many wheel designs have a lot of openings in them.

Do not stand with your torso or head exposed in the window glass of the passenger cabin because a bad guy can just shoot you through the glass. Avoid staring through the windows to watch what's going on as if were the windows at an aquarium; take brief glimpses instead. When moving around a vehicle for a shot, stay low and creep around corners. Slice the pie.

Shoot and observe from under the vehicle if you can. On the other hand, be aware of this danger. A hit in the feet or legs is still a hit that can lead to death through blood loss or allow you to shoot the target in the chest/head once they fall to the ground. In fact, this is how LAPD ended the North Hollywood bank shootout. Officer Donnie Anderson fired his AR-15 at robber Emil Mătăsăreanu from beneath his patrol car, although it took the suspect over an hour to die of blood loss from two shots in the thigh, of 29 total, gunshots to his legs.

Vehicles tend to draw a lot of suppressive fire because the targets often can't be seen or easily hit, so volume of fire is used in lieu of accurate shots or in an attempt to penetrate the car body.

With enough fire, if you sit still and with no one engaging the bad guy, a bullet will get you eventually. Remember that cars are small, the protective areas are actually tinier than they seem, and there is a lot of open space that surrounds the engine block.

Keep moving, keep looking, and keep fighting! Get away from the vehicle and move to better cover (i.e. a wall) if it is nearby. Don't just take cover behind the fender and wait for the bad guy to come around the car. If you do that, he probably will get the drop on you.

A shot-up vehicle may not be functional so moving away from the car lessens the chance of it being hit and disabled. These days, a hit in some random component may force the vehicle to shut off or go into limp mode, preventing you from returning to the vehicle to flee in it should the opportunity arise. A ruptured battery, punctured fuel tank, or blown fuel line may mean a fire. Burning cars can explode. Have a plan to fight, escape, and evade on foot.

### Hood/trunk

Bullets tend to skip or deflect off the flat body panels (or the ground) and travel parallel to that plane, especially the horizontal surfaces. Do not hug the body panels of the vehicle. Stay back a few feet. This will help protect you from rounds skipping over the hood or trunk, give you a better view, and offers the same protection if you are up close. Resist the urge to rest your arms and weapon on the hood. This will expose too much of your body.

Turn your rifle on the side to shoot over the hood. This is because there is a one to two inch offset between the barrel and the sight. You might be able to see the bad guy through your sights, but your muzzle could still be in line with the vehicle. Turning the rifle on the side puts the sight and the muzzle on the same vertical axis, eliminating the possibility of shooting the hood or decklid. This can also be done to get low and shoot underneath the vehicle without the magazine hitting the ground.

## Shooting from inside

If you have to shoot inside a car you may suffer irreversible hearing loss as gunshots are magnified by confined spaces. Be mentally prepared for tinnitus and eardrum pain. Family and passengers will probably start screaming. Reduce the trauma to your ears by rolling the windows down, at least two. The more shots you fire, the more likely you are to hurt your ears.

Gun gasses will be noticeable in the vehicle. Use quality ammunition that burns as efficiently as possible. Dust and dirt may be stirred up, depending on where you're shooting, what you're shooting, and how messy the interior is. Rolling the windows down may help reduce the reflection of the soundwaves and will also vent any gas or dust.

Draw an imaginary angle out the front window and do not engage any targets outside the passenger side window if someone is in the front passenger seat. No one wants a gun shot off in their face. If at all possible, have the passenger engage any right side threats. If possible, divide the forward area of responsibility into right and left. When in motion, the passenger may have to fire at threats ahead of the vehicle. Even when in motion, passengers should not attempt to shoot perpendicular past the driver's face or body.

Stay low in the vehicle whenever possible. Front occupants may want to try and put their body in position where the B-pillar provides some additional protection. Keep your legs and feet in the car whenever possible because exposing them could present a target to a bad guy or a ricochet may hit them.

When sitting properly with one's face away from the glass, shards and chunks of glass broken out by bullets should not injure the eye. Normal glasses and sunglasses should provide adequate protection in extremis. I've seen a lot of car accidents in my time and glass in the eye causing a serious eye injury is uncommon. Obviously full eye cup protection with ballistically rated lenses are preferred.

You probably will flinch when the glass breaks and pieces hit you in the face. This is a natural reflex. Glass will get everywhere when a car is shot up, but again, it will not be much of a hazard. Clean up will be necessary and you will want to check your clothing to make sure any glass has been removed from it.

## Shooting through a windshield

You can easily shoot through a windshield. Way back when, CHP had this stupid theory for its officers to stand in front of the A-pillar looking in at the driver because they assumed that no one would shoot out his own windshield. Bullets will hit targets with fair accuracy, depending on the shooter, when fired through a windshield. There will be some deflection, but at near distances, not enough to matter (more on this later).

The first round through a windshield will likely have the most trouble penetrating; this can be true of any shots that go through undamaged glass. Make your first shot a good one, well placed on the target without consideration to the deflection the glass may cause. Don't try to adjust your aim based on the bullet holes/impacts on the glass. Pick an aimpoint on the target, keep your aim steady, and fire at that spot. Your intent should be to saturate your target with bullets to get a hit. Even if your shots are less than square range accurate, they may provide a suppressing effect on the bad guy if he isn't expecting to be shot at.

Particularly with rifle, if you have the ammo, blow out a large enough area of glass to shoot through the resulting hole. Since you're so close it's going to be easy to make a hole in the glass large enough to keep shooting out of. Enlarge that hole. This is called "porting" and it typically takes three to four shots to make a hole large enough to shoot well out of.

Shoot out of the hole you made and each bullet will fly to the target true to your aim. Your muzzle will probably be only inches away so it won't be difficult, even under stress, to do this. Close up, this is your best bet to quick, accurate shots when precise accuracy matters. Within typical pistol distance, your shots, if well aimed in the first place, will not deflect enough to matter. Keep in mind that shooting holes in your windshield makes it weaker and a little easier for incoming bullets to hit you.

Don't just "aim low" when shooting through the windshield "because the first round will go high." The first shot (going out) will likely deflect high, but your subsequent shots, unless you are shooting through undamaged glass, will generally not behave the same way. Shots will behave randomly depending on this or that variable—did the bullet catch the edge of the glass? etc.—but will land within center of mass if that's where you're aiming.

## The effect windshield glass has on bullets

**Note:** Much of this is academic. Bullet deflection is a problem when precise shots are made a long range (minor deviations at the muzzle create large deviations hundreds of yards away), but at handgun distances, say a few yards, it does not practically matter. Don't worry about up/down, inside/out deflection as your own aim is more important on the bullet/glass interaction.

Copper jackets will separate from the lead in a bullet almost always when hitting glass. Jacket fragments may impact the target, passengers, or bystanders. Bullets may be deformed and have reduced performance on target, including keyholing. This is where contact with the glass causes the bullet to yaw in flight impacting the target sideways at lower velocity, producing a hole that looks like a keyhole.

Windshields are angled to deflect the wind. The degree of slope varies between vehicles. This slope affects bullets because when the bullet enters, it will make first contact either high or low. That is, the "top"[29] of the bullet will impact the windshield first going out, since the slope makes the high side closer to the "top" of the bullet. Going into a vehicle, the "bottom" of the bullet will make contact with the bottom of the glass first. This is what causes deflection.

---

[29] Top and bottom are relative because a bullet is spinning.

Shooting out from inside, the bullet will go high because of this effect. Conversely, when shooting into a vehicle through the windshield, the bullet will go down and strike low. This is why some trainers tell students "Aim low when shooting out and aim high when shooting in." In practical terms this doesn't matter. Unless you are a sniper or taking really long shots that *must* be precise through unbroken glass, you shouldn't concern yourself about this.

This doesn't apply to the nearly vertical side windows which are not as thick or tough as laminated windshield glass. Windshield glass is laminated and side/rear window glass is tempered. Windshield glass tends to hang together rather than breaking apart.

Rear window glass may be angled but shatters the easiest (due to escape/rescue reasons). Note that a lot of quality side glass won't immediately shatter into little pieces when shot but will tend to remain intact up to a point where the structural integrity of the pane is lost. Your mileage may vary.

Side window safety glass breaks into chunks instead of shards. These chunks are difficult to get cut with even on purpose. Windshields are the most resistant to damage and are more likely to spiderweb than shatter. Holes will form and bits will come off, but they almost never will shatter in your lap.

## Rifle

As said earlier, wedge your long gun between the seat and the center console while you're driving. Passengers can always just hold a rifle. Rifles will be hard to maneuver to the side in the front seat. When raising your rifle, bring the butt up and over your shoulder, keeping the muzzle pointed forward. If you are right handed and in the passenger seat, it may help to bring the butt over your left shoulder and transition to the right to avoid sweeping the driver.

When using a rifle, shoot a hole in the glass using the porting method mentioned above. Once you've created the hole, push the muzzle through so that the bullets' flight is not affected by the glass. This also gets the muzzle blast out of the vehicle. You will still be able to use your sights or optics through the glass if the spiderwebbing isn't too bad.

## Shooting at a moving vehicle

Don't shoot at a moving vehicle if you can at all help it. Shooting at a moving vehicle is a bad idea. It's even worse if you're in front of it. People driving vehicles who also need to be shot like to run over the people shooting at them. Potentially lethal "warning" shots fired at a vehicle should be first fired at the engine compartment, then at the driver. Please note that any shots fired at a vehicle may injure or kill innocent people in the vehicle and misses may strike bystanders.

You are not going to instantly disable and stop a moving vehicle. Even if the driver is killed instantly, the vehicle has inertia and will continue until it loses that energy. A vehicle traveling downhill, or if a disabled driver presses down on the gas, will ensure the vehicle keeps going. An out-of-control vehicle with a dead or wounded driver is a hazard to the defender and anyone else around. Innocent passengers and bystanders might also be wounded by misses.

Get out of the way. If you must shoot at a moving vehicle from the front quarter, do it from behind solid cover that can stop a vehicle like a section of K-rail. Only take shots at moving vehicles when there is no other reasonable means available to stop the vehicle and the threat it poses. You should also avoid shooting at parts of the vehicle, like wheels and tires, to try and disable it. Shooting at moving vehicles is rarely effective due to the combination of a moving target, the relative protection that a vehicle affords, and stress affecting aim.

Be aware that innocent people inside the vehicle can be killed or wounded when shooting into it. A partner at my station once shot into a vehicle that was dragging him and he unintentionally wounded the girlfriend in the passenger seat. The suspect who was trying to flee with a deputy attached to his car got charged with his girlfriend being shot because it was him that precipitated the shooting. Lesson to women: don't have felonious boyfriends who try to run from cops and your odds of being shot by one will go down dramatically.

### Disabling a vehicle

Vehicles can be stopped (or forced to turn around) in the following ways:

- Shooting the engine block: an effective shot will disable the engine and the vehicle will stop once it runs out of inertia.
- Killing the driver: the vehicle may not stop until it hits something or runs out of inertia.
- Hitting a vital component in the engine compartment: the vehicle may continue running until it catches on fire, overheats, or something fails that kills the engine.
- Shooting the tires: can keep driving on flats or the rims.
- Shooting at the vehicle generally: you're basically scaring the driver and relying on either his survival instinct or cowardice.

Most shot up vehicles stop because the driver wills it to out of fear, injury, or malfunction; not because bullets magically make it stop. As just discussed, don't stand in front a vehicle that wants to run you down, even if you have a machine gun. Get out of the way and behind solid cover that can stop a vehicle *and* bullets. Your AR-15 or pistol isn't gonna make that car stop on a dime no matter how good your aim.

Shooting at the tires is very difficult to do without a high volume of fire (like from a real machine gun), although it is effective. Shot tires will probably just leak air instead of immediately failing catastrophically. Note that when one tire is blown out, the vehicle will yaw in the direction of the failed tire, but it will still keep coming. Vehicles can drive for surprising distances on flat tires and rims, even more so when not all four tires are flat. Also consider if the vehicle has run-flat tires.

A .50 caliber rifle is ideal for stopping vehicles as it can penetrate engine blocks and major vehicle components including lightly armored vehicles. The problem is the weight of these weapons, many are single shot or bolt action, and they are typically intended for longer range shots with telescopic sights. You're not slinging a Barrett M82 from low-ready and sending 11 well-placed shots into the engine block.

If you must, the minimum caliber to shoot at and potentially disable a vehicle is 5.56mm M855 62gr Light Armor Piercing (LAP) rounds. The difference between hollow points and "ball" Full Metal Jacket (FMJ) rounds is negligible. If you have to shoot cars or think that will be an issue, use light armor piercing rounds like the M855 5.56mm round from the AR-15. Most bullets will penetrate car sheet metal but this will give you a little better performance.

7.62mm NATO M61 armor piercing is better but rarer. For an M1 Garand .30-06 M2 AP rounds are probably the best round that is easily accessible (for a price). This is the cartridge that is tested against NIJ Level IV body armor. Tracer ammunition and specialty incendiary or even high explosive ammunition can occasionally be sourced as well.

Plan to use a full magazine or even multiple magazines, fired by different shooters at different angles. With AR-15s, as most people will have, you will probably get lucky enough to shoot the battery, hit the alternator, or damage something like the fuel lines. Major repairs will be necessary. The vehicle might not be able to continue on that day. On the other hand, you may blow up the master brake cylinder and that vehicle is only stopping when Newton's Laws say so.

A high volume of fire needs to be directed into the engine compartment to destroy the radiator, damaged vital components in the engine compartment, and possibly damage the engine block. The larger the caliber, and preferably with armor piercing bullets, the better. If someone in your group has a semi-auto .30 caliber rifle, they should be tasked with anti-vehicle duties. If you can, have a rich person buy an actual machine gun.

## Shooting from a moving vehicle
Shooting from a moving vehicle is not ideal and firing on

another moving vehicle is another bad idea. The most you are really going to do is send back suppressive fire and *maybe* get a lucky shot that kills a bad guy or disables the vehicle. Remember that you don't have to apprehend these people. All you have to do is survive and make them go away. If you can do this by letting them get away, let them.

The odds of disabling a moving vehicle, particularly when shooting from behind it as in a pursuit, is much lower than any other angle because the bullet has to go through so much of the vehicle to disable a vital component. It is more likely that you will kill or critically wound the driver rather than hit something that will render the vehicle non-functional.

You will also rapidly deplete your ammo supply, which means you have to reload while driving—a two handed operation. Accidentally shooting yourself, a passenger, or something important like a radio in your car also becomes a serious problem. Return fire can be deadly. Remember you're fighting inside of something whose effectiveness of cover depends mostly on the random chance of a bullet striking something hard enough to stop it.

Should you absolutely need to return fire while in motion, don't stick the gun out the window if you can help it. If the gun is knocked out of your hand and it is outside the vehicle, it will be lost to you. You may not be able to recover it from the floorboard while moving but dropped in the car is better than dropped on the road.

Shots from a moving vehicle into a moving vehicle, all while the shooter is trying to drive, is a recipe for inaccuracy. The vehicle is moving, you are distracted, the other vehicle is moving, the road is uneven, etc. While the gunfire may have suppressive effects and might hit the intended vehicle or target area, the risk of stray shots injuring an innocent person goes way up.

If someone tries to ambush you that way, but instead of driving right alongside them to try and return fire, why not hit the brakes and let them go flying by? You can then evade or assume the tactical advantage. If you are doing the shooting out the door by choice, remember that the door offers you the least protection and endangers everyone else in the vehicle. Only idiots or people with no options participate in a running gun battle from car to car.

Collision, either by loss of control because hands are busy elsewhere or through distraction with the gunfight. Your primary duty when driving a vehicle is to drive it. Preferably have a passenger who can shoot for you. Remember that if you hit and disable a driver the vehicle is still going to continue until it runs out of inertia or it hits something.

### Stationary targets

Shooting drive-by style is stupid and dangerous. Sure, you might have to do sketchy offensive stuff in a dystopian future, but this is the suburban *defense* series, remember? Don't do it. Desperate suburbanites antagonized by domestic conflict and privation are likely to respond as inner-city gang members do and may retaliate in kind.

As far as training, I really don't have any advice. I remember a briefing in the mid-2000s when a sergeant made the point that some gangbangers in LA were training harder than we were. The video he showed us was of some cholos in the desert driving around a barrel while they took turns shooting at it while moving.

Travel at a low speed, five to ten miles per hour. Actually aim the gun and fire multiple shots. A good shooter should make several center of mass shots but all across the torso. You are aided by the fact that the target is initially (probably) not moving which makes tracking them as the vehicle moves easier. Remember that most ghetto drive-by shootings are by people who can't shoot, use a high volume of fire, and generally get lucky. After the first shot, if your target is smart, they will duck and try and run away.

One man should shoot out the driver's side (not the passenger side; don't shoot across the vehicle). In the two man version, the passenger can use both hands to shoot and has extra time to acquire the target and aim. The most accurate tactic is to stop, shoot, and then drive away but this will expose you to the most danger. Rapid deceleration will also create a whipsaw motion that will affect aim.

## Drive-by shooting characteristics

If America goes pear shaped criminal gangs, rival militias, or just disaffected people are going to try and kill others. A really easy way to do this is the drive-by shooting. In a more military context, it makes sense for a bunch of dudes in a pickup truck to mount a hit-and-run attack without even dismounting if they can help it. For this, we can look to gangland for some understanding of this kind of attack.

Drive-by shootings are popular among the criminal class because they permit an attack made with the element of surprise. The idea behind a drive-by shooting is to attack an enemy and escape before they can react. A vehicle allows a relatively stealthy approach as it blends in with traffic or the environment, only revealing the shooter at the last minute. A properly concealed vehicle shooter will not reveal himself until he is about to begin shooting, making detection of a drive-by unlikely. They are essentially mobile ambushes.

Drive-byes occur with little warning and subtle signs. Attacks are often unanticipated by the victims. One pre-attack characteristic that defenders should be prepared for is that suspect vehicles often do a dry run to recon the target prior to the shooting. They may return the same way after circling the block or make a U-turn to travel back in the opposite direction for their attack. If a vehicle heads back after driving by, go to code red.

Other attack features are:
- Vehicle approaches rapidly then stops suddenly.
- Doors open up while the vehicle is still moving.
- Someone with a gun is visible in the window or a gun pops out of an open window.

Targets must be in close proximity to a road, alley, or parking lot. Individual homes or groups of persons out in the open can be targets. Specific individuals outside and near the road can be stalked and killed as well. Favored "terrain" characteristics for attackers are unobstructed wide streets and easily traversable roads that permit quick escapes to main thoroughfares (arterial streets, highways, and freeways).

Effect on target depends on the skill of the shooter with firearms. Urban criminals typically use handguns because that's what they have available but in a SHTF situation rifles, carbines, submachine guns, and machine pistols can be expected. Non-criminal elements engaging in drive-by shootings will likely have greater firearms proficiency and access to better weapons.

### Defense

When pre-attack characteristics are noted, defenders need to resume an immediate danger posture and prepare to respond. Families and non-combatants need to take shelter. Defenders should already be standing behind solid cover, and if not, immediately move to bullet resistant fighting positions. As soon as hostile intent is confirmed, defenders should peremptorily engage the threat, not waiting until shots are fired. Concentrate and overwhelming amount of firepower in to the passenger compartment although careful shots should be taken at exposed attackers.

Sometimes the vehicle will stop and the attackers dismount to shoot with less hindrance. For a prepared defender, stopping the car and then getting out is one bad idea followed by another. This gives you better presented targets who are suddenly lacking the minimal protection of the vehicle. Shoot them before they can take cover behind the vehicle. Disable the driver and the vehicle so they can not flee.

Barricade strategies should be used. Traffic barriers that restricted avenues of escape were shown to reduce drive-by shootings and violent crime. LAPD used K-rail to close off intersections to major arterial streets creating artificial cul-de-sacs. This was done across the immediate neighborhood to create one vehicular access point. Traffic was channeled onto roadways that were not conducive to stopping, such as a continuous high volume traffic flow.

Removing visual obstructions to allow better visibility from homes, businesses, and for pedestrians denied anonymity of suspects by creating more opportunities for witnesses. It's unclear that without police that this strategy would be effective. In fact, without police, the fear of apprehension is non-existent. The only fear for those attackers who got away would be reprisal.

## Vehicle bullet resistance

Vehicles offer minimal ballistic protection and greater psychological protection in the event fire is returned. Remember that doors and body panels are not bulletproof. Don't bet your life on the hope that a bullet hits something inside the car and is deflected. Cars are actually surprisingly better cover than is commonly believed but a huge element of this is random chance. Even so, don't lock yourself into this mindset that you are going to die if someone shoots your car.

Bullets aren't going to automatically penetrate vehicles, but they can. There is a lot of stuff in vehicles behind panels, in doors, etc. that are enough to deflect or outright stop bullets. Some cover from a car is better than none, however, don't bet your life on it. You aren't going to automatically die taking shelter behind the trunk of a car. Not all the rounds will penetrate, but never count on being lucky.

Ballistic penetration of a vehicle isn't always effective at injuring/killing people inside or taking cover outside because of:
- Volume; there is more open area than there is space occupied by you.
- Solid components; bullets hit something they can't penetrate like a window motor.
- Energy depletion; the bullet doesn't have much velocity left once it flies through the windshield, the front and rear seats, the trunk floor, and the bumper.
- Deflection; bullets hit a solid component and are redirected away from you.

153

Anecdotal evidence shows that about half of the bullets fired at a vehicle will fully penetrate but the ones that do tend to still be lethal and can be deadly inside the car.

Obviously, the best protection a car can offer is behind metal wheels and the engine compartment. The roof pillars are also relatively bullet resistant, but due to their thinness, are kinda like trying to hide a fat man behind a lamppost. The curvature of the windshield and the A-pillar can be combined for additional protection from shots coming laterally across the vehicle's narrow axis.

# Avoiding Victimization In or Near Cars

## Vehicular self-defense basics

In *Suburban Defense*, we looked a lot at driving through crowds. Much of that chapter also covers basics like avoiding the area where trouble is. Here, we're focusing more on criminal situations like robberies and kidnapping attempts. A collapsed country will feature carjackings, robberies, and kidnappings on its highways. This is not something that you will be able to totally avoid as you might with a riot.

A breach of your vehicle is someone forcing their way inside for any reason, such as breaking a window or pulling the door open. In a future country where violent vehicular robberies and carjackings are the norm, shoot people trying to get into your vehicle. Your exact rules of engagement depend on factors like the political make up of you area, how the prosecutor views self-defense, and the effectiveness of police.

All self-defense laws apply until there is no rule of law. In most states, you cannot use lethal force to protect private property, which would include car theft, however if the thief has to take you *out* of the car this becomes a violent felony. You must be able to articulate why you thought you were in danger, such as "I was afraid that he would break the window out with the crowbar then crush my skull with it," etc.

Ordinarily, you should only shoot those who actually are a danger to you, such as someone with a crowbar breaking the window or someone trying to drag you out. In these situations, many states extend "castle doctrine" privileges to your vehicle. This allows you to defend your vehicle against a violent attack the same way as someone breaking into your home (i.e. riotously, tumultuously). Without the rule of law you would be within your rights to shoot someone who *threatens* to force their way in.

# Home

In third world countries like South Africa, many homes have fenced and gated courtyards that vehicles can pull into before entering the garage. Many attackers have hit drivers as their garage door came open to enter or exit. The most vulnerable time in these countries is waiting for the gate to open and close when going in and out. Criminals like to lie in wait where the view is obstructed by a wall or landscaping and ambush the driver.

As you get home, get rid of any distractions like turning off the radio. Check your mirror to see if anyone is following you. Start watching traffic and the surroundings as you go home. If you see suspicious circumstances, get help, don't just go home.

Be wary of unfamiliar vehicles following you through your neighborhood. If you are worried about what a vehicle is doing, pull over and let them go by. Watch them as they pass. You can do some "dry cleaning" and go around the block or make random turns to see if they follow. If you are being followed, don't go home.

Do not attempt to enter your driveway, gate, or garage if there is any suspicious traffic nearby that could follow you in or ambush you. In most residential neighborhoods, there is very rarely a lot of traffic so let any cars go by before turning in.

Scan the approach to your home before turning in. Wait to turn in and open the gate/garage if there are suspicious people walking by. If there is anyone hiding or loitering on your property, drive off. As with being followed, go to a police station or a secure location where friends, relatives, or fellow defenders can "scratch your back" and drive off the person following you.

Be vigilant during the entry/exit process as doors and gates open and close. Watch for people trying to get in the perimeter to assault you. This is turn your head and check all your mirrors time. Do not put the vehicle into Park as the doors may automatically unlock and it will be harder to get away. Keep your vehicle locked with the windows up until the gate and/or garage door is safely closed.

Keep the door from your garage to the house locked. An attacker may get your keys but with the door locked they *have* to have the keys instead of running straight in. Remove any vital necessities from your garage or lock them up in secure cabinets. You don't want someone grabbing your generator or survival food and loading it up. Place security cameras inside your garage and outdoors to cover any blind spots so you can check them remotely before going in or out.

If the gate or garage door suddenly malfunctions, it could be a trap. Scan the area and look for persons potentially hiding in ambush. If you have any suspicions, do not get out of the car and attempt to troubleshoot or bypass the problem yourself. Call for help so that you have security overwatch available incase it is a trap. Parking is an excellent time to have an armed passenger exit and provide exterior overwatch and security. Relatives, friends, or neighbors can also provide this function from the house itself.

Vary your route between common destinations or on regular commutes. Don't use the same entrance and exit to your neighborhood every time to frustrate any plans based on "regular" behavior.

## Parking

You pull into the parking lot of Big Chain Restaurant to spend way too much fiat currency on a hyperinflated meal. Feeling lucky, you pull into that spot at the front of the restaurant that takes a little wiggling to get into, but the lack of a walk to the door more than makes up for it. On your way out, you are confronted by an aggressive duo of robbers. You jump into your car to flee.

The robbers don't like this and they draw guns to order you out of the car. You're trying to do the arm over the passenger seat thing while you look over your shoulder while being shot at. As your family is screaming, glass is flying around you, and you wish you had a free hand to draw your pistol, you turn too sharply and slam the left fender into the rear of the car parked next to you. In your panic, you stop the vehicle once you've backed out, but you forget to shift from Reverse to Drive and are surprised when you hit the gas and smash the rear bumper into a parked car.

Park like a cop. Back in to parking spaces or pull through so that the nose of your vehicle is facing out. Cops are trained to do this because it is far easier and faster to simply drive forward under stress than it is to try and reverse out as the anecdote illustrated.

Choose a parking space in an open area of the parking lot where possible. Open space around your vehicle is a safety buffer where potential assailants can be spotted. It makes maneuvering the vehicle and getting in and out of the car easier. Park near or at least facing the exit. If something goes bonkers and the entire parking lot is trying to leave at once, or you need to get out of the parking lot ASAP, it's a lot easier to do so if you have a "head start" on getting out on the street.

Pay attention to where you park. Don't park next to the sketchy homeless guy's tent on the sidewalk or the group of urban youths on the corner. Assess the behavior of people near the parking space; do they look suspiciously as if they are trying to appear that they aren't watching you? The same thing goes for natural hazards, like underneath a pine tree shedding skull-cracking pine cones on a windy day. Also consider the space itself; is it a parallel-parking space where you could easily be blocked in?

When you park, you will be distracted with the details of shutting off the vehicle, gathering your stuff, and locking it. This is a prime moment for an attacker to strike. Have your stuff ready to go. Never leave the vehicle idling with the keys in the car. Stop and get out of the vehicle quickly. Don't put your head down and futz around. Also, keep the doors closed except for the brief entry/exit time; open doors invite temptation and trouble.

Let's talk about purses; women, don't dig around in your purse trying to find your keys. SHTF isn't the time to be messing around with your purse. If you must carry one at this point, all you should be doing is putting it on your shoulder. Keys and phone go in your pocket because if your purse is snatched, the means of calling for help and getting away are *not* in the purse. We've discussed it before, but it bears reminding again. DO NOT PUT YOUR GUN IN YOUR PURSE!

Cops get out of vehicles quickly by habit. Men tend to also get out of cars quickly. Ladies, it often takes you a longer time than males to get out of the car for many reasons. Break this habit if you have it. Parents need to travel together. Dad provides security overwatch while Mom gets the kids or stuff in and out.

Don't park next to vans. We all get the creepy child molester vibe from panel vans but minivans can go in the same category. Avoid panel vans and ones with tinted windows because they could be hiding attackers or kidnappers. Don't walk near them and be very wary if they pull up to you while you are on foot.

Vehicular burglary is a sad common fact of life these days. Nowhere is safe and toilet bowls like San Francisco are worst of all. First off, never have irreplaceable things in your car. Sure, I'd miss my tool bag, my blow-out (medical) kit, my spare magazines, and holster, but I can replace them easily and relatively cheaply. Anything valuable goes with me. If this is a major concern in your area, leave nothing in the car to tempt thieves, valuable or not. No bags or boxes that "could" to a junkie's or tweaker's eye hold something worth stealing. Remove it, put it in the trunk, or cover it up with a cargo cover.

## Leaving

Between your car and your destination, your attention needs to be on what's around you. You should do this anyway unless you are planning to be a professional plaintiff living off insurance settlements. Again, no digging in your purse, looking at your phone, or talking on the phone. Predators are looking for distracted targets.

Be vigilant.

Walk down the sidewalk as far as you can from a place where people can grab you. This may be along a flat building wall or closer to the street. Landscaping or alcoves that could conceal someone or next to parked cars are danger areas. In parking lots, walk down the center of the aisle. Avoid cutting between parked cars where you could be ambushed or grabbed.

Assess your car from a distance. Is there someone lurking around nearby? The far side wheels are a preferred hiding place. Did a strange vehicle park next to your car? Large vehicles with tinted windows and occupied vehicles are worthy of more scrutiny and concern.

Use this time to do a quick scan of the tires and undercarriage for anything underneath the vehicles or to deflate the tires. Be sure to check the bed of a pickup, the rear seats, or cargo area in the event someone found a way in and are concealing themselves; most of this can be done through the windows before you get in.

When leaving a destination, reverse the parking procedures. Should things be really bad, travel in twos. Grocery store thefts will probably be a thing with thieves striking as groceries are being loaded in the car. You've got the stuff outside, with easy accessibility to "load and go" into a suspect vehicle in the aisle, and you're distracted while frequently turning your back.

This is where two people shine. One person loads while the other provides security. Adult 2 could be sitting in the driver's seat ready to go, as well. If kids are involved I'd really love to have three adults; a driver already in the seat, the child-wrangler, and the security adult. If at all possible, in SHTF avoid taking the kids to places like the store.

A two-parent situation goes like this in my mind; family and cart arrive at vehicle. Dad provides overwatch while Mom buckles the kids in. Mom gets in and starts the car, waiting in the locked vehicle while Dad loads the groceries. Mom is scanning the area looking for suspicious circumstances and Dad has his head on a swivel. If things go sideways, Mom can drive off while Dad fights. Dad should put the cart away while Mom follows behind in the car. Then Dad gets in.

If you are alone, keep the keys in your possession. You can use the keys as a delay/bargaining chip to either let the kids get out and to safety while you hand over the keys or use them to quickly negotiate getting your kids out of the car. Never let the keys go until the kids are out and safe even if you have to fight or die first. Most carjackers don't want your kids but don't take that chance.

Get in the car fast. Have your keys out in your non-dominant hand so your gun is free. Practice this if you need to. Do not be distracted with your phone, etc. Make sure your gun hand is free; don't have stuff in that hand. Remotely unlock the car only when you are arriving at it, not across the lot. The beep-and-flash might give away your car's location to an attacker. Use the panic button if an attack happens.

In the event you are attacked, don't focus on just getting in the driver's door or having everyone get in through their proper door. In an emergency, use the closest entrance you can manage through. Loading groceries, this may be the liftgate or buckling kids in their car seats and crawling over the kids. Better some protection in a locked vehicle than outside.

Inside the car, lock the doors then start the engine, followed by releasing the parking brake and shifting into Drive. Immediately scan the mirrors and any cameras to make sure that no one is trying to ambush you at the moment you just got in the car.

Do not rely on auto-lock features that activate/deactivate on Drive/Park. Your vehicle is now secure and ready to drive off in an emergency. Keep your windows up until you are in motion. Learn to put your seatbelt on while you are driving so you can easily get out if you need to and you aren't looking down while stopped.

If you must fiddle around in the car, like putting stuff away, yelling at your children, adjusting seats, mirrors, radio, HVAC, etc. pick a safe place to park. Safe places to park are empty stretches of curb away from any visual obstructions or the middle of an empty parking lot. You want to see anyone approaching from far away and be somewhere they have no reasonable business stopping. Look up and around regularly to scan for threats. If a car or person approaches you out in the middle of nowhere, leave. Do the absolute bare minimum you need to and leave. Do not get locked into your phone or whatever you are doing.

## Driving

Avoid traveling at night. If you must go out at night, park only in well-lit and well-trafficked areas. When you are pumping gas, day or night, put your head on a swivel. It is not cellphone time. Put your back to the vehicle or the pump and look around you constantly.

Travel with a partner. Two people makes defense more effective and complicates things for unprepared attackers. Virtually all carjackings are of single occupants. Two people outside of the vehicle, one pumping and one doing security, is the best option. Gas up in daylight and keep your tank at least half full so you aren't getting gas at sketchy places with the Empty light blinking.

Any time you are in traffic, stop where you can see the rear tires of the vehicle in front of you. In almost every case this will give you enough room between the vehicles to maneuver away, such as a U-turn, if you have to. Maintain a minimum of one car length between vehicles and two is preferable. If you can stop, in traffic, where there is a driveway, alley, or cross-street you can turn around even better.

Try not to stop in the middle lane of three or more so that you are boxed in by cars on both sides. The far left and right lanes give you the best opportunity to turn out and take evasive routes. Drive over/on medians, sidewalks, lawns, etc. until you are safe. If you have to drive down the shoulder or the suicide lane, do it. Just be aware of turning vehicles and white knights that are looking to block you because they think you should sit in traffic (and danger) like them.

Ideally you live in and are traveling in places without sidewalks or a median barrier. The new trend in suburbs is to have a raised median with curbs and either landscaping or stamped concrete in the middle. A high ground clearance vehicle can jump the median (or curb) and give you a better chance of driving on the non-road portions of a highway. Do not be afraid to drive in an unconventional manner to save your life.

A vehicular assault could be personal violence, theft, carjacking, robbery, or kidnapping.

- Vulnerable "moments" for vehicles are:
- When stopped in heavy traffic, often at traffic lights.
- Entering traffic at a driveway where someone has to stop.
- When occupants are getting in or out of a vehicle.
- In the middle of a protest.
- ATMs and drive-throughs.
- Gas stations and car washes (the vehicle is usually unlocked and the key in the ignition).

Minor traffic collisions or "bumping" are often caused as a pretext to get you to stop at which point you are attacked. If it is SHTF and a minor collision occurs, specifically if you are not at fault, do not stop to exchange information. Get a license plate and call 9-1-1 immediately. Don't let a potential attacker from a staged collision follow you home. If things are so bad that insurance companies are insolvent or no one carries liability coverage anymore, don't bother trying to settle the damages.

Indicators of a potential vehicle attack include:

- A vehicle that does not move forward at a green light.
- Doors of a vehicle ahead/behind you opening up and people getting out.
- A vehicle ahead reversing into your vehicle, known as "air bagging."
- Being lightly struck by another vehicle in a deliberate collision.
- Someone in another vehicle trying to flag you down to get your attention.
- People running into traffic.

- People standing in traffic, potentially armed, attempting to get you stop.

Common ruses beyond minor, intentional collisions to get you to pull over is someone yelling about mechanical issues. Make sure that your vehicle is functional and if anyone starts trying to get you to pull over for anything wrong with your car, don't. Pull over only in a safe, public place.

One anecdote I have is a shift partner I worked with once made a traffic stop. Days earlier, we'd been briefed that air bagging was a common thing and it was being done by cartel members looking to kill cops. So my partner finds himself stopped on the freeway behind this car when suddenly it reverses into his unit. The airbags didn't deploy (they only do so under very specific, and usually confidential parameters) but two Hispanic men get out of the car really fast. As my partner starts to unholster his gun, the two men hit their knees and start begging for forgiveness. Turns out the driver was just an idiot.

One trick in areas with low traffic are fake accidents that block the road to force traffic to stop. Staged accidents often feature one or two cars parked so as to block all or most of the roadway. They are often stopped at odd angles that wouldn't result from a collision in that area. Look for damage on the vehicles and debris on the road. Don't worry about rendering aid; keep going.

Additional obstacles might be laid in the road, like trees, telephone poles, or rocks. Do not stop for these. Back up, turn around, find another route. Blind curves are popular ambush sites. So are places with ditches or a lot of thick vegetation on the side of the road. Vigilance and low speeds are the trick to seeing the signs of an ambush in time.

Stops are not always caused by objects in the road. A red flag is someone outside your door or in front of the car demanding that you stop. Do not stop. Run them over or hit them with the body of the car. In a Bay Area pursuit, the suspect ended up on foot on the freeway and was trying to carjack people. He had no weapon and his endeavor relied entirely on fear and physical force. A middle-aged man stopped, rolled down his window, and engaged with the suspect at length all while the police helicopter watched.

In that case, the man was removed by the suspect without harm. Other cases have been much more violent and resulted in death or injury to the driver. There is no need to talk to someone running in traffic; let the police handle it. Keep driving, even if you hit them or run over them.

Do not stop to talk to people on or near the roadway. You are not AAA or the Highway Patrol. A common ruse is people who are lost, claiming they ran out of gas, need a ride for X emergency, or their car broke down. Ignore them. Keep your window up and keep going. Do not be the naïve, stupid good Samaritan who rolls down their window for the raving lunatic in the street.

In lightly trafficked areas, try and time your stops so that you slow down and roll to a red light, which hopefully turns green before you reach the limit line. Keep moving and never stop for threats just to obey traffic laws or signs; only stop to avoid collisions. Run red lights and stop signs or outright drive illegally if you feel threatened. Use reverse to your advantage. Very few attackers will expect you to reverse out of danger. Practice backing and turning at high speed in empty lots.

Compliance is generally up to you. *Never* comply if you have kids in the car. In ordinary criminal carjackings, the intent is to take the vehicle with a minimum of fuss. Violence is used to ensure that the victim complies and doesn't put up a fight. Usually that violence is a beating, brandishing a weapon, threats, or physically removing the driver. Conventional wisdom is bail out and let them take the car; fine enough for "normal" times carjackings.

Post-SHTF or in a real WROL apocalypse, taking someone's car may be akin to stealing a man's horse two hundred years ago. That car may be your lifeblood to your job or losing it might strand you miles from home in dangerous territory. Shooting someone over property theft is contraindicated by law in "normal" times.

If you are taken hostage, do not allow the kidnapper/carjacker to take you anywhere. Odds are, they will take you to what's called, after the fact, the "second crime scene," and kill you or worse. Fight them or escape at all costs. You may well succeed at getting away or forcing them off.

If you are forced to give up the car, one opportunity to kill the attacker is as he is getting in the car. His attention will be on getting seated, starting the car, putting it in Drive, etc. This would be your opportunity to turn around, draw your pistol, and blow the guy away. Of course you will sustain broken glass and blood stains in your vehicle. I would only recommend this if your kids or a loved one is still in the car. Technically, this is kidnapping and a perfectly defensible use of force in "normal" times.

## Road trips

Try and avoid traveling alone for distances that require sleeping at all costs. Getting a room is one thing but sleeping in the car is a terrible idea. A predator coming across a car with a single dozing occupant in the middle of nowhere is a killer's dream. Have a traveling partner so you can sleep while the other drives or at least have one person sitting up and doing security.

If you must travel alone and sleep, I'd recommend finding a way-off the beaten path place far from any town or major highway. Like a place so remote that no one will go hunting for victims there. Camouflage your vehicle. Sleep in a camouflaged shelter well away from the car so that even if they find the vehicle, they can't find you.

## Non-violent protestors blocking traffic

Obstructionist "non-violent" protestors getting in the way of your car or traffic? You can't run them over or shoot them. The problem with dragging them off is that you have nowhere to take them to and they will just return to the street. Yet waiting for them to get up and leave of their own will is not always possible.

Consider zip-tie handcuffs. Place a cuff around one of the wrists of the protestors and drag them away to the sidewalk or wherever. Force both hands behind their back, but the secret is to do this with their back up against a pole of some kind. If you don't have zip-cuffs, but you have large zip-ties, drag the person (who hopefully just goes limp) and zip tie them to the pole.

Be prepared for them to fight you when being drug or cuffed. When you secure the cuffs to both hands, their arms are wrapped around the pole and they cannot get free without someone cutting the cuffs (or zip tie). Because the plastic ties or cuffs can be cut or broken, this isn't a long term solution, but may give you a short window needed to pass through.

Their compatriots may free them or have more protestors waiting in the wings to take their place, so have a plan to deal with this. You may need to use a degree of non-lethal force to keep them compliant or prevent escape attempts. Such as shooting with paintballs any would-be rescuers or persons trying to fill the gap.

Never leave a running car alone while doing this. Lock your car and take the keys. A two or three man approach is best. Ideally, a driver stays with the vehicle who can immediately exploit the gap made in the line. Two people can do the protester wrangling and split security as well.

# What Police May Do During an Insurrection

You know a day that starts off with your partner flippantly warning you to "watch out for a large, angry black ex-cop" who killed some people is going to be an interesting day. I took the warning in stride because it sounded ridiculous and being murdered was a regular job hazard. The day got even more interesting when I found out he had a connection to the area I was patrolling and might even be there. Around 1000, I got called back to the station for a special briefing.

This is when the AM radio reports of Christopher Dorner's February 2013 night of rampage I'd been listening too on and off started to make sense. Turns out he had a loose tie to my jurisdiction and given the fact that the night before two cops were shot, the situation had turned from a local curiosity to a real threat. It was the ambushes that startled everyone (mostly the brass). We in the field felt a little unsettled and "checked six" more frequently.

Operations changed. The mostly elderly Citizen Patrol was taken off the streets. All unarmed, uniformed staff was as well. Motorcycle deputies were put in cars. To prevent a car shortage, some people had to double up on patrol (usually we ran one-man units).

This was not an unusual response from San Diego to Central California. Similar modifications were made to patrol operations across the Southland. LAPD went on "tactical" alert or 12 on 12 off (my agency used 12 hour Panama shifts.) Non-emergency calls were handled by phone or at the station. Traffic enforcement stopped. Institutional fear was real.

Individually, we were more wary than afraid. There was a kind of tense excitement in the air like before a hurricane. Every cop in Southern California was on high alert. The public felt sympathy for law enforcement like after 9/11. Briefings started with the latest info that usually had already been leaked to the press.

Over the weekend Dorner was no longer believed to be in our

area or a threat to us, so we went back to normal operations by Monday. Briefing included warnings not to try and start our own personal investigation as cops all over the LA basin were doing. This came to a head when he was finally cornered in the mountains.

The San Bernadino Sheriff literally had to say "no thanks, stay away" to other agencies because so many cops were rushing to the shootout scene. Traffic was becoming congested and cops were getting in the way of the *actual* investigators and apprehension team. Every SWAT team in SoCal wanted a piece of him. It all resolved when Dorner barricaded himself in a cabin he burglarized and shot himself when SWAT arrived.

Dorner was an aberration in law enforcement. He wasn't cut out for the job and turned his failure into excuses and a crusade. LAPD doesn't have a sterling reputation of integrity but none of that justifies what Dorner did. Remember, to start his spree he murdered the daughter and her fiancé of the attorney who represented him. Next he shot at officers investigating a sighting of him, and after that, he ambushed two Riverside police officers before going on the run.

The larger response that Dorner's actions generated is what I want to look at. Cops were tense and more alert than usual. For the first few days, it felt like we had a special mission just to look out for this guy whether or not we were directly participating. LAPD cops I know described it as more of a feeling like they had a target on their back, though the odds of them being personally targeted was small.

Institutional panic was something else entirely as command staffs put their agencies on the defensive. Non-essential operations were chopped back for 20 million citizens. Manpower shifted to guard details and extra officers on patrol, costing lots in overtime pay. Who knows how many hours were wasted as extra-curricular investigations went on? This was all because of one man.

Though I cannot personally comment on what the situation was like after the Boston Bombings, during the search phase we saw what effective martial law was like. Americans will *not* like door-to-door and house-to-house searches. Lockdowns won't be like with COVID but enforced by soldiers and cops with bad attitudes. On top of all of this, the media will be panicking the public. I'm willing to bet a future insurrection will also target civilians of differing ethnicities and ideologies, not just police and government folks.

Widespread such attacks will paralyze American law enforcement. Department heads will err on the side of caution, even if the officers want to be brave. Directly affected agencies will want revenge and have their resources stretched by the investigation and response to the attacks. At-risk agencies will change their operations to provide for greater officer safety at the detriment to policing for the public.

Without a known suspect like Dorner, everyone will be a suspect. Those panicked cops that shot up a random Toyota? Yeah, that'll be common. Average traffic stops will be more tense for both parties as officers are more circumspect about safety techniques. Officers will probably be more aggressive when resistance is shown or they perceive a threat. Yes, they will be more trigger happy.

2020 is a good example in terms of encouraging criminality of what happens when police pull back. Homicides went from aberrantly low during the lockdown to a quickly rising tide. In LA, police pursuits went through the roof in early summer. I remember one night there were several going on *at once* and TV news couldn't get choppers on them all. "Sideshows" where street racers take over an intersection were a scourge as well.

All this will take is perhaps a team of a few cop killers out there, never mind a general insurrection. The evidence for this is that in 2020, officers were at perceived great risk of political persecution if they used force suppressing the riots. Liberal policies also permitted this to go on. The attitude then was "If they want to tie our hands, this is what they will get." Now imagine cops being killed. Yeah, they'll sit on their hands.

Cops accept that we might be killed in an accident or by a

criminal, not that we're going to get assassinated. Police forces are not like the military where desertion can get you shot; a cop can quit or call in sick. There are ways of collecting one's check by half-assing it and hiding all shift if necessary. Whatever the result, the public will pay the price with an increase in crime as crooks take advantage of officers' distraction and demoralization.

All of this is a recipe for a poop sandwich because more crime, less traditional policing, and actual danger from the violence of an insurrection will frustrate and scare people. Official overreaction tends to polarize people and America is already on the edge. Heck, agitators would love to strike against the criminal justice system and even try to pit the people against the police.

## How a police attacks might drive a break down in law enforcement

How I imagine a national level insurrection going involves someone who simply has had enough, probably acting alone and with little in the way of a plan, if any. For those who recall the Whiskey_Warrior_556 (Alex Booth's Instagram account) standoff before Thanksgiving 2019, I believe this is the pattern by which a patriot v. police battle will occur. The true background of the standoff is immaterial here; what happened is what is important.

Mr. Booth began putting information out on social media about the standoff, claiming that this was a "red flag" gun confiscation type situation. This angered many patriots across the northeast and social media reports indicated that many patriots were coming to his defense from all around the area. Police found themselves overwhelmed by people simply congesting traffic, to actively demonstrating, and even attempting to interfere. It seemed like there was a real fear that armed patriots would arrive and this might lead to a gun battle.

So in my scenario, police conduct some sort of activity; an arrest, a warrant service, "red flag" confiscation, etc. The individual resists and calls for help from likeminded individuals. This call is heeded. Because people have been pushed so far in the past year and a half, the police are engaged by the patriots.

Police being fired on by armed citizens, especially multiple ones, would draw a response from every cop in the area. In Dorner's final moments, the lead agency had a serious problem with cops from other agencies trying to get their piece of him. In our scenarios, this help will be welcome or necessary. Even the FBI's Hostage Rescue Team may get into the act.

As others have posted, this would probably lead to a Boston Bombing style cordon and search. Depending on how far the police or National Guard go, it could get a lot worse. A harsh crackdown, especially with unconstitutional searches and/or arrests, would probably incite patriots to retaliate. The city in question would have to lockdown. As we saw with the Bundy Ranch standoff in 2014, a massive effort to stop armed citizens from flooding in to engage with government forces would have to be mounted.

Creating a perimeter causes a much larger problem, even if the initial conflict ends. As long as police maintain any sort of lockdown, people will push back. Expect highway patrolmen manning checkpoints looking for weapons in vehicles to be ambushed or sniped. Those who get through the outer perimeter will be able to strike government forces anywhere within the inner perimeter, turning the city itself into something like Northern Ireland.

Using the highway patrol as an example, a good tactic would be to create stress on the system outside of the main area of operations. Massive numbers of officers/troopers would be required to maintain the blockade, so attacking a barracks or station during briefing or killing officers across the state is akin to attacking the rear.

Such attacks scare the highway cops, reduces their numbers (not effectively), and causes them to invest resources in defending stations, doubling up on patrol, etc. Suddenly the highway patrol is unable to effectively do traffic enforcement and their blockade mission is stress-tested.

What accelerates this is active participation by police in unconstitutional or immoral activities; Australia's recent tyranny is an excellent example. The atrocities committed by police Down Under would be violently resisted here. I'd bet that respect for police in Oz is at an all-time low. Once police are painted as the enemy and demonized it is far easier to kill them.

Now imagine a situation where police enforcing political unpopular ideas become targets. Police are seen as the enemy and killed. Attacking the highway patrolmen from the earlier example is basic strategy, but the situation will grow out of control as criminals and those with vendettas look to settle scores. Some will kill police because of a simple hatred for "badged orcs" and others will do so to ensure there is no government opposition to whatever evil they have planned.

There will be all sorts of excuses used to kill the police that are not directly related to the *causus belli*. The traffic and parking cops will be killed because everyone sees tickets as "theft." Hardcore criminals might go after the detectives that arrested them. Thieves will kill cops to stop them from going on patrol so they might rob and loot with impunity. Deputies serving eviction notices will be killed.

## How police might react to an insurrection or insurgency based on Dorner

### Individual officer's responses

- More aggressive officer safety protocols were followed than normal, i.e. ordering persons out of a vehicle for a weapons search.
- Officers from multiple agencies began their own investigations, often without official sanction.
- Officers would respond to reported sightings unbidden under the guise of "mutual aid."
- So many cops responded to the final standoff that roads were clogged and the incident commander had to tell uninvolved cops to leave.

173

- Officers became less proactive and tried to have less contact with strangers; i.e. staying in their vehicles.
- Traffic enforcement went down (good or bad, depending on how you look at it).

## Agency responses

- Normal policing operations were disrupted across Southern California in unexpected ways.
- Numbers of officers on the street shifted variously; more officers in some places, fewer cars as officers doubled up, etc.
- Civilian and volunteer staff were pulled out of the field.
- Training and time-off was cancelled.

## Police-public interaction effects

- Police became jumpier, for example the LAPD detail that shot up two newspaper delivery women in a totally unrelated vehicle.
- Stops of suspected vehicles were more tense and cautious than usual.
- The public was not really affected except in the mountains when he was finally "cornered" and on the run in the snow.
- Citizens/officer interactions became a little more adversarial as officers took a more safety oriented approach vs. public relations.

## Police behavior changes in a future scenario

- Policing will be less proactive as officers seek to have less contact with the public and less physical exposure.
- Officers will not want to get into an ambush setup by a deliberate, egregious violation in front of them and thus will ignore more criminal acts.
- Police will favor officer safety versus courtesy and may employ pat-downs, vehicle searches, and handcuffing for minor offenses when they didn't before.
- Officers will be more aggressive and more likely to quickly resort to force, including deadly force.

- More officers will respond to incidents in case they go sideways or for general security purposes.
- Fewer officers will be able to respond as they are tied up with investigations or security details.
- SWAT team responses will be more common to lesser circumstances.
- Operations involving actual or suspected insurgents will generate a *massive* police response with SWAT elements. This may further drain resources from other areas.
- Increased use and deployment of special weapons or hard plate armor.
- Lockdowns and roadblocks, enforced by arrest, may be common.

## Risk to citizens in a future scenario

- Citizens will be at greater risk of being caught in the crossfire of police or insurgents.
- Trigger happy or jumpy officers with poor emotional discipline will likely shoot innocent people under mistaken circumstances.
- Officers will be less tolerant of challenges to their authority, even if the citizen is in the right, posing a risk of "contempt of cop" incidents.
- Citizens may be caught up in lockdowns, roadblocks, subject to searches, etc. as a precautionary measure.
- Unhappy citizens exercising their constitutional rights or legally going about their lives may be harassed by police/military while in martial law type conditions.

# How Policing May Collapse

Earlier, we looked at what effect the Christopher Dorner (the ex-LAPD officer who went on an anti-law enforcement rampage) manhunt had on Southern California police. The conclusion I made there is that targeted killing of police, even on a small scale, will have a huge effect on how police operate from day to day. In a SHTF-future, citizens assassinating police will have deep repercussions.

I predict that "normal" people are going to start shooting cops over things like evictions, foreclosures, and repossessions. As this behavior expands and mutates, it will eventually result in the breakdown of law enforcement. This is probably the most likely cause of a loss of the rule of law, not the aftereffects of a nuclear war or EMP. In the more extreme SHTF scenarios, overzealous policing is less of a threat but the effects are perhaps more dire. It is a case of pick your poison, although we won't get that choice.

## Under what circumstances might people turn on police?

The economy will collapse catastrophically eventually. We get closer everyday. When it does hit its peak, payment processing may be impacted, savings may be wiped out, and businesses will go under. That means that millions of Americans will suddenly be broke. What is left of banks will probably seek to foreclose on debtors, repossess their cars, and landlords will evict tenants. Government stimulus checks will not save the day.

Take your average person who did everything right. They paid their mortgage, rent, and bills on time. They trusted the government, saved money, invested, and didn't welsh on their obligations even when things got hard. Then, the inevitable Really Bad Economic Collapse happens and all the Zerohedge doom predictions come true. Banks become insolvent overnight. Investments and savings disappear. Hyperinflation begins. Jobs disappear as businesses go bankrupt overnight.

Someone who has done everything right will (and should) be angry if they are put on the street through no fault of their own. Economic conditions beyond our control resulting in a catastrophic downturn will take people over the edge. I predict that attacks on law enforcement will coincide with this mega-depression starting with reprisals or resistance against civil processes? What civil processes? Those pertaining to repossessions, evictions, and foreclosures. Deputy sheriffs, bailiffs, and constables will be killed when they attempt to serve these things.

Now, I don't want some repo man or civil deputy to lose his life over a repossession or eviction. I'm flat out leaving morality off the table. Yes, it is your moral and legal duty to pay your debts. I'm not going to nitpick when it becomes morally acceptable to stiff the bank. Murdering people just doing their job is wrong. That being said, this stuff will happen and the questions involved, morally, politically, and economically, are too voluminous to discuss.

Armed resistance works when the person coming to do the immoral, evil, or illegal thing is killed or wounded, thus preventing them from accomplishing their design. In 1775, the Massachusetts militia shot the regular soldiers who came to confiscate powder. The powder was not confiscated. Deputies won't be serving warrants if they are being killed in the process. "Forget this," will be the order of the day (although it will probably take killing to get to this point).

The people responsible for the whole chain are politicians and the bankers that made the donations and pushed the policies. Striking back at them is beyond the ability of most people, so they end up killing the "soldiers" at the ground level effecting the policies. In a symbolic sense, much isn't accomplished by killing a humble repo man or cop. Yet it does have the effect of demoralizing the "soldiers." As General LeMay said, when you kill enough they stop coming. When the soldiers refuse orders, the policies are a dead letter.

It will begin with isolated incidents. Cops will be killed serving foreclosure notices or showing up to do evictions. This will expand independently as people snap, then mass media notice may make it go "viral." The first riots and looting in Minneapolis in 2020, broadcast by mass media, showed the country that police were unwilling to step in and stop the chaos. Thus we saw spontaneous and independent looting riots spin up all across the nation with only media driven grievances as a supposed catalyst.

Desperate, irrational, and criminal people will start the ball rolling, but once desperation comes to everyone's door and the media coverage blows up stories of "resistance," the idea will take off. The numbers don't have to be large, but just large enough to put fear in the hearts of cops and sheriffs. Cops will follow orders up to a point. They are not going to die over eviction notices, repossessions, or foreclosures if everyone is hurting.

De-policing in the last few years is the evidence we need that cops won't risk their lives for things like this. Start killing a lot of cops over eviction notices? Cops will just refuse to serve them or "keep the peace" for banks or whoever. Sheriffs will refuse to do it out of political reasons or to keep their deputies safe.

All of this is predicated, of course, on the crisis being bad enough that people are desperate enough to kill and that they do. If we're lucky, the American attitude will be enough that politicians won't *allow* banks to foreclose and evict people because the political blowback and risk of insurrection will be too bad. Hopefully, sheriffs or legislatures will get smart enough to prevent evictions and foreclosures for simple non-payment.[30]

Moving on, let's assume that every day or so, we're hearing about a repo man, process server, cop, or bank employee being popped. A Robin Hood idea will take hold that it is morally justifiable to resist repos and foreclosures kinetically. Should this tactic prove effective, and especially if killing of police continues, the reasons

---

[30] Please note I don't approve of the 2020-style rent deadbeats that screwed up the rental market and penalized small landlords.

*why* police are being killed will expand from acting as the banking system's toadies to "I just hate the police."

In a world where it has become popularly justifiable to kill cops to keep your house, others will see this as an excuse to attack police for other reasons. Some grievances are arguable, others aren't. I hate Washington State Patrol's habit of "hiding" to pop people going 5+ over, but it's nothing to kill over. But people will use the background events as license to exercise their personal grievances or fantasies.

The scary part of this is the normalization of violence against police to stop bank actions will metastasize into revenge attacks for all sorts of perceived injustices. Police will be ambushed on the side of the road writing tickets. Traffic enforcement will stop. Cops eating lunch will be shot and killed for no apparent reason. Police will be lured into reverse SWATing incidents. Stations will be bombed.

## Officers aren't getting paid any longer

This one is pretty easy. Would *you* stay on the job if you weren't getting paid? I know that waiting for that bi-weekly paycheck feels like an act of faith some weeks but when it doesn't show up, all the danger and abuse isn't going to be worth it for the overwhelming majority of cops.

Officers will probably need more than a rumor that they aren't getting paid to walk off the job. They have robust unions that can ensure money keeps flowing or even pay the officers for a missed period, although it would be virtually unheard of and very alarming if a major government entity couldn't make payroll. Cops will assume they will be paid eventually and can probably get along for at least a month expecting that their employer will pay interest or a penalty.

In a world where the risk factor has exploded exponentially, cops will not stay for no or low pay. And anyone not getting paid will need to get paid, so there will be an exodus to other agencies or jobs. We're already seeing that effect in low-paying agencies today. However, the hiring process, even between agencies, can take several months, so shuffling of cops between departments isn't easy or automatic (normally).

Once the paychecks actually stop coming, all bets are off. Let's say NYPD can't make payroll because reasons and even with a court order for the city to pay up with interest and penalties, no checks come. Probably more than three-quarters of the officers stop coming to work. You legally cannot make someone work if you aren't paying them and firing them would tend to alienate them once you can pay again, so many cops will still have their badges and authority. This works to their benefit and maybe yours if you live next door.

Let's be honest; there are a lot of cops who see the job the same anyone else sees a job they happen to not hate. The paycheck and a good retirement are the reasons they stay. Take that away, and they'll go home. Other factors in this chapter may accelerate that. Very few cops are so dedicated to what they'll do that they will stay behind if the figurative end of the world is happening.

The scenario I wrote about in my novel *Blood Dimmed Tide* is not what I would actually expect to happen in such a situation. Deputies would not be holding out at the police station simply because of honor. My plot line of the rural jail being turned into a fort and the deputies staying in, only reluctantly leaving on a mission, is more realistic. Unpaid cops are not going to risk life and limb for honor's sake.

The short version is, if officers aren't being paid, they aren't going to protect the public for the love of the job, honor, "law and order," or for weak people of society. Cops aren't in it just for the money, but money is a necessity and a huge motivator for a large portion of the force.

For most cops, we take our sense of duty a lot like parents. Yes, you voluntarily decided to have a kid (in most cases) and love them, but sometimes you really wish you didn't. It is a reluctant obligation that you've come to love. Okay, you don't really cut kids off from love at 18 or kick them out in this economy, but cops don't do their jobs for free. The ones that do are very far and few in between, and modern policing is impossible just using the volunteers.

A lucky situation is some officers do remain to answer dire emergency calls on a volunteer basis. A skeleton force might even be paid. Proactive policing may disappear and anything short of life-threatening may be ignored. They are basically only keeping people from being horribly murdered or whatever out of a sense of honor. I only really see this happening in small communities where the officers are residents, sort of like a volunteer fire department.

Police may return if the financial problems keeping them from being paid is affecting everyone. Cops will hold it against bureaucrats and politicians if their malfeasance or incompetence affects their wallets and quit or find a new job. If everyone is hurting, once the pay restarts, the officers can forgive and start working again. It's gonna be a lot harder if a callous mayor or whoever starts criticizing officers who won't work for free.

## Too many cops are being killed to make the job safe

Policing will break down as officers cannot safely respond or simply quit. Those with a vested interest in chaos will keep this up until they achieve their desired goal, such as a major metropolitan police agency becoming non-mission capable.

This harms us all because police act as a moderating influence in our society. Without that moderating influence, crime and disorder goes up, just like in the cities that shat on their officers or "de-policed." Suddenly, you're on your own. That sounds well and good until the gang members and real predators in society see that there are no police to interfere with them. Police do act as the security net for many people in our communities who are unable or unwilling to protect themselves. We all benefit from this protective effect.

Police will eventually stop doing their job if it is too dangerous. Remember, they are people too who will also be facing their own financial difficulties. Public safety is not worth being assassinated over when the world has gone stupid.

My personal fear is that the criminal justice system remains extant but is dysfunctional enough to deny the benefit of police protection but allow prosecution and persecution of disfavored groups. Without the rule of law, every man for himself will be better because at least then civilian mutual defense groups can operate as necessary, instead of with one hand tied behind their back. Naturally, biased policing in that form would only spur further reprisals as the government cracks down on those who defend themselves.

Backing up, initial attacks will be treated as a local, isolated cop-killing, maybe with a copycat element. As attacks become coordinated and sophisticated, the Feds will get involved and use it as an excuse to start political persecution. If things get too widespread, military forces will be required to engage in counter-insurgency operations. At that point, we'll already be in a civil war and the soldiers will have to decide what side they want to be on.

However it does shake out, the future is one without police. You will be on your own and you and your neighbors will have to figure out how the peace was kept ages ago. For those unable or unwilling to defend themselves, things will be very bad as they are at the mercy of the bad guys. Prepare for an interim period of street terrorism, rampant crime, and just enough police to catch *you*.

## Cops stay home to protect their families

Police officers can go to work in jurisdictions distant from their homes because those officers know that their local cops will be watching over their families. Not personally, of course, but cops just as dedicated will be proactively patrolling and responding to calls. That's how a cop living in Staten Island can police the Bronx. If local law enforcement is not present at the officer's home, the odds are greatly reduced that he will be willing to leave his family to give his protection to strangers.

This system of trust is what makes modern policing work. Even officers who work for an agency that has within its jurisdiction the officer's home might not be assigned so as to watch over their own neighborhood. Even then the officer might be too busy to protect his family. So all cops rely on other cops to provide that coverage for their neighborhood.

In an emergency that's so bad that officers cannot trust their local cops to police their neighborhood, officers will not come in to work. Why should a guy from the suburbs commute an hour to risk his life protecting the ghetto while no one from the suburban PD is on the street or answering 9-1-1?

Most cops don't want to live in bad neighborhoods or big cities where they work. They can afford to live in the suburbs or nicer neighborhoods and often do. The areas that are impoverished, have a lot of violence, are outright ghettos, etc. will probably have no policing. If its that bad, no cop is going to risk his life for low-class people in an area infested with gangs, drugs, and crime. Inner cities will become war zones and that disorder will spill over into the lower-middle class and middle-class bordering areas.

High-income residential areas will likely be able to purchase police or other protection, whether that is a straight monetary transaction or involves politics. Officers might no-show in a violent precinct but show up for work in a wealthy area.

So what does this mean for the average citizen? Areas home to a lot of cops will have a lot of off-duty cops available for neighborhood defense. Their participation will vary. Off-duty officers who don't work for the local agency will probably not be acting in a public capacity. My suggestion to agencies would be to re-deploy staff to patrol the areas where they live and absorb any non-local officers into the agency structure.

If you don't have a lot of cops where you live, you will need to handle the policing, if your officers are staying home. Here is one example close to me. LAPD officers living in Simi Valley[31] can go to work protecting Los Angeles because they know Simi PD and Ventura deputies will (figuratively) watch over their homes and families when they are gone.

This is hugely important because safety in many communities relies on officers that don't necessarily live there. In large cities or counties, officers who live within their agency's jurisdiction might not live on the beat they patrol. I've been assigned to the beat with my home in it and also worked in an entirely different patrol division across the county. But I knew that if there was a big earthquake or some other Really Bad Thing, even if I was across the county, dudes I could count on were keeping the streets safe at home.

Going back to 1992, when the Rodney King riots erupted, this trust in the cops back at home was a big deal. Simi Valley was where the LAPD officers were tried due to a change-in-venue from LA County. I worked with deputies who were present at the courthouse when the acquittal came down and the situation was tense. There were scuffles and a lot of angry people who had to be dealt with, but being 1992 and not 2020, no one burned down the courthouse.

Today, Simi Valley would have been ground zero for the riots. Major disruptive protests probably would have already been happening. As it was, Simi Valley and the Ventura County residents that acquitted the officers were accused of being racists. A real worry was that rioters would come up the freeways into Ventura County and cause problems there. LA basin cops had their concerns, but for us in Ventura, no one worried about rioting at

---

[31] Simi Valley is just over the hill in Ventura County from the San Fernando Valley. It is a popular place to live for LAPD officers who don't want to live in LA County. Downtown LA is about an hour away in pre-dawn traffic (if you're lucky).

home.

Rioting began in South Central LA and was generally confined to that area (for various reasons). We did not see opportunistic looting in upscale areas across the LA basin or into other cities as we did in 2020. While there was sympathetic rioting and unrest in other cities across the nation, none of it was to the scale of the George Floyd riots. The relatively confined nature of 1992 meant that local law enforcement could be concentrated on the riots and mutual aid requests could be fulfilled from other California agencies.

In 2020, while the rioting went national, mutual aid was still able to be utilized. Most residential areas were safe, as were the suburbs. So while society hadn't totally collapsed, we did see bad actors exploiting the unrest to loot malls and stores with relative impunity as many major police agencies effectively "stood down." Using Ventura County again, the Oaks Mall in Thousand Oaks and the Camarillo Outlet Mall (both 40-60 miles west of Downtown LA on US 101) were closed and guarded by deputies.[32] Nothing happened at either, but most cities in Ventura County during that period experienced some form of protest.

What I'm getting at is that police resources were not totally strained to the point that areas went without police coverage. A lot of cops in Southern California personally increased their own personal readiness posture at home just in case, but no one called in sick to guard their families. Law enforcement across the country was strained but did not collapse. Officers had trust in their brothers and sisters.

In a breakdown of law enforcement this trust goes away. Individual officers are too fearful for their families to leave them undefended. If the world ends, no way is an LAPD cop going to leave his family if he doesn't absolutely know that a Simi PD black and white will be there for his loved ones.

Our own families and our tribe—be that our neighbors, friends,

---

[32] Both malls were already effectively closed due to the COVID-19 lockdown and had just barely begun reopening their stores.

or just our small part of the world—are more important than strangers. Asking a cop to prioritize strangers all the way across town to the actual or potential detriment of his family and tribe is a losing proposition. Without someone keeping the peace in his neighborhood, an officer will struggle to remain attentive and effective at his duties on his beat. Put another way, why does an LAPD officer care about stopping a riot in the ghetto when rioters are driving up to Simi Valley and invading homes without police intervention?

Again, a collapse of policing hasn't really been seen in America. During the George Floyd riots, police, usually for political means, didn't intervene to stop the thefts and vandalism. Yet riots were somewhat contained (usually) and ordinary law enforcement and police protection went on elsewhere. 9-1-1 was still working. During Hurricane Katrina, we did see officers totally desert or abrogate their duties. In the latter situation, could one fault an officer staying home to protect his house and family knowing that there was a very low chance other cops would respond?

## Jails and prisons

American jails now are technology dependent for security, surveillance, ventilation, and movement. One of the jails I worked at had very few sets of physical keys; the other had a single elevator bank to move between floors. Neither had natural ventilation. The old jail was converted into city offices. The honor farm, last I saw it, had old fashioned bars and stuff, but that has probably been removed by now. Modern jails sans electricity will be unsafe for staff and any court system will find that stuffy, smelly, and hot jails with no water are cruel and unusual.

A grid-down world means there are no jails for those reasons above. In an extreme emergency, an outdoor jail or some sort of makeshift facility might house the worst of the worst. Staffing, logistics, and space will make it difficult to house the number of inmates that jails house today, so any grid-down jail will be holding only the worst of the worst. The misdemeanors that now, and for two hundred years, landed someone in jail for a few months will go out the window. We don't have the facilities that we did 100 years ago that functioned without modern utilities.

Prisons will probably be in a worse position. They are more technology dependent than any jail and require far more staff and supplies. It is well known among prison inmates and guards that "if the world ends" many of the inmates will be slaughtered to prevent them from escaping. Others will be locked in and left to die. That remains to be seen and few scenarios are as sudden and catastrophic enough to warrant such a thing. Even if this doesn't occur, prisons will be as problematic as jails and likely follow the same path.

## Conclusion

Law enforcement administrators need to not send their officers on suicide missions. Staying away from things like politics and evictions is necessary to continue the basic role of public safety. Traffic enforcement might have to be cut back. Average people are not in a position to defend themselves and strong criminals will exploit the weak. The only way some sort of order can be maintained without a lot of bloodshed happening first is if the criminal justice system retains some basic level of functionality.

# Martial Law in the United States

## Legal background

Martial law is not a term found in the Constitution nor is well defined within US law. People like to throw around "martial law" anytime the National Guard is called out, whether or not the troops do anything more than provide logistics or a show. True Martial law is when the military enforces civilian law and administers justice (courts) or enforces operational military regulations on the public (exclusion zone, blackouts, etc.). The military acts as law enforcement *and* military order is enforced on civilians.

That is, troops are arresting civilians for not only civil law violations but violating military orders. Civilians may be turned over to court martial or other military tribunals in lieu of ordinary courts. This is *supposed* to only happen in times of war (civil or foreign invasion) and civil unrest so bad the normal course of criminal justice has been disrupted.

### The Constitution

Article 1, Section 9 of the US Constitution allows the suspension of habeas corpus, usually a hearing on whether or not the authorities can continue to jail someone, only "when in Cases of Rebellion or Invasion the public Safety may require it." President Lincoln did this controversially during the Civil War.

This power was supported in part by *Ex parte Milligan*, 71 US 2 (1866), a Supreme Court decision that found Lincoln's suspension of habeas corpus was illegal in those areas where normal courts still functioned. Specifically, a condition of war, including civil war, for the purposes of martial law, "cannot be said to exist where the civil courts are open."

The court found that two types of military jurisdiction could apply to civilians on US soil. A military government, in the case of a foreign war or invasion, or "martial law proper." "Martial law proper" applies "in times of insurrection or invasion" in those places "where ordinary law no longer adequately secures public safety and private rights."

## Insurrection Act

The Insurrection Act can be invoked when:
- There is a rebellion within a state (or against the United States itself);
- Law cannot be enforced through the ordinary criminal justice process; or
- Civil unrest is so bad that it is interfering with the protections of the 14th Amendment (equal protection of civil rights) *and* that state authorities can't or won't ensure that protection.[33]

The president may use federal troops to suppress the insurrection or to restore law and order and constitutionally protected rights. Most recently, this has been done in response to the 1992 LA Riots, after Hurricane Hugo in the Virgin Islands, the 1967-1968 riots, and in the civil rights movement. Earlier, it was used in early labor strikes.

## Posse comitatus

In 1878 the Posse Comitatus Act was signed into law and laid the framework for prohibiting the military from enforcing civil law. This applies only to federal troops, that is, not the National Guard, unless they have been federalized.

In 1992, President Bush federalized the California Army National Guard (already deployed) and regular Army troops with the Marines to keep order. Federal troops were *not* allowed to act as law enforcement in this case, but to provide mainly equipment and other assistance.

In 1906, federal Army troops were pressed into service as law

---

[33] 10 USC §251, 252, 253

enforcement after the San Francisco earthquake. Under *posse comitatus*, this would be illegal for them, but appears to have happened anyway. It is not impossible for local authorities to "deputize" federal troops ostensibly deployed domestically for other purposes.

## Military government vs. martial law

**Military government** is the term used in *Milligan* to describe when the military issues necessary orders to the public to conduct its operations. Where the military assumes control of the government; this would be known in foreign countries as an occupation government. In the United States, WWII was the best example of this and is a mixed bag.

During WWII, civil government was suspended in Hawaii until 1944 and rather draconian measures implemented on the populace. Mail, radio, newspapers, and long-distance phone calls were censored. The army took control over labor, wages, employment allocation and opportunities; you couldn't change jobs or quit without army permission. Civil courts were briefly closed and civilians subjected to military tribunals for criminal violations. Wide swaths of the islands were closed to off to the public and let's not forget what happened to Japanese-Americans.

In California, restrictions were not nearly as bad, but the Japanese were still interned[34] and other restrictions existed. It is acknowledged that in a time of war, the military commander may make any and all regulations necessary to effect his military duties. This includes things like evacuating areas for military operations or security, restricting travel, or creating regulations (like blackouts to frustrate enemy air raids).

**Martial law** is distinguished in *Milligan* by essentially military law enforcement and tribunal because ordinary civilian law

---

[34] By Executive Order.

enforcement and courts are non-functional. Generally, this would be because the court system and local authorities are absent, dead, or destroyed. This also has included situations where things are so corrupt the system is effectively non-functional.

In Russell County, Alabama, in 1954 the National Guard removed local law enforcement and assumed the duties to end political corruption combined with organized crime. Courts and elections were compromised and totally corrupt. Under civil rights protections, federal troops can act to enforce civil rights, as was done in the 1950s by President Eisenhower in the South.

In a civil war type situation, a military force sent in to restore order may act as police and establish tribunals to replace courts. Again, as in the military government section above, this essentially puts the military on the honor system to truly act in the best interest of the public to reestablish justice. A tyrannical government could easily abuse this in its interest to suppress those it considers rebels or enemies.

## What has martial looked like in the United States?

Earlier we gave examples from the mid-20th century of military government and military administration of justice (at the state level). In the late 19th and early to mid-20th centuries, Guardsmen were involved in labor disputes, again making mass arrests and occasionally getting into gunfights or massacres. These were bloody affairs that are typical in third world countries today, like the 2021 Myanmar Coup where troops fired on civilian protesters.

In more recent decades, military assistance to civil authorities has generally been in the nature of assistance rather than a primary role. Most frequently the military, in the form of the National Guard, steps in to assist with riot control, mass arrests, or assisting police with guard duties or crime suppression patrol.

In 1992 in Los Angeles, one of the major roles of the National Guard was to patrol with police, effectively lending heavy firepower to local cops. During the 2020 riots, the National Guard did very little as they were held back by political decisions. Guardsmen performed logistical duties, assisted with surveillance, and guarded buildings. They had very little to no interaction with actual rioters. In fact, using troops for riot control is rare in recent history.

Military aid during modern unrest has largely been patrolling to deter crime, apprehension of offenders, transportation/guarding of offenders, logistic support, and guarding of critical infrastructure or other government facilities. Typically the National Guard does not like engaging in making arrests or guarding/transporting prisoners, preferring to leave this to police. Guardsmen provide heavy fire power to police and escorts to law enforcement.

## Surviving martial law

Martial law is not your friend, even if it is against your enemy. One would hope that if a foreign war came to American soil, we would rally behind the troops and our flag as we did in 1941. Today, Americans are more skeptical and rebellious towards the government, so strict military restrictions on the public in the homeland are likely to be flaunted or violently resisted. This is a bad combination and it has the potential to flare up into a rebellion against the government.

For our purposes, we consider a situation where military troops are peacekeeping during *really* violent riots and lawlessness or are engaged in suppressing a local insurrection (civil war). Remember that a civil war doesn't necessarily have to be directed against the government, but it can be citizen on citizen, like a genocide. Basically, the soldiers (and Marines) are there to keep people from killing each other *or* are dealing with rebels (not you) and the crime situation is out of control. In either case, if you start lighting up people on your street, the literal cavalry will be coming.

Any use of force is likely to be responded to or investigated by the military, which may have a "shoot first, ask questions later" policy. Soldiers are likely to be on a shorter fuse than law enforcement, especially in a civil war situation. Any instructions or orders you are given need to be obeyed immediately and without questioning. Know that soldiers are probably expecting, if not already facing, an insurgency against them by someone.

Even if the military is present to keep the peace, they may not take your side. They may have orders to be equally harsh to anyone who instigates their own offense or defense. Even if not, how do they know that you are "friendly?" Or perhaps the army is there to safeguard the angry mob from you, a politically unfavorable group.

Weak "neutrality" is a possibility. In Northern Ireland, the British troops were biased against the Irish-Catholics and towards the Protestants. The official policy was neutrality, but the main insurgency was from the Catholic IRA and most British soldiers were non-Irish Protestants. While the soldiers were reasonably professional, Catholic neighborhoods received a far heavier hand than unrest in Protestant neighborhoods.

Understand that you may be under surveillance from hidden observation teams or even drones operating at high altitude. You may be under surveillance long before a ground element contacts you. While in a major, all-out national civil war the advanced elements of the US military will be short staffed and simply can't cover the whole country, in regional flare-ups all the assets used against terrorists in the Middle East will be used here.

That means telephone and radio calls will be intercepted. Snitches and informants will mean that it will be difficult to trust anyone. Interaction with authority figures could make you a suspect. In some third world countries and insurgencies, being seen talking with police/soldiers could make you "guilty" of being an informant and subject to murder.

Be prepared to evacuate on your terms rather than be interned or removed by the military. You may be temporarily removed from your home for reasons mentioned above like being too near a target or in a combat zone. It's not impossible that a rogue government decides to put the "deplorable" citizens in concentration camps.

### Future expectations

Using the Guard or the regular military to suppress riots or perform law enforcement duties is probably politically unlikely unless it is a political move to suppress an insurgency. A repeat of 2020 style rioting will likely follow the same pattern of police not engaging and the Guard held back. The example of the post-January 6, 2020, use of the National Guard to guard the US Capitol probably signifies a future pattern of creating "green zones" for government operations among a hostile American populace.

Should a revolt or insurrection develop, then military troops may get involved as a primary role to suppress a domestic rebellion. This would entail massive issues with troops refusing to attack those with whom they may share political ideals. This would be a civil war type situation and the military would probably become combat ineffective due to desertions.

Now I fully expect that in the case of a war with China, the West Coast will be attacked with cruise missiles and possibly Chinese special forces engaging in acts of sabotage. Pacific Coast Highway may be closed, for instance. Civilian pleasure boating may be stopped to deny Chinese frogmen covert insertion platforms.

Disturbingly, this essentially puts the military on the honor system of restricting civilians for the good of national defense. One might not object to being removed from their home because it is likely to be obliterated by artillery but being forcibly dispossessed of one's home because it is "too close" to a military base would enrage the public. There is a certain limit for legal and political reasons (as long as those limits are respected).

In a civil war, if the military is able to dominate an area, they can enforce what they want. This is literal rule at the point of a gun. If you are on the side the military supports, it would be a minor inconvenience. For enemies of the government, the military could literally do whatever it pleases under the excuse of military necessity.

An anti-constitutional military will almost certainly be under the control of a Democratic government; sorry left-leaning readers, but Republicans weren't the ones calling for draconian lockdowns, vaccine mandates, and vaccine passports, nor does the American right have a history of engaging in totalitarian behaviors, your MSNBC fantasies aside. This will be a danger in areas of active rebellions or "blue" regions controlled by Democrats.

Should things go pear shaped and the military get involved in the fight on the side of a totalitarian government, anything goes for them. Martial law would become outright tyranny and oppression, the pretense of the law aside. If you are caught in this situation, reaction and survival is a matter of personal choice, capability, and morals.

# Body Disposal and Avoiding TrashINT

**Note:** This chapter discusses disposal of dead bad guys or large numbers of dead strangers, not disposal of "your" dead. You will obviously treat your loved ones and friends differently. The health protocols and technical aspects will also apply to the burial of loved ones.

In my discussions of less-lethal force and crowd control, I advise against "just f---ing shoot everybody" as a tactic in all but the direst of circumstances because lots of dead bodies have to be disposed of. In Iraq, oftentimes the wives and mothers of dead insurgents would come out to claim and remove their loved one's body with help from family if Coalition forces didn't take custody of the dead for intelligence purposes.

Conventional wars have burial details that take care of dead soldiers. Burial details can be to temporarily put the dead underground to deal with the problems of a rotting body. Later graves registration teams disinter the bodies and remove them to a memorial cemetery or send them home. These details can include recovery from far flung battlefields.

In a grid-down SHTF situation, no one is coming to clean up the bodies. Not the coroner, not the mortuary, and probably not even the relatives. It will be up to you. The main issues with disposing of decayed bodies are the odor, the fluids, and the ease with which bodies can be dismembered with movement. Manpower will be necessary to collect, move, and dispose of the bodies. Digging graves will be another major energy expenditure.

You will not have a team of soldiers to remove and bury the dead. Let's face it, moving dead bodies is terrible. They stink, they bleed, there is urine and feces that leak from them. Depending on the state of decay they can fall apart. It may not even be a body any longer but instead bits and pieces. No one will volunteer for this duty and even the loved ones of the dead will struggle with it.

You, however, will have to dispose of the bodies. Body disposal will be necessary because of the stink, the carnage, and the potential of disease. Another factor is psychological; its not healthy for your defenders or your uninvolved neighbors to be looking at bodies all the time. You will be motivated for comfort and health reasons to move the bodies out of the area.

There may be some merit to using corpses as a warning. Until modern times, dead bodies were often hung or gibbetted at prominent places often with signs explaining what the offense was. A mound of corpses may have the same effect; however, I think it would be incidental and contraindicated by hygienic concerns. Plus the OPSEC violation of advertising that people are around *and* what you have done does not seem like a good idea to me.

Leaving a dead body of a bad guy could be construed by his friends as disrespectful and a reason to come back to avenge them. Consider that leaving dead bodies where they fell may cause others to think you are a monster. It would be bad public relations and could be exploited as propaganda against you. Word of mouth about an engagement that killed a large amount of attackers may be enough for your purposes.

## Ceremony

Ceremonies and memorials are for the living, not the dead. Death is easier for people to accept and understand as they live if they know that they are not going to be forgotten by those they leave behind. The dead don't care if they have a tombstone or a funeral. These things are to help the mourners who don't want to just unceremoniously lay their dead loved one to rest. Certain cultures engaged in burial rituals as superstition because they did not understand death.

As far as any ceremonies for bad guys, it is not necessary. These people were coming to harm you and died because of it. You owe them or their relatives no obligation to record their deaths or burials. Doing so would be a courtesy. If you choose to do so because of your religious or personal convictions, that is up to you. Prayers or a ceremony of some sort *may* serve to ease the psychological burden on you and your defenders.

## Innocent people

History has shown us that in any domestic conflict, innocent people—civilians, women, children, the elderly—are often killed. This may be through the effects of warfare, disease, or massacre. Genocide is not impossible. Defenders may be faced with the unpleasant task of having to dispose of large numbers of bodies of those who were not their enemies. Obvious in this case, more deference to courtesy and ceremony should be paid out of respect to the loved ones and for the emotional care of the survivors.

- Photograph the area of any atrocities including injuries to bodies, any graffiti, evidence, etc. Attempt to identify the bodies by name, when possible. If unable to positively identify, note general physical characteristics, any marks, scars, or tattoos, describe the clothing they were wearing or any personal effects they may have had. Photographs of the face or any identifying features should be taken.
- Individual body records should include the above identifying information, cause of death, and the location of burial.
- Allow any surviving friends or relatives to participate and mourn insofar as possible.
- A ceremony of some sort may ease everyone's emotional trauma and allow some closure. Note that enemies may exploit a funeral service for further attacks.
- Bury the bodies whenever possible out of respect for the survivors and to make later recovery post-crisis or for forensic purposes easier.
- Record and mark (when possible) the place the persons are buried. Picking a space that can be considered sacred ground may ease survivors' psychological burdens.

# The putrefaction process

When a person dies, they will continue to bleed as a function of residual pressure in the circulatory system and gravity. However, the heart is no longer pumping blood so the volume being discharged is less. Body temperature will fall about 1.5 degrees Fahrenheit per hour until the body assumes the ambient temperature.

With the lack of circulation, blood will pool in the low parts of the body due to gravity causing these areas to appear reddish (post-mortem lividity or livor mortis). Skin will turn white (blanch) as the blood drains away. The areas that have blood pooling in them will be a red to purple color. Note that blood in the first hours to days has not yet coagulated and may leak from wounds upon movement.

As muscles relax upon death, the bladder and rectum will be emptied of urine and feces. It is not uncommon to find that the deceased have soiled themselves after death. This depends on what they've consumed recently and how long ago they last used the toilet.

Rigor mortis, the stiffening of muscles, takes place beginning about two to four hours after death and the process is complete within six to twelve hours. Limbs in rigor can be very difficult to manipulate. Rigor begins to decrease after about 36 hours and ends after about 72 hours. Note that rigor will make it difficult to move bodies.

If safe and possible, adjust the position of the body into one that is easy to move; legs straight, arms down by the sides, and lying flat. Extremities may have to be wrapped or restrained as muscle contracture could cause them to extend even if pre-positioned. Lower temperatures cause rigor to set in faster and last longer while warmer temperatures have the opposite effect.

Bloating will occur within two to six days of death. This is variable based on temperature with warmer temperatures promoting decay. Gaseous build up is most notable in the abdomen and in the face which may cause the eyes to protrude alarmingly. The gases are not released until five to twelve days after death. Fluids will begin to drain from the body during this process and the body may rupture from the gas pressure if handled roughly.

Note that after a few days, the skin will begin to separate from the layers of tissue below and may slough off under handling. This is why clothing of the deceased should be grasped, a two-man lift used, and the body wrapped when possible. As the decay progresses, the body will increasingly turn fluidic.

Bodies subjected to a traumatic injury such as a gunshot can smell right away. The first scent will be the coppery smell of blood often followed with feces if the intestines are ruptured. People in combat or who sustain serious injuries may also defecate from pain/fear. Any artificially opened orifice will allow the purification process to accelerate and thus will begin to smell sooner. The process is variable depending on injury and temperature but can take up to 24-72 hours for a foul odor to be noticed.

If you ever wondered what a dead body smells like, imagine the putrid odor of roadkill. That's it and often you're smelling a relatively small animal. The odor from a dead human is far worse and probably the most offensive and distressing thing about bodies being out in the open. The scent can be incredibly overpowering and has been documented to cause major psychological trauma among survivors. This alone should be the major motivating factor in putting bodies underground.

### Disease

For certain diseases, like cholera, to be spread by the decay of a dead body, the deceased must have been infected with the disease first. Many third world diseases are (currently) very rare in the United States due to our healthcare system. Unchecked immigration from the third world with little to no public health screening threatens to allow the introduction of rare pathogens. Biological warfare or a future, virulent pandemic might change this.

Infectious diseases that may be encountered on a corpse are tuberculosis, streptococcal and gastrointestinal infections, hepatitis, HIV, and hemorrhagic fevers (Ebola). For an infection that the deceased died of or with, the threat is relatively short lived. The main source of pathogens found in dead bodies are bacteriological versus viral. As bodies deteriorate, they dry out and the temperature drops, which kills off host bacteria, making transfer of that infection difficult. Viruses also have similar problems.

Typically, bodies are not a major risk of spreading disease *unless* they are contaminating water sources with feces or a particularly dangerous disease. If the person died of trauma (i.e. you shot them) they will likely pose little risk of contamination. Chances are, if they were sick, they wouldn't be able to fight. However, since gastrointestinal diseases are present in feces, someone who recently had a stomach bug could pass on an infection that way.

Rotting bodies in contact with a water source are a disease vector because of potential pathogens that may flourish in the decaying body (as they might with any similar growth medium). These would be introduced from the environment or from a scavenging animal that then transfers via a vector to the population. Dead bodies in drinking water can impart foul tastes or odors to the water that are not necessarily deadly.

Remember that in a grid-down situation superstition, fear, and folk beliefs will hold sway. People will not have Wikipedia, YouTube, and Google to answer their questions for them. Newscasters will not be interviewing experts to reassure the public. Bodies will need to be buried to allay people's fears of disease and to get offensive and visual and olfactory sensations away.

In a general sense, untreated sewage contaminating a water source is a greater threat than the dead body of a healthy person. Disgust is the major factor with bodies and is the strongest contributor to perception of infection risk. This psychological factor should not be underestimated. Without locally endemic disease, the risk of a dangerous infection is low. Waterborne diseases, like giardia, are more likely to be a problem than a disease ridden corpse.

## Procedures

**Note:** This is *not* how to dispose of the bodies of someone you murdered. Instructions here are to provide for the sanitary removal and burial of the dead.

Embalming is out. You are not a mortician and preserving a body to put it underground is not a good use of resources even if you could. Freezing a body for preservation is also out. Freezing should only be done using outdoor temperatures and snow/ice until the ground thaws for burial. Loved ones are an entirely different matter, but again, preserving any dead body in a survival situation is not a good use of resources.

Be sure that any cleanup and removal is done under security overwatch. Persons dressed up in PPE and dealing with the bodies cannot effectively provide security and fight. There should be at least one defender per body handler. For example, if two people are digging and dumping the bodies, two people need to be armed and watching the surrounding area. Nothing says that the two groups can't switch off. Anyone going outside the perimeter needs to be armed and on alert.

### Equipment

- PPE: N95 mask (minimum), eye protection, disposable gloves, booties or bagged shoes, and preferably disposable coveralls. Ponchos or trash bags can be used to protect the survivor and their clothes from any contamination from the body. Any clothes or reusable equipment should be thoroughly disinfected and washed.

- Vick's VapoRub on the upper lip can help mask odors although full filter respirators should be used against odors.
- Disinfectant, deodorizers, and soap/washing.
- Trash bags for contaminated items and other things that need to be disposed of.
- Thick plastic sheeting to wrap bodies (preferably black).
- Duct tape.
- Wheeled transportation, preferably large two-wheeled carts that can be pulled or towed long enough to carry bodies lengthwise and can be titled to dump. Carts should also be easy to clean. Bodies should not be moved long distance by hand when possible due to possible disintegration and psychological issues.
- Shovels, hand tools, and wheelbarrows.
- Rocks, rubble, or other debris to place atop the grave to keep animals from digging.

Removal

Make a careful search of the battleground for any bodies that are not obvious. A person may have died behind or under cover. Their bodies may be hidden or camouflaged. Bodies may be buried under rubble, tangled in wreckage, or burned beyond recognition. Don't wait until the body starts to stink to find it. Remove and bury the bodies as soon as it is safe and practical to do this. The less decay that has occurred the easier it will be.

Cover the bodies as soon as safe and practical before removal. This will make it easier for survivors and person living in the area. Cloth or plastic covers are for visual and hygienic purposes. No one wants to look at a dead body or get covered in the gore coming off it. They are not necessary unless the body is severely decayed or dismembered.

If using plastic sheeting as a body bag, place the body in the center of the sheet and fold the ends inward. Corners should be folded over and taped up if there is a concern about fluids leaking. The opening should face up to help retain fluids inside the plastic.

Tape or tie the opening shut.

Bodies should be handled by two persons at each end to avoid lifting/strain injuries or putting too much tension on a damaged body that could result in dismemberment or rupture. When possible, transport bodies out of the view of others while covered.

The ground surrounding the body may be contaminated. In addition to blood or other bodily fluids and materials, there may be urine and feces. If possible, use high pressure water to wash away the effluents into storm drains. If not possible, remove any large chunks of tissue. If water is not available, use dry soil, sand, or kitty litter to absorb bodily fluids which you can then sweep away. Leave any puddles or stains covered in a light layer of your absorbent until they naturally disappear.

## Intelligence

Post-attack intelligence can be gathered from the bodies of the dead enemy. Note the demographics of the persons who attacked you. What do they have in common, if in a group? What does the condition of their health tell you? Well fed; healthy; emaciated and starving? Check for tattoos or jewelry that may indicate gang or an ideological affiliation.

Search their clothing and any bags carried for anything of intelligence value, such as documents, items, or equipment carried. What are the types and condition of the weapons that they carried? Does their kit indicate they were well-supplied and disciplined or just a ragged assemblage operating on the logistical edge?

If you have concerns about identification of the bodies being later used against you, sanitize them as best as possible by removing any documents, personally identifiable items, and any clothing or equipment. Forensic examination can later identify the bodies but at least these measures will make it difficult for (example) a looting gang from easily identifying their dead once the corpses have rotted to become unrecognizable.

## Sanitary burial

Burial is the easiest way to dispose of a body and cut down on the smell rotting flesh produces. Due to the energy expenditure when digging graves, mass graves and vertical stacking may be preferable. A deeper grave with several bodies stacked on top of one another might be the most efficient.

Bodies should be buried at least five feet down. This is to help alleviate the ground settling, makes it difficult from scavenging animals to dig down and eat the flesh, and prevents the bodies from inadvertently being uncovered due to incidental digging in the area.

Absolute minimal burial depth depends on the soil conditions. Under optimal conditions, 18" of heavy clay could be sufficient to prevent escape of odors, but three to four feet is better. More depth is always best for the above reasons. A layer of rock, rubble, or hard debris should be buried to discourage digging scavengers. This is important if the bodies are buried shallow. Barbed wire can also be used for this purpose.

In freezing conditions, bodies can be left above ground and covered with snow until the ground thaws sufficiently to bury the bodies. Bodies should be covered with cloths or tarps and the location clearly marked for when the thaw comes. Burial should happen as soon as it is feasible and before the bodies begin to decay further.

Bodies in body bags or wrapped in plastic sheeting keeps the bodies separate from the soil. If bodies are not individually wrapped, layers of sheeting can be placed above and below the bodies. Coffins are unnecessary and a waste of energy and resources.

## The burial ground

Pick a location preferably through community consensus for a mass grave. Sites should be isolated from development and adaptable for the purpose. Fields not likely to be used for cultivation on the outskirts of town or in the center of undeveloped areas are excellent. If parks must be used, the center of sports fields far away from playgrounds and homes can be used.

Burial grounds should be located at a minimum of 150 feet from the nearest water source and a quarter mile from homes, preferably further. Transportation as far away as feasible from you and anyone else is the decent thing to do and makes discovery or investigation of the corpses by an enemy less likely. A burial ground right behind your housing complex might make it easy for the allies of a looting gang to surmise you killed their friends.

Identification, beyond intelligence purposes, is unnecessary. If you choose to do it for personal reasons or for post-conflict purposes, consider if doing so may allow someone to track the burial down to you for the purpose of revenge. You have no duty to memorialize the death of someone who wanted to kill or exploit you. Consideration should be given to secrecy and inaccessibility. Truly motivated bad guys may disinter their dead to identify them or use the bodies as propaganda.

Mark the burial ground minimally as containing dead bodies to warn others for health concerns. Marking and recording the area may be necessary for later disinterment for reburial in more suitable location after the crisis is over. One ideal as a deterrent or marker is along the lines of "Rape and pillage gang buried here; you loot we shoot." This could serve as something to explain the mass grave to archeologists or if all survivors who know about it are dead.

Because disinterment and reburial are processes few people will want to engage in, try to avoid "battlefield" burials and remove the bodies to a more permanent disposal area. Avoid dumping bodies in random places. This is an OPSEC violation and is disrespectful to others who may encounter the bodies.

## Cremation and water burial

The intense heat of cremation calcifies the bones so that they eventually crumble. The "ashes" left after a mortuary cremation are the remains of the bones, not from the bodily tissues. The tissues dry out and burn away completely in a proper crematorium. Certain bones do not always breakdown and may need to be crushed; the bone fragments that remain are then ground down into the commonly known ashen remains.

The process usually takes one to three hours and the oven reaches between 1400 and 1800 degrees Fahrenheit. These are gas fed ovens specially designed for their purpose. A field cremation will not be as effective. The smell of burning flesh will be noticed. Note that a fire will attract attention and the unique scent created by it will tip off potentially hostile individuals as to what is being burned.

The bodies will require a lot of fuel (either petroleum products or wood) to completely consume the bodies. Human bodies burn poorly on their own. Over six hundred pounds of wood is required for an effective cremation outside of a crematorium. Cremation *in extremis* is not recommended.

Do not dump cadavers into bodies of water. Water decomposition can be slow and particularly disturbing. Fish and other aquatic creatures like to eat soft tissues first and this often results in corpses washing up that are quite upsetting to see. The risk of disease is also greater in a water source as well. Anyone drinking the water doesn't want to taste or smell rotting flesh in their drinking water.

**Do not:** Attempt to dismember a body, dissolve it in acid, feed it to animals, or dump it in a water body. Bodies should only be buried or cremated.

# Security garbage disposal

This section isn't about getting rid of solid waste so it doesn't stink up the neighborhood, although we'll touch a bit on that. What this section is about is information security (INFOSEC); in other words, safe trash disposal so it can't be traced back to you. We're talking about two kinds of sanitation; hygienic and INFOSEC. More specifically, how to avoid exposing important information about yourself or your group via TrashINT or trash intelligence.

Put simply, this is trash digging that reveals information about you. Right now, criminals dig through garbage to look for personal information to exploit for identity theft and fraud. Recyclable collectors going through the neighborhood are not a big deal unless you are a busybody but persons scavenging through garbage post-SHTF could stumble across something that might lead them back to you. The last thing you want is a desperate person coming to your house because they found out you have an abundance.

Garbage analysis can be used to gather intelligence on you. At the simplest end, your neighbors could look through your trash bag and see that you are still eating canned food when they are making broth from the bones of their dog. A more astute inventory of your trash could reveal the number of people that are in your family or group or even your health.

Right now, if you were going to do some illegal dumping, you'd be stupid to include personally identifying information inside the trash bag. Idiots who leave their junk mail with their address get busted all the time. If you are attempting to conceal the source of the garbage you must be certain that nothing can be used to directly identify you. This means *not* disposing of old mail or personal documents in your SHTF trash.

Garbage will pile up when collection stops. Trash removal is inconvenient because people aren't going to know what to do with their garbage or want to deal with it. Suburbanites drop the bags (hopefully they use bags) and then forget about it when the can is on the curb. Garbage strikes have shown that people will just leave the bags on the curb and hope the trash fairy will come pickup the bags.

In SHTF, people are going to be unlikely to properly dispose of their garbage. People are lazy. This tendency will be made worse by fuel shortages and by a lack of food. Proper garbage disposal takes effort and energy that people won't want to expend. Even the people who might drive trash to a dump won't have a pickup truck and will pale at the thought of cramming stinky, dripping trash bags into their SUV.

If you're lucky, your neighbors will cart the trash a few blocks to empty land or a parking lot and dump it there. Commercial and government dumpsters will quickly overflow. Holes will probably be dug in public parks as well. Want a great post-SHTF business idea? Haul trash away to a dump somewhere. Mixing your garbage in with the neighbors is a good way to disguise the source of your rubbish.

Desperate people will raid dumpsters for cast-off food. If this isn't possible, the more savvy among them will analyze garbage to try and find out the source to beg or steal. Anti-prepper laws might allow governments to seize food stores giving them an incentive to inspect dumps. Remember that once garbage has been put on the curb, courts consider it "abandoned" and a warrant is not required.

Tear off and burn labels. Wash out and/or burn out food cans until they're black. Burn any combustible food containers. Compost organic (plant) waste and burn, bury or discard any or meats, fats, oils. Bag your garbage or security wrap it. Reuse plastic containers or melt them down.

### Best practices

Dispose of your garbage as remotely as possible to anonymize its source. When dumping it, try to avoid being seen to be identified as the source should an observer decided to track you. Group dumping may confuse any rubbish detectives so there is some merit to a collective trash run.

Reuse, burn, and compost as much as possible to reduce the size of your "signature" that your garbage will produce. Compost fruits and vegetables; do not compost meats, fats, oils, or processed food. When possible, bury your organic and non-combustible garbage. Since this takes effort and energy, a lot of people will not do this.

Burn combustible garbage. Cans can be hygienically sanitized and anonymized by burning also, although the cans themselves won't be consumed. Garbage can be burned in steel drums, repurposed washing machine drums, or pits in the ground; not a fireplace. Screens may be needed to keep embers and ashes inside. Be sure that combustible items are burned completely. Don't be the inconsiderate jerk burning his trash openly in the street.

Use a garbage dump site that is as remote as reasonable from homes, water sources, or where food is grown. Dumps will attract vermin and scavengers—both human and animal. Rotting garbage will produce a minor disease concern and one very large smell, especially if unburied, as much of it will not be.

# Communications

## ComSec basics

Communications security (ComSec) is about denying intelligence to your adversary. This goes beyond solely information denial which you accomplish through encryption or frequency variation. Even if your enemy can't understand what you're saying, knowing when, from where, and how frequently you transmit can give them valuable intelligence. Each time you key up, a sophisticated enemy will be able to triangulate your position and map it. Over time, this will reveal a pattern.

Patterns of life are important to consider. Imagine someone analyses your cell phone data over several months and maps out where you usually go. A large diversion out of state to Grandma's house or the beach is not unusual, but suddenly going out of your way to an area where others being monitored are present is a clue. Even if you turn off your phone a mile out from the super secret whatever, the investigator can guess where you went. On the other hand, if your phone stays home, someone will have to physically be observing you.

Electronic Warfare (EW), also known as communications surveillance and interference can be targeted or general. In the targeted sense, your adversary knows you are out there and actively hunting your signals and monitor them for intelligence. This enables them to track you, learn from you, avoid you, and harass you.

For instance, a sophisticated looting gang knows that your neighborhood has a radio plan could have mobile units to recon the surrounding area. More generally, an adversary is not looking for your specifically, but monitors the electronic spectrum (airwaves) for signals. These signals are analyzed to produce intelligence. For instance, your neighborhood's ham radio guy hears a bunch of bad guys you weren't aware of chatting away on their radios.

Militias and opposing partisan forces will likely be targeted by government, military, or powerful non-governmental organizations. If they know you exist, they will be checking to see if you are emitting electronic signals. Once they know that you are, they can then target you for EW. Cartels in Mexico do this to each other and it is not beyond the possibility of well-funded or equipped groups in a major collapse situation to develop these capabilities in America or the first world.

For most people, general monitoring of the electronic spectrum will likely reveal "interesting" radio traffic. This will eventually lead to the discovery of someone or a group that is deemed worthy of monitoring. For the average survivor, this will be how we will learn of a threat using radios, etc.; we'll hear the bad guys on a scanner. From this casual capture of signals, further work reveals more info. Triangulation leads to locations. Message analysis leads to discovering identity, mission, methods, etc.

EW can be a great asset or a great liability. However you may use it against an enemy, it can be used against you.

### High technology won't save you

Technology has given us tremendous advantages in processing data and making everything we do easier. There are several apps for cell phones that act as tracking and coordination devices for tactical type teams. The military calls them "blue force trackers" and they are basically a map with the location of your friendly units. These apps enable communication, sending intelligence, storing maps, and assisting in navigation. For civilians, this is something that was impossible to get prior to smartphones.

These are a major bad idea for any civilian trying to coordinate a defense or something. Anyone who can hack your phone will know where you are. Gangbangers and looting gangs not so much, but the would-be militia types facing off against the military, UN troops, or Chinese marines are gonna die. Entrusting your life to a third-party, who may be hacked or compromised, is a terrible idea.

If these apps are broken, your enemy knows where you are, who is with you, and what you're up to.

In Ukraine, Russia was able to triangulate artillery troops because they were using a cell phone app to calculate their shots. Militaries spend a lot of money developing electronic tools that are very difficult to detect and hack, let alone electronically eavesdrop on specifically so the enemy can't do what Russia did. The soldiers got lazy and died for it.

Second, even if there is no government or foreign military trying to kill you, these apps are totally reliant on third-parties to work. Namely, functioning cell phone towers and GPS. In any war with a major military (China or Russia), these systems will go down or have major reliability issues. Heaven forbid an EMP occurs or something to take out those systems. If you're lucky, you'll have downloaded maps on your phone, but at that point why not have paper which doesn't need charging?

Remember, your phone navigates via GPS and cell tower triangulation. It downloads maps using Internet data via the cellular signal. Excluding Bluetooth or near-field communication, your phone does *not* operate like a two-way radio in close proximity to other phones. In a civil war, you're handing the government a win as the Taliban did with their satellite phone calls to each other.

I have to say that the problem with many of these apps is that they are "turnkey" solutions. That makes them attractive to the average person who wants the advantage and solutions they provide, but without the technical knowledge to create something similar. There *are* other devices and solutions that do something similar but aren't dependent on cellular networks, Internet data, and GPS. Communication is achieved via radio. These do require electrical, computer, and ham radio skills, however, so if you don't like the idea of homebrewing and tweaking programs and electronics, they may not be for you.

## Cell phones

Do not rely on cell phones. Cell networks can be easily overloaded in large emergencies. Anyone in earthquake country can tell you even the old phone system was overloaded after a quake. You picked up and waited for a dial tone. Crowded areas often get very poor cell reception because there is too much traffic for the node to handle. In an insurrection or major social upheaval of some sort, cell towers may be shut down entirely.

A disaster may render the cellular network impotent, such as if the backup generators eventually run out of fuel. A major regional disaster coupled with a fuel shortage may cause this. A war with China or Russia would also probably see major infrastructure hacking and even damage to the GPS system or satellite communications, which would wreck cell towers' ability to connect with one another. Sat phones aren't an answer either; just imagine a war where satellites are deliberately targeted.

Your cell phone is basically a tracking device that you willingly carry in your pocket. The systems in place are capable of revealing your location within ten feet (that's how 9-1-1 finds your location on cell phones if you don't know where you are). Even with degradation, one hundred feet to one hundred yards is very common. So don't think that a dedicated enemy with the resources to do so can't find you easily by your cell phone signal.

Cell phones don't even need to be making a call to give you away. As you move around, they "register" with towers. Data is transmitted by apps without you knowing it. All of this happens innocently for your convenience and the best signal, but it is bad if you are being hunted or monitored. Devices known as "Stingrays" can spoof cell towers and not only track your phone but can vacuum up all phones in the area that try to connect with it. Federal law enforcement has been known to fly planes over cities to monitor one person or a small group, hoovering up the signals of innocent citizens.

The only time a phone is truly safe is when it's off. Even this can be deceived if the government is really out to get you. A phone that may be used against you needs to be in a metal box that prevents all signals from getting out, known as a Faraday cage. Many people use metal ammo boxes or repurpose old microwaves instead of buying purpose built products out there, such as metal mesh bags.

If you are doing or discussing something you don't want someone to hear, don't take your phone. Again, taking your phone is like taking a personal tracking beacon with you. Turn it off, leave it at home. And don't assume that just because it's off, Wi-Fi or cellular data is turned off, or you have it in a Faraday cage, it isn't spying with you. Assume the microphone is secretly switched on and the spyware is just waiting for you to give it a signal again so it can transmit what it recorded.

Cell phones can be tracked remotely from the comfort of an office, should the government or an adversary want to track them. Yes, the field is possible too, but it's most likely someone is in an office. For radios (especially low-power, short range radios), someone physically has to be in the field in a van or toting around a backpack with antennas on it and a computer inside. Physical electronic interception sites are possible, but less likely. They can't fill the Rockies, the Cascades, or Appalachia with towers to catch every Baofeng out there. Remember, America is still by no means a surveillance state, even if we have the capability.

If the government is actively prosecuting patriots, don't talk about anything the government would disapprove of except face-to-face. And face-to-face conversations must be need-to-know between absolutely trusted individuals who are well-known (for many years) to each other. Not online, not using some "secure" app, not over some secret squirrel radio protocol, but in person. Even then, there is the possibility that someone has been compromised and will report the conversation back to the authorities.

Should the government be ill-relevant and have no means to prosecute you (even for less legally dubious things like organizing a neighborhood defence), "secure" electronic means can be used. Again, keep in mind that there may be some degree of compromise or that an interested party with the means to do so is listening in. Apps like Signal might be okay to keep communication secure from a sophisticated looting gang but not from the NSA.

## Your radio shack for interception and intelligence

Radio traffic interception will be the bulk, if not the entirety, of your SIGINT and COMINT duties. You'll do this by scanning radio frequencies or sweeping whole bands. I recommend having multiple scanners for this, 2-3. It's very difficult for a person to pay attention to three sources of information at a time and what I consider the maximum aural attention span for an average person. If you have the skills, a device like a Software Defined Radio (SDR) or Hack RF One could be used.

A tape/digital recorder can be used, set to the VOX or voice-activated setting, to record only voice traffic for later review. This will not get you real time intelligence but the recording can be analyzed later. VOX modes will also condense the recording to only transmissions without extensive dead air.

### Normal times

In normal situations, monitoring only or primarily law enforcement and emergency radio is good enough for general situational awareness. During the 2020 riots, I had a scanner listening to local police. I heard the marches and the police traffic of not only the location, but the behavior of the crowd. Had things gotten violent and moved towards my location, I would have become more concerned and considered broadening my listening profile.

Monitoring the "easy" frequencies (see below) If riots, protests, or other sportiness kick off nearby, I would start adding these in as incidents begin to develop hyper-locally. Remember that probably only organized groups of professional agitators or really bad people are going to be using the "easy" radios. Groups of random looters, rioters, and young troublemakers will communicate via cellphone and apps.

Here's the thing; short of large Antifa rallies, political violence, or organized banditry, radio communication between bad guys is not going to be a thing. Your average thug who wants to tag up a wall and steal a pair of Nikes isn't going to own, let alone know how to use, a Baofeng. This is a little different if you have a townhouse a few blocks away from an Antifa besieged federal courthouse.

Next, we'll be talking about scanning whole swaths of allocated frequencies, or bands, for when we don't know *what* frequencies will be in use.

### SHTF

When you have nearby bad guys coordinating via radio, it's time to make the primary emphasis of your radio interception their traffic. You want to know what the bad guys (or other defenders) are doing and where, not what the police are doing or how they plan on reacting. Heck, the police might not even be functional and your safety could be all up to you.

The primary frequencies your scanners should be checking are: 1. GMRS, FRS, and MURS; 2, 70cm/2m ham; 3, CB radio. These are all the easiest and cheapest radios to get and the most likely frequencies that bad guys will be using to communicate on. Next, scan outside the approved bands on the frequencies Baofengs are capable of using ) 136-174 MHz and 400-480 MHz). As I discuss elsewhere, traffic can be "hidden" by using non-standard frequencies illegally because it's less-likely anyone is listening. Next I would consider adding in other radios people might be using surreptitiously, like marine UHF.

Military traffic can be a source of some intelligence. The military will encrypt anything but the most boring, least important traffic. I would not put it past a savvy psychological operations officer to deliberately transmit false information in the clear to trick guerillas or insurgents into action. For defensive purposes, you might be able to pick up on basic movements in your area, like motor pool or maybe arrangements for food distribution.

When you determine a frequency is being used, set a dedicated scanner to that frequency to monitor it. Scanner cycles can be several seconds long and might miss a very short transmission of a second or two, like "Execute!" or "Go! Go! Go!" that might be important to hear. You'll want a faster scan time that can pick up short, but vitally important, transmissions.

## Beating radio interception

Never assume that anywhere you went or anything you did in the past is a secret. Who knows how long cell phone or Internet data is actually kept? Our best defense is a high signal to noise ratio; if they are keeping everything, we have to hope that there is too much data in a non-cataloged fashion for them to make use of. Hope is not a plan, so assume that someone watching you knows.

Assume that everything you say on the radio is being overheard. The red flashlight filter under a poncho solution doesn't truly exist for radios, but other ways to minimize your radio signature can be utilized.

The first is encryption, which is illegal on ham bands and not accessible to most radio users. Using code names, codeword, and messages sent in cypher are all viable. This obfuscates who is speaking and what the conversation is about but does not lessen the chances of interception, signal analysis, or decryption.

You have two ways of obfuscating your radio traffic; encrypt it or hide it. Hiding radio traffic means getting off the most commonly used and monitored frequencies to a frequency your adversary does not expect. Encryption makes it impossible for anyone but the NSA to know what you are saying. The transmissions sound like electronic noise.

Encryption is like cutting up a letter into puzzle pieces and then reassembling it on the other end into a coherent message. If it is intercepted, all one gets is jumbled and pretty much no one except the government can decrypt the message. It's not at all like hiding. Anyone can hear and locate the source of your encrypted transmission; they just won't understand it. An encrypted signal is like walking around a mall with a sign written in an unknown language; everyone can see the sign but they can't read it.

For most of us, encryption isn't gonna happen. We can't afford the radios and legal use of encryption is not permitted for amateur use. Digital modes are, but those aren't encryption. Digital radio is transmission of data versus voice. The radio turns your speech into data, transmits it to another radio, and the receiving radio turns it back into speech. A radio that is not able to decode digital signals or not properly configured to decode your transmissions will just put electronic noise out of its speaker.

Digital would be a good middle ground halfway to encryption because pretty much all but the government and very skilled hams would be able to decode your transmissions. A gang sophisticated enough to monitor those frequencies would probably be using a consumer grade scanner that would only get electronic noise. Now digital is not foolproof, but it is the closest that the overwhelming majority of us are going to get to private radio transmissions. The caveat though is that everyone you want to talk to digitally all must have properly configured digital radios, which is a tall order.

## Misusing other bands

Most radios are locked into a set of frequencies (typically your big box store radios) or a particular segment of the radio band. This means that a lot of people are using a small number of frequencies. Imagine for a second you're in a car trying to travel or escape undetected. You'd choose a backroad instead of the freeway, right? You can do that with radios as well. Uncommon or non-voice frequencies are like the backroads of the airwaves. The fewer radios using that frequency, the fewer ears listening. The trick is you need a radio that will access a wide range of frequencies.

If you have a VHF/UHF radio that can transmit all over the band, such as the popular Chinese Baofeng UV-5R model, you have a spectrum of potentially 136-174 MHz and 400-520 MHz (depending on the model). Being able to transmit outside of the amateur bands is, in this case, a good thing. This idea is only applicable to SHTF as it would be illegal otherwise.

Take for instance something in the 156 MHz range. Those frequencies are allocated to licensed commercial or government users and maritime VHF radio. 137 MHz is to communicate with satellites. On the UHF side, there are similar allocations. What you would do is find a set of unused frequencies in your area, basically outside the range of other radios or what bad guys would logically be scanning and talk on those. It's illegal misuse of those frequencies, but if your life is at stake in a without rule of law situation, it's an option.

If you're in the middle of Arizona or Colorado, where no one is using marine VHF radios, the likelihood of interference or intercept is lower because fewer people are likely using or monitoring those frequencies. Using frequencies that don't ordinarily carry voice communication is another way to go undetected as ordinary scanners and radios might not pick up that frequency.

The caveat is that the FCC can detect your traffic being used improperly outside of the proper allocation. Skilled hams can do the same thing. A scanner that covers the frequencies you are using can pick up your signals as well. A microchip controlled device that is monitoring everything, just in case, could turn out to be your worst enemy. What you are doing is not making your signals undetectable but making them harder to detect.

An analogy I'll use is this. You veer your car off the highway and take a path down a dirt road. Someone driving down the highway may never see your car on the side road. On the other hand, someone flying over in a helicopter looking for you can easily find you or discover your car where it doesn't belong.

Finally, using non-allocated frequencies in a non-without rule of law situation can land you in a heap of legal trouble. Hams may *hound* you and report you to the FCC just for the pleasure of it. You could also cause interference with navigation devices (very bad), satellites, critical business communication, or emergency services. One example is careless Mexican fishermen using repurposed equipment with very powerful transmitters. Their conversations bled into the sheriff's channel and a Spanish speaking dispatcher would have to attempt to get them to change frequencies.

### Unpopular bands

Want to gain a little more privacy and lesser chance of interception? Use unpopular or uncommon bands. Most ham and consumer radios operate in the 2m VHF (140 MHz) and 70cm UHF (440 MHz) bands. These are the most popular FM frequencies because most cheap radios (Baofengs) utilize them. The underutilized bands are 1.25m (220 MHz), 6m (50 MHz), and 10m (28 MHz).

I personally would recommend 1.25m (220 MHz) because it's so similar to 2m (140 MHz) VHF, but with a lower noise floor. 1.25m is not widely used and none to very few commercially available radio scanners are tuned for these frequencies. Because few people have these radios and it's highly unlikely any civilian will have a scanner that can pick up this band, there is a low, but not zero, probability of intercept. Baofeng sells 1.25m handsets and a variety of mobile and rack units are available.

6m (50 MHz) is another uncommon band, but HT units seem to be rare, so this would be limited to vehicle or home mounted usage. 10m (28 MHz) is quite similar to CB radio in characteristics and it is usually within the ability of commercial scanners to monitor the frequency range. Again, HT units are uncommon as this is more of a rack or vehicle mount, but more easily sourced than 6m HTs. 10m radios are going to be found mostly in the hands of serious hams and scanners for everyone else.

Please note that repeaters for these bands are uncommon and should not be relied on. In fact, no repeater should be relied upon. A high-quality antenna mounted as high as possible using the most powerful legal transmitter you can buy is the best option with line-of-sight FM communications. You will need a 2m/70cm radio if you want to talk to most mobile hams.

Again, if you decide to go with an unpopular band, such as 1.25m, be aware that your communications are *not* secure. They are *less* susceptible to intercept than other frequencies simply because there is a lesser chance that someone is listening. These are not secure channels but are the equivalent of having a private conversation in an empty room with the door open. Someone could walk right in or be listening just outside the door. All emission control (EMCON) and communications security (COMSEC) procedures still apply. You are transmitting in the clear.

To truly decrease the chance of interception, the lowest transmission power to get the job done coupled with a directional antenna (horizontally polarized) should be used. Low power is analogous to whispering to defeat an eavesdropper. Antennas are discussed in more detail below.

## Alternate callsigns

If the rule of law and the FCC hasn't collapsed yet, but you need to talk on ham radio without a license or don't want to identify yourself, borrow someone else's callsign. Note that this would be illegal.

Find an active callsign in the Technician (entry level) or General (intermediate) classes from an entirely different region. Record or memorize the callsign, the person's name, and the city and state they're from. This way, if anyone looks up the callsign, you can accurately give the correct name and area while you claim to be traveling.

Alternatively, find a callsign that's similar enough to yours to be easily confused, such as a letter or number off. You can just pretend to be a total idiot if caught, though this would be easier to trace to you.

Obviously do not use your real name or any personal info. Never transmit from your home or from the same static location. I cannot stress how important this is; the FCC and experienced hams can determine where you are transmitting from. Change up the callsigns as well but keep in mind someone with a good memory might notice the same voice using multiple callsigns, doubly so if they have a recorder.

## Antennas

Most radios will come with a cheap, six to nine inch "rubber duck" antenna, their length often 1/8th of the frequency at that wavelength. This should be immediately replaced with a longer antenna. For common VHF/UHF radios, this will be around a 19" antenna. Flexible and folding antennas exist for easy storage, mounting in a belt holster, or on load bearing equipment.

When using common handheld radios (handheld transceiver, or HTs, also known as "handy/walkie-talkies") hold the radio with the antenna in the vertical. This applies to your 2m/70cm ham radios, GMRS radios, and most consumer two-way hand-held radios (which will be FM transmitters). Do not angle the antenna back as feels natural (or you see everyone on TV do) as this will reduce its effectiveness by half. Turning it horizontal will be even more detrimental to your signal. Keep the antenna pointed straight up by talking into the microphone as it is held right in front of your face.

To properly use these radios and antennas, they need to utilize a ground plane. This is why antenna angle is important. Think of the ground plane as a giant reflector of radio signals. The signals are radiated from the antenna in roughly all directions. This "sphere" of radio waves does much better if it can "bounce" off the ground plane and up into the air.

Vehicle mounted radios often have their antennas mounted on the roof or trunk because the metal enhances this effect; even a baking sheet at home can help. In your hand, your palm is acting as an indirect ground plane (a weak one). In handheld fashion, the ground plane can be improved by creating what's known as a "rat tail" or counterpoise to make a dipole antenna which is more efficient.

A rat tail is a piece of small gauge wire (22 gauge and higher on the number line) looped around the threads of the antenna base where it screws into the radio. This will be cut to a length of your antenna multiplied by 1.05, plus an inch to wrap around the threads.

Note that the length of your antenna will *not* be how long it is, but how long it *should* be electrically. Don't measure the antenna because wire may be wrapped around the inside beneath the insulation to make it electrically longer. Look up what wavelength the antenna is, either on the packaging or the manufacturer's spec sheet. Yes, the antenna might actually be physically as long as the actual fraction wavelength it is advertised as, but don't take that for granted.

So, if the antenna is a quarter-wave antenna, that is one-fourth of the wavelength for the frequency band. 2m VHF is 78" or, at one-quarter wavelength 19.5"; 70cm UHF is 27.5" or, at one-half wavelength, 13.75". Using the above examples, the respective VHF rat tail would be cut to 21.5" and the UHF cut to 15.5."[35] A little extra is fine, but in this case, more is not better.

The looped end needs to be bare, but the rest can be insulated. Some operators use crimp-on rings to make better connections than just wrapping. There are a lot of different ways to

---

[35] Note this is just an example. For UHF, a half wavelength antenna is given, but you'll likely be using a quarter-wave antenna and the length will be 7.75."

do it and a little Googling will be a lot of help to you.

When using your rat tail, the wire should be allowed to hang straight down from the radio towards the ground when the radio is held in a vertical orientation. This is a dipole antenna in one of its most basic forms. Because the rat tail is loose, it can be easily stored in a pouch, pocket, or pack. And yes, it looks just like a piece of wire dangling from your radio. It's low tech, cheap, and it works. You can use it for the cheap basic antenna or use it on your upgraded quarter or half wave antennas to make them even more effective.

A vertical antenna allows omnidirectional transmission and receiving. Vertical means perpendicular to the horizon or pointing straight up into the sky. Antennas can be held in the horizontal position (parallel to the ground), like you are pointing it at your intended recipient, to get a stronger signal and decrease the signal interception area. The standard single element antenna (one thing sticking out) is not the best for this, but it can be done.

For this to work, both antennas have to be in the same plane (horizontal to the ground) and preferably aimed at each other's direction as closely as possible. A vertical and horizontal antenna will not be in phase with each other as their polarities are in different orientations; this is what makes interception difficult as most antennas are going to be vertical. A multi-element antenna that looks like an old TV antenna (Yagi) works best.

## Talking

Think first, then talk. No one needs to hear silence while you key the mic and think about what you want to say or listen to "um, gee..." If you need more time to respond to someone, ask them to standby so others can transmit.

Unless you are using an external microphone, shove your face into the HT when transmitting. The body mounted mics are not great and need to be close to your mouth for best performance, especially on Baofengs. Just keep it far enough away that you aren't spitting on it.

Be aware of your microphone button, especially if it is a remote mic. Open mics, hot mics, or stuck microphones is a condition when the transmit button is depressed but no intentional transmission is being made. This is really annoying to listen to and potentially embarrassing when people hear what you are saying off-air. Additionally, this can cover up actual radio traffic. So pay attention to where the mic is and that nothing is inadvertently pushing the button; you probably won't notice it until you shift just enough for the button to be released.

## Repeaters

During a large disaster, such as a hurricane, major earthquake, or Godzilla, repeaters may be your only way to communicate over medium distances. I would actually endorse repeaters for disaster communication. However, that all changes when the world become feral. Use of a repeater in a SHTF situation is not always a viable proposition.

Repeaters transmit over a wide area as part of their purpose. The bigger the area receiving, the more people who are listening. Additionally, savvy repeater operators can direction find (DF) your location when using a repeater (anyone can ordinarily, but using a repeater just makes your traffic that much more obvious). For tactical communications, repeaters should not be used for these reasons. It's like switching on a white light on a very dark night and waving it around.

## Distress calls

Most normal rules are suspended when sending emergency traffic. This includes transmitting on unauthorized frequencies, without a license, or without regard to transmitter power (wattage).

Aircraft have a special distress frequency, known as the "Guard" frequency, the same as CB channels 9/19 or Marine VHF

Channel 16. For amateur radio, the common calling channel[36] for whichever band can be used for this purpose and should be monitored in a grid-down scenario. Most traffic now centers around repeaters but if repeaters go down, these frequencies should be used to establish contact then move to other frequencies.

The Wilderness protocol for amateurs in remote areas is to announce their presence at the top of the hour, every three hours, from 7 AM to 7 PM. Ships at sea maintain a silent listening period for distress calls for three minutes at the top and bottom of every hour. These periods allow persons to connect with each other when they might not otherwise be listening to the radio.

The proword for an emergency is "Mayday," usually repeated three to six times. Information that follows should be location, nature of emergency, persons in danger, help needed, and callsign. Remember to speak slowly enough to be understood. In an emergency situation, you are likely to talk fast, stumble over words, and speak in a higher pitch than normal.

If a "mayday" is transmitted:

1. **Do not transmit.** The mayday/emergency traffic takes precedence over everything else. Only those transmissions related to resolving the emergency are permitted. The person in distress has priority over any helpers.

2. Record the details, either with a recorder or by writing it down. If you record the audio, write down the information anyway. This includes callsigns, frequencies, locations, the nature of the emergency, and who is involved.

    a. Saving information makes it easier to understand what is said and pass it on later.

    b. Writing down the information allows you to accurately pass it on and verify information.

    c. Written records of the emergency can help rescue efforts or later investigations.

3. Provide what help you can. If you are in a remote area or if this is SHTF, there may be no calling 9-1-1. You may be the rescuer or the only lifeline to someone capable of providing aid. The golden rule applies here.

---

[36] For example, UHF ham 70cm band is 446.000 MHz.

a. For many operators, summoning help or coordinating a response is all that they will be able to do.

b. In a potentially violent environment, be aware that distress calls could be hoaxes to trap responders.

4. Monitor the frequency until you are no longer able to, someone else who can handle the emergency assumes control, or the emergency is over.

A net control station working the emergency can request radio silence. Example: "All stations [your callsign], emergency traffic this frequency. Impose radio silence." Periodic reminders need to be broadcast periodically. You may wish to give an update to anyone who is listening but hasn't heard all the emergency traffic. Once the emergency is over, transmit something to the effect of: "Emergency radio silence ended. Normal traffic may resume." There are no strict guidelines on imposing radio silence or what needs to be said on the amateur or GMRS bands.


## Jamming

Radio frequency jamming is as simple as broadcasting a powerful signal on a particular frequency or across a broad portion of the radio spectrum to overpower legitimate signals. This often happens on accident via the open/hot mic situation where someone is, for example, sitting on their microphone pushing the transmit button. This happens A LOT in police cars. For malicious purposes, this is used to deny the benefits of radio communication against an enemy.

Currently, jammers (the people) do this mainly out of spite. A lot of the cases are from some unhinged loony who wants to go on political rants. Others want to show everyone how smart they are so they build a remote jammer unit and hide it. As is common on CB radio, some people like being asses and swear or yell over the radio for the same reason people act like fools in public. On the criminal end, organized crime will occasionally use these units to jam cell phones, GPS, or police communications, although this is quite uncommon in the United States.

## Power

The first method of effective jamming is using a powerful transmitter, preferably with more wattage than your radio. Militaries have radio sets with the power to simply overpower and burn through jamming.

## Proximity

A close transmitter is as bad as a high-powered transmitter. A 5-watt radio immediately outside your perimeter will make it very difficult to hear transmissions from far away and may make it impossible, even with a very powerful transmitter, to overpower the near signal.

Jamming can be accomplished with any radio simply by holding down the mic. It's more effective if something is being transmitted, like a recording, but someone with a portable radio can cause a lot of interference over a wide area.

The good news is that consumer radios being used as jammers can only target a single frequency at a time. That means the jammer himself has to be listening to you and key up when he hears activity on your frequency. Since there are many different frequencies to use, he would need a separate transmitter for each frequency he wants to jam. Since most persons are nuisance jammers, the easiest defense is to just switch frequencies.

A savvier jammer will be listening to a scanner and hear you on the new frequency, but then he has to tune his jamming radio and key up, buying you some seconds to transmit. This is cumbersome, but frequency hopping can be done. Military radios do this automatically, however, you will have to have a pre-arranged plan. You will need to be communicating with a trusted friend or member of your group for this to work. Any instructions transmitted have to be encrypted so the jammer cannot hear it and switch frequencies when you do.

A malicious and technically proficient jammer can build a device that can transmit on multiple frequencies or automatically detect traffic and key up. Or they can build a spark gap generator and blast whole portions of the electromagnetic spectrum. Thankfully, this kind of jamming will be rare as it involves special skills and most people with those skills don't do that kind of thing. Also other skilled operators can direction-find the jammer and make his day go poorly.

Jamming antennas are often vertically polarized because a vertical antenna is omnidirectional and the easiest way to go. One way to defeat this is to try and turn your antenna 90° from the vertical to the horizontal for both you and the receiver. This out-of-phase transmission may allow you to receive signals from the other antenna now that both of you are in a different polarity orientation from the jammer.

Direction finding will reveal the location of a static (non-mobile) jammer. A dedicated team could even localize a mobile repeater in a vehicle. All you have to do is triangulate and follow the signal. Jammers have to be switched on to be effective. Eventually, a jammer can be located and physically disabled. In SHTF, if the jammer is *not* sitting all by itself on a mountain peak, but in someone's house, I'd expect the operator to be in physical danger.

In reality what will probably happen is shortly before an attack, a 50-watt mobile unit mounted in a vehicle will key up near the target site. This tactic makes it difficult for defenders to coordinate by radio and call for help. The jammer operator will have a scanner to hear what frequency defenders are using to target those frequencies on the fly. If they are smart, they will have conducted communications surveillance to determine what frequencies you operate on.

### Counter-measures

- Protect your group's frequency plan as restricted information.
- Use uncommon bands, like 1.25 meter.
- Switch frequencies, preferably in a known to you, but unpredictable pattern to the jammer.
- Increase your transmission power to overcome jamming and lower the power to decrease the possibility of interception.
- Use directional antennas (i.e. horizontally polarized).
- Retaliate by sending the police/FCC or other WROL only means.

# No Warlords; Guarding Critical Infrastructure to Prevent Criminal Opportunism

## Criminal opportunism

A criminal opportunist is a person or group that seeks to benefit in times of war or disaster through illicit means without regard to morality, laws, or any other considerations beyond their own power or gain. They seek to profit through the suffering of others primarily by exploiting the critical needs of a population in a time of crisis. This is often done through exploitation, theft, profiteering, extortion, kidnapping/ransom, black markets, or smuggling. Violence is often used to support these ends.

Opportunists can be individuals, small collections of criminally inclined persons, street gangs, drug trafficking gangs, international cartels, the traditional mafia, or foreign state elements. While street gangs, drug cartels, and mafias are the most likely source of organized opportunistic criminality, any person who is amoral enough can end up exploiting a community. Typically this is seen in fiction as an "evil" individual who amasses power and control for a nefarious purpose.

The lack of effective police or military deterrence during times of instability enable opportunists to operate with little resistance. In societies with little to no civilian ownership of arms, it is easy for criminal gangs to extort and control the local population. Historically mafias have used the isolation and naivety of immigrant populations, along with a lack of a tradition of arms and availability of weapons, to engage in various rackets such as protection.

Most often the purpose is simple material or financial gain. In my EMP series of novels, I wrote that Mexican cartels began to dominate and enslave the local Hispanic population for their financial gain. Access to water and food was controlled along with physical violence to keep that community "in line." Without giving too much of the plot away, the "gain" aspect was to salvage valuables from post-apocalyptic America to sell in the third world.

Extortion efforts can also be much simpler and in reality much opportunist behavior is small-scale. An example that fits with many historical narratives is charging a tax to use a water source. If one cannot pay the tax, they cannot draw water, and any attempts to draw anyway would be met with force. Typically the population does not have the ability to neutralize the opportunist.

In a SHTF or WROL situation, criminal opportunists will become a major problem. Limited water sources may be captured and controlled by armed groups. Food distribution points or centers could be captured or otherwise regulated to the benefit of such a gang. Critical infrastructure may be captured and held hostage or disabled.

I predict that this will be a very real threat in any major catastrophic event in the United States, particularly in Hispanic communities. Cartels already exert a great deal of influence south of the border and even within the United States. A failure of government to police cartel activities will leave them unmolested to extort, exploit, and ultimately control populations within their sphere of influence. Historical examples have shown that disparate ethnic or national groups will victimize others if there is a weakness.

In the American Southwest, Latin American gangs and cartels will likely consolidate power within the Hispanic communities and form the equivalent of an insurgent state. Neighboring predominately European ancestry communities will be targeted for violence, kidnapping, theft, and exploitation due to the lack of organizations with similar structure, leadership, and propensity for violence.

This phenomenon will not be limited to Latin cartels. Basically any gang of criminals that exists now will have the potential to morph into outlaw and warlord groups. Opportunists who may have no criminal involvement now may find themselves willingly or unintentionally falling into those roles. A particularly ruthless businessman may find that he can profit by supplying or protecting his community, suppressing dissent with violence.

This doesn't have to be some wide-ranging conspiracy that requires a local motorcycle gang deciding it wants to be the next marauding army; it can be as simple as the only guy with a gun in an apartment building who forces women to have sex with him in order to have access to the water cistern spigot. Where this becomes a concern for the suburban defender is mainly protection of critical infrastructure.

## Guarding Critical Infrastructure

Survivors of a SHTF event or those living in a world without the rule of law (WROL) will need to guard critical local infrastructure to prevent its exploitation from malign actors. I wrote two books about my agency (a SoCal sheriff's office) surviving an EMP. One of the major duties I gave to surviving police is simply guarding local water wells to prevent them from being captured by gang members. In a real grid-down situation, I do not expect *any* peace officer to actually take up this duty, so it is up to the community to prevent vital infrastructure from falling under the control of any one group.

What I was getting at in my writing is that the good guys have a vested interest in maintaining open public access of vital infrastructure. Practically, this means water, transportation routes, and logistical venues (stores and markets). Without water and commerce of daily necessities and food, people will die. Monopolization of critical infrastructure by bad guys subjects everyone to the whim of the bad guys. Do you want to be extorted just to shop at a local farmers market or women selling themselves to a dude with an AK just so she can draw water?

Practically, what I mean is that good guys will need to take turns guarding things like wells, substations, pumping plants, etc. The community will need to act to prevent armed forces from extorting businesses, farms, or markets (or customers). Transportation routes may need to be routinely patrolled to detect and eliminate ambushes on traffic. Barons in Europe used to stretch chain barriers across rivers and tax boats that came through, impeding free trade and increasing the costs to everyone.

In the Old West, horse thieves were hung not for the economic value of the animal, but because a man's livelihood was being stolen. Without a horse, that farmer might not be able to plow to sow his crop and he would starve to death. Death by hanging for horse theft, proverbial or not, served as a powerful deterrent to that crime. Survivors and patriots in a world gone pear shaped must be prepared to make the penalty for certain offenses so harsh as to be unthinkable. I can certainly guarantee that the evil, desperate men who want to victimize others will resort to terrorism to further their ends.

## Basic concepts

1. Secure vital infrastructure. This includes wells, water and food distribution areas, and places of commerce. Guard these locations using a neutral force and ensure that the public knows any able bodied person is able to join the guard so it remains impartial.

2. Patrol important transportation routes to maintain open roadways and eliminate any person or group seeking to obstruct, rob, or tax.

3. Eliminate any persons or groups that attempt to extort open markets or their customers, and producers of foodstuffs or goods.

4. Make the punitive costs so high to anyone violating these norms that it is not worth the effort (or the lives) of bad guys to mess with your area. In other words, kill these people, their friends, and anyone else who might try to avenge them.

5. Publicize your efforts. Europeans gibbeted the dead bodies or heads of criminals as a warning to others. Roman crucifixion had a similar purpose.

6. Maintain a credible response force to not just eliminate these threats, but to head off reprisal attacks from a vengeful enemy (or purge the enemy entirely).

7. Forget any notions of fairness or that certain things are uncivilized. Your enemy won't be honorable.

Let's say a small gang takes over a well and is asking for food, valuables, and sex for water. If I was a mafioso or a cartel member who could no longer sell drugs, I'd look to sell access to vital necessities. Your team doesn't try to intimidate the guys or bargain with them; you kill them. You mount their heads on pikes with a sign "death to extortionists" and when/if you hear of their family members complaining and plotting revenge, you kill the males who might attack in revenge.

If positive (morally good) control is maintained over critical public infrastructure, it requires the *enemy* to be on the offensive, rather than good guys to *defensively* react and re-take that point. The public knowing that there is free and safe access to X resource is going to buy you and your friends a lot of brownie points and raise the community's consciousness about keeping important things open and free.

Some readers might wonder if this bears mentioning at all, but I think it does. We're naturally inclined not to stick our necks out so our plans consist of protecting our homes and neighborhood. They are reactive. Well, those plans need to be broader than what to do if a looter gang drives up to your barricade or a riot shows up. Offensive operations against an antagonistic force may be a bit too much for many, but a proactive defense of guarding infrastructure isn't. Preventing a takeover is half the battle.

Your measures may start off with your defense group or even just a competent, proactive group of neighbors, but this effort has to be picked up on by the community at large. With community engagement in the tasks of peacekeeping and guarding critical infrastructure, the ability for one person or group to monopolize a resource is complicated. If a everyone takes turns protecting X, no one is burned out with constant guard duty, everyone feels like they have a stake in the defense, and regular guards don't have the chance to "get ideas."

Security must be a public undertaking, it cannot be monopolized by a single group because control, even if it starts out as good in the beginning, can metastasize in the end. If virtually anyone can participate in the security operation, it means that no one person or group is the access broker. Constant variation of guards helps prevent clicks from forming and decreases the risk should a guard be compromised.

A constantly rotating guard or observer force may be hard to achieve, but even the idea of no one messing with the well or blocking the road can be something that is maintained by the public. Anyone can challenge anyone else who is attempting to monopolize or control a resource. Preferably no one tries it because all attempts have failed or it is too hard to beat the defenders, constant surveillance, etc.

As far as who does this, any able-bodied male can be a guard or respond to a take over attempt. This is original community policing; you don't dial 9-1-1, you deal with it because wrong is wrong on its face. In my novels, police are the ones to do the work of securing the critical infrastructure. I was writing to encourage my brothers-in-blue to step up should a major grid-down SHTF occur, but in reality I fully expect a 100% desertion rate when things get far enough along.

What static infrastructure guards' duty will be is to maintain a visible presence to deter any exploitation of X. In a contemporary context this might be a security guard in a park who runs off troublemaking kids that might graffiti walls. You can detail a rent-a-cop for this instead of putting the SWAT team out. Someone competent to defend themselves will do for guard duty.

Save your SWAT team for the offense and rapid-reactions. Few of us will have pre-organized defensive groups and those who do will probably be dealing with more serious problems than guard duty. You don't take a bunch of ex-special forces guys and have them stand around running off scumbags who are trying to get people to trade a can of food in return for five gallons of water. This is something that ad hoc, post-event, volunteer groups should be able to handle.

## Guard duties

- Maintain a visible deterrent presence.
- Crowd/traffic control.
- Ensure equal access and use of the facility (rules enforcement).
- Repel any attempt to monopolize or destroy the facility.
- Have the capability (skills, will, and weaponry) for at least self-defense.

Put another way:

- Stand around looking tough (and preferably with the training and mentality as well) to give confidence to the public using the facility that they are safe and deter threats. Make the bad guys want to go somewhere else.
- Keep the crowd orderly and in line.
- Permit equal, open, and free access to the facility but disallow anyone who seeks to violate the "rules" like taking more than their allotted ration. No one wants to be the kid who counted time out loud as others drank from the water fountain, but someone will have to be the narc.
- Have the ability and willingness to drive off or kill anyone who attempts to seize control of the facility or victimize consumers. If you can't do that, be able to protect yourself to get away and call your rapid reaction force.

## Commerce

Vital infrastructure includes things like markets, stores, and swap meets. A concentration of people, stuff, and potentially money is an easy target. Such markets could easily be controlled and "taxed" by a mafia-type organization, raided by bandits, or plagued by thieves.

In my novel *Blood Dimmed Tide*, in the aftermath of an EMP, one of the scenes is set at a rather pathetic community market. The few remaining sheriff's deputies are there to keep order and provide security for what could be a lucrative target to bad actors. Any place selling or trading anything has always been a target for theft or robbery. Customers with large amounts of money or valuables to trade can be robbed going to/from the market. Sellers could be extorted by violent gangs. In order to effect safe post-SHTF commerce, the security of the market (i.e. economy) must be maintained.

An open, free market that all peaceable people are welcome to is a benefit for everyone when conventional stores no longer exist or can operate. Assembling buyers and sellers in one place and time is efficient for everyone especially when transportation is difficult. Sales go up with "window shoppers" acting on impulse. Both merchants and customers gain security through safety in numbers.

However this convenience is easily exploited. Today, farmer's markets and swap meets often charge a nominal cost to defray operating expenses. Renting a public space (or private property), security, portable toilets, etc. is not likely to be a concern for survivors setting up a flea market in a park or empty lot.

Given that a market is a concentration of wealth and people in time, they are prime targets for crime. At the low end of the spectrum, it's defrauding people (talcum powder instead of flour) and petty theft. Moving up, robberies of vendors and people leaving the venue. A bold and savvy gang may attempt to control the entire premises, extorting protection fees or helping themselves to the goods for sale.

Buyers and sellers need to be armed. Everyone should theoretically be at parity of arms with one another. Any sort of venue that is a "gun free zone" even with trusted security should be avoided and altogether shunned. Security screening is unlikely to be effective or complied with post-SHTF despite anyone's best efforts. Even screening by a trusted force, like the police, could be co-opted.

Punishment for petty theft should be immediate and public. The victim and witnesses should state their case before the crowd and attempt to reach some consensus before punishment.[37] Punishment should be proportionate to the crime; i.e. a good thrashing for stealing food vs. amputating the hand of a first offender for snatching an orange. Too harsh of a penalty may radicalize thieves to retaliate and it may cause the public to feel inappropriately merciful to the offender.

### Protecting vital commercial establishments
- Ensure security at the venue from external threats.
- Maintain surveillance for thieves or acts of extortion.
- Remove fraudsters from the venue.
- Have a dispute resolution mechanism for buyers/sellers.
- Make sure that the market is hosted in a neutral venue.
- Have a way to punish thieves.

Some degree of vigilantism may be involved, but historical examples have shown that when the community isn't acting out of bias (racism) and there is good evidence or testimony, the court of the mob often made correct judgements. If there is no legal mechanism, this may be necessary in order to provide a deterrent effect. Giving the judgment and punishment to the community present at the time of the crime may also have the best shot at fairness as well if there is no rule of law to take over the judicial and punitive element. A neutral, group based (civil) dispute resolution system can help keep grudges from festering or cheaters getting

---

[37] England once had market courts (Court of piepowders), intended to quickly settle disputes between people who might live far away and only meeting at the market.

away with fraud.

## Roadways

Roadways are vital pieces of infrastructure by virtue that we all need to use them. Actively protecting them and patrolling them in a SHTF situation may be tricky and the exact how-to is a little beyond the scope of this chapter. Suffice it to say, roadways will need to be patrolled to remain open, free, and safe.

- Regular usage maintains the right-of-way from neighboring property owners who may wish to close the road.
- Regular traffic can discourage criminal attacks; however, busy roads have always attracted bandits.
- Challenging extortionary or unnecessarily exclusive road blocks prevents denial of road access to neighbors or legitimate through-traffic.
- Patrolling the roadway is a visible indicator of security activity that:
  - Gathers intelligence;
  - Encourages public morale to make people feel secure ("showing the flag"); and,
  - Patrols can discourage bandits and discover traps, ambushes, surveillance, etc.

I encourage you to think beyond protecting your home or your rural retreat. Mowing down the mob and shooting roving gangs is only part of life in SHTF. We need to think about how lazy people with no compunctions about exploiting others would want to gain during SHTF and defeat them. This part of post-apocalyptic survival may not be sexy as pumping 37mm rounds into a riot or patrolling in the woods, but it will be important.

# Rethinking Evacuations

What I don't like about many bug-out-bags is that they are loaded down with unnecessary items because they are trying to be many things at once. That's because the "advice" out there and packers follow the spirit of some weird formula that's part wilderness survival, part guerilla, and part disaster recovery. So much of the concept is done with the fantasies of hiking on foot from home to a remote location, evading zombies, or "heading to the hills" and camping out in mind.

That needs to be re-thought. What exactly you need in your bug-out-bag or survival kit is a big discussion. In "normal" times you aren't going to be fleeing before a barbarian army with just the stuff on your back. And when the barbarians do come, you are probably going to have time to pack a better bag than just the kind of stuff you can afford to leave forgotten in the dark.

The concept of the bug-out-bag exists as the idea that a person who is forced out of their home will be able to live from the contents of a single backpack. So these backpacks take the form of food, water, and shelter, all too often filled with cheap camping and survival items. These collections of matches, space blankets, and wind-up flashlights are great if you are forced to involuntarily camp and want an easy "forget it" solution but will leave many buyers disappointed.

My bug-out-bag sat in the hall closet and always got in the way of the vacuum. One day I looked through it and decided it was too heavy and a lot of the gear wasn't oriented towards any one scenario. It wasn't ideal if I had to run from a fire and rebuild my life from my parents' house nor was it adequate as a wilderness survival pack. Frankly, I wish I had it on a recent camping trip because a few of the bits and bobs would have been nice to have.

If my home burned down and all I had was this bag, it would be barely adequate for a night at a hotel until I could get to Target in the morning. If I got lost camping, well it would be at home, but would have been quite welcome, except there are a lot of things I would end up dumping to save weight. It was a mix of portable chargers, a solar panel, old socks, lifeboat food, pocket survival kits, a .22 pistol with ammo, etc. The bag was a collection of things I might need on the run.

What it turned into was two bags; a camping oriented bag I could use on actual camping trips with extra survival mixed in and the kind of bag you might pack for an overnight trip. The camping bag gives me extra functionality and survival capability when I camp. My "soft" bag is perfect for having to relocate to my parents' place or a hotel if my house is uninhabitable. Pajamas and a tube tent don't mix in the same bag.

Some readers may be horrified that I don't have a single bag. More horrifying to them will be that my bags take a minute or two to "round off" in an emergency. I am not a big believer in any kind of SHTF emergency that will require you to run out the door at a moment's notice with just your bug out bag. What could possibly realistically happen with such little notice that you only have time to get dressed and grab a bag without thinking? Sure, the actual arrival of said event might be zero notice, but there almost certainly will be indicators to start prepping beforehand.

As the risk of disaster and the potential duration increases, so does the breadth and depth of what you carry. A Californian might need only worry about packing like for a vacation, whereas a tornado victim in a freak December storm might need shelter and warmth right away. In fact, barring someone on the Pacific Northwest coast in an isolated community after a tsunami, I struggle to think of a disaster that will strike with zero to minimum preparation time where extensive survival outdoors would be required.

Earthquake country is fairly temperate and even in the intemperate areas like Alaska or mountainous regions, houses are unlikely to totally fail. Same for tornados. There will be someplace to go and someone to offer basic help. You'll be on your own for a few hours before the Red Cross or someone shows up. You'll probably have a car, money, and working local infrastructure.

What I'm getting at is that for the vast majority of us, a survive out of your bag scenario is highly unlikely without a lot of notice, such as the total collapse of civilization, first. Domestic catastrophes like a housefire are far more likely. Even in these cases, you're going to a hotel, a relative's home, or a Red Cross shelter.

Someone reading this right now is freaking out saying, what if you need to escape and evade for weeks on the run with what you just have on your back that you had only a minute to grab? Barring SHTF having already happened, what could possibly happen that I would have zero warning to up my game and pack a bigger bag?

Nuclear war? EMP? Genocide? Flooding? There will be signs and warnings of war, major weather events (beyond tornados), and you'll know if the neighbors are planning on massacring you. If you are so stupid that you miss the build up to a nuclear war or so totally ignore the news and/or the sheriff telling you to evacuate, you probably aren't going to survive no matter how much gear you have.

There will be more than "get out right now" time for these events. When you have ten minutes, an hour, or days to prepare what you pack up is a lot different than when you run out the door. What I'm saying is that if you are alert you will modify your emergency gear and packing for the conditions you are facing. Camping gear does little more than take up space if your apartment catches on fire and you have to walk to your in-law's house a mile away.

A disaster that requires camping gear will almost always have more notice and time than just "BOOM!" in the middle of the night. Given five minutes, I can get my camping gear out of the garage and into the car. If I need a bivy bag not to die, it'll be packed already. What I'm getting at is pack your bag realistically. Don't overstuff a bag to the point it is cumbersome because of "what if?" fears.

A single bag to cover all bases doesn't have to be the answer.

It may be the wrong answer for you. One bag gets you out the door in an immediately life-threatening situation in "normal" times. Another provides essential survival items when you are surviving out on your own with no social safety set. Addons give you greater comfort and longer survivability depending on the situation and your transportation.

## One Minute Plan

- Your house catches on fire.
- Tsunami.
- Tornado.
- The mob is down the street and torching houses.

In this scenario, getting out of the house in a minute or two is the difference between surviving and dying. You should be grabbing a bug-out-bag, tossing the last-minute items in it, and getting out the door. This is assuming that you put on clothes appropriate for the weather, your shoes, grab your wallet and pocket or purse miscellany, and holster up your gun.

Your shelter plan is the Holiday Inn or Red Cross shelter in the short term and in the long term, staying with friends/family. If you don't have the money to stay at a hotel and have to rely on charity or shelters, and if you don't have friends/family, you are going to want to pack differently if your conditions are going to be more austere. A night or two at a shelter will see you bringing more creature comforts that would otherwise be available in a hotel or at a loved one's home, like extra blankets.

This bag is the absolute bare minimum level of necessities and survival gear. It is tailored to the evacuation scenario and personally configured for you.

Bag contains:
- At least one change of clothing (until you can buy more)

- Toiletries
- Medications
- Spare phone and electronics chargers, including battery packs
- Important documents backed up on a USB thumb drive and/or paper copies
- Flashlight
- Knife/multitool
- Snacks
- Water (one liter absolute minimum)
- Radio (AM/FM or handheld transceiver with FM bands)
- Trauma/first aid-kit

To this you can add in a hurry:
- Your laptop or iPad and charger
- Important document folder with paper originals
- Jewelry box or that one Really Valuable Thing
- Comfort items like pillows and blankets
- Books and other entertainment items
- Extra clothing

Kids will need to be packed differently. Toys and games will need to be included. Not only will they need more entertainment to divert them from fear and boredom, but they also aren't going to be able to tough out cold or inclement weather as much as parents. Babies will need diapers, bottles, and formula (what if Mom is incapacitated?). Pets will need leashes, bowls, and food; don't tell me in a fire that you're going to have time to hit the hall closet for the leash.

You'll want clothes in your bag in case you have to leave so suddenly you can't gather anything or get dressed. Even if your house burns down you won't want to go into Target in PJs and slippers. Pack enough toiletries and medications to get by. This becomes more important for those in sudden disaster areas where stores won't be open right away.

Its not a bad idea to have cash, spare credit cards, or copies of your wallet cards (ID, etc.) in your bag. However, I think in most situations where you can grab a bag you have time to grab a wallet or purse as well. This is why these items, especially purses, need to be kept in the bedroom at night or in a location that you will pass while evacuating.

I don't need MREs to survive in a grid-up world. A snack would be handy to have so that you aren't at the mercy of others and children who get hungry can be placated. Absolute worst-case scenario if my house burns down on Christmas Eve and everything is closed and no one cares, I go hungry until dawn when McDonalds opens. Now for our friends who might be stuck on a hill waiting for tsunami water to recede, more food is better.

Some basic survival items are good to have. A knife of a multitool in a hotel room is a good thing in any situation and there might be a disaster. A first aid kid is also a must for disaster related injuries.

Survival items like matches and tents can be a consideration considering your weather. Do you live in a very cold or rainy climate? Might you have to make a fire in the yard to stay warm or build a shelter to stay dry? In SoCal, an earthquake isn't going to be so devastating that there isn't a building nearby of some kind to shelter in, nor is the weather going to be that bad. For someone in Washington or Oregon who just watched a tsunami sweep their town clean in the middle of winter, it becomes a lot more important.

Attached to the basic survival items are ancillary things like cordage, tinder, fire starters, and tent pegs. Urbanites will have little use for a water purifier or tablets short of a boil water order (cuz if there ain't no mains water, there ain't no water), whereas rural folks in watered country will.

Basically once you're dressed and you have the bag, you can grab secondary items of great value (sentimental, financial, or personal) and save those with the understanding that should conditions become too dangerous, like the smoke becomes overwhelming, that you abandon your hasty packing and get outside.

## Seasons

You may want to consider putting a warm jacket or other seasonal clothing in your bag. This way, if you don't have time to dress up like a deep sea diver for the below zero temperatures outside, at least there is long underwear and a parka in your bag. This is the same principle as packing your vehicle for different seasons. Carrying tire chains during summer is a waste of space.

## SHTF minute plan

If you are reading this, you shouldn't be the kind of person that is buying a commercial bug-out-bag, stuffing it in the back of the closet, and forgetting about it. If my home burns down tonight, a tube of waterproof matches and a cheap, plastic tube tent are not going to help me if what I need is an iPhone charger and a pair of pants. Yet if a firestorm burns down my house after the world has already collapsed, I really will want a bag that is strongly oriented towards outdoor living.

If we can adjust our bug-out-bags for winter and summer, we can adjust them based on circumstances. So if we have a bug-out-bag set up for a house fire or tornado with our sheltering plans being a night at the Holiday Inn, you will pack differently than if you are expecting to take shelter underneath a freeway overpass.

The changeover from having homes, charities, and hotels to rely on will be as gradual as the changing of seasons but a lot less definite. A situation could slowly decline over months or weeks but then turn into a nightmare overnight, sort of like a sudden cold snap, except you won't have a calendar to know about a coming dictatorship like you would know that December is coming. So changing over your bag may be an incremental process and requires paying attention to the times, not just swapping things out like smoke alarm batteries because it's the equinox.

In SHTF, you will need to plan to shelter outdoors and provide all of your basic needs. Your bug-out-bag will be your life and your sole source of supplies. Not news to those who have bug-out-bags, but from the above concept, this is something different. This is your SHTF bug-out-bag bag.

Since you aren't staying at a hotel, this bag will need to cover shelter, warmth, cooking, food, water, and personal needs. You will need to have the hotel and Dennys on your back. This bag will have a tent, a sleeping bag, fire starters, cook sets, freeze dried foods, and a water purifier. Exactly what goes in will vary by your situation, as discussed further above. For this bag, you can take all the advice for life on the run.

### Survival bag

A survival bag is more oriented towards general survival gear rather than personal items. Mine is my camping bag. This would be a multi-person bag for the whole family. As an example, when I was a kid we had an "emergency backpack" that was a Plano medical case stuffed into a camouflage backpack. It was filled with all sorts of interesting equipment like fire starters, compressed towels, a crappy plastic tent, finger bandages, and a plastic compass. It was a mix between incidental camping gear and survival tools cobbled up in bulk from a camping equipment supplier.

This backpack would have been more useful to a stranded hiker or plane crash survivor than a suburban family. Most one and done survival kits are like this; camping gear repackaged to give the buyer more peace of mind than functionality. "This fits in here," is not the criteria you should be using.

First, what disaster are you realistically facing? For most of us, this would be some sort of loss of our home with no place to shelter. In an SHTF world, there is not likely to be a Red Cross or much in the way of charity. For others, it may be short-term survival in bad weather. We'll start with basic needs that can be adapted based on your circumstances:

- Staying warm and dry.
  - o  Tent in wet or unsheltered areas.
  - o  Sleeping bags, blankets, or survival bivy sack.
  - o  Matches, lighters, and fire starters.
  - o  Portable heater or chemical warming packs.
  - o  Towels.
  - o  Rain gear.
- Food.
  - o  Snacks for short term, freeze-dried foods or retort pouches (MREs) for long term.
  - o  Lifeboat or other long storage food for emergency long-term situations.
  - o  Stove and fuel for cooking food or warming water.
- Water.
  - o  Stored water for immediate drinking.
  - o  Water purification tablets and/or filters.
  - o  Water storage containers.

Staying warm and dry in a big city doesn't require a tent, though someone waiting in a rainstorm until the river goes down might want a tent. For single person cold weather survival, a small bivy sack made of aluminized material and an outer layer might be the perfect lightweight addition to warm clothing. Alaskans and Canadians might want a full -30° mummy bag and mountaineering tent.

You might want ground cloths, tarps, plastic sheeting, and cordage to tie things off. Towels and rain gear make working in the weather a lot more tolerable.

Food is really a question of how long you might be stranded before resupply, assuming you can't get to your survival food storage. Three days is a good answer because you can carry it easily without taking up too much space or weight. Two weeks is too hard to carry and more than enough time to go through rubble, find an alternative source, or get official help in most non-nationwide emergencies.

Freeze-dried food is great if you have an abundance of water. It packs well, stores a long time, and is lightweight. Things like MREs require little to no water and less preparation, though they are heavier and bulkier.

Cookware, stoves, dishes, and utensils come along with food. I'd recommend going as simple as possible such as: reusable sporks, lightweight combination backpacking cook sets, and Esbit stoves or cooking over a fire. If you can eat directly out of the package, even better from a weight/space perspective.

Water depends on where you live. Phoenix residents probably want to have gallons available whereas a Seattleite could get by with a bottle to drink right now and some means of purification. I do think some means of purifying water, regardless of where you live, is a good idea in case mains water becomes contaminated.

Can you see the train of thought here? You don't just throw a compass into a bag because someone told you to. Compasses are great and all, but one shouldn't be put in a bag because you were told to or when that space, weight, and money can go to a piece of gear that is going to get used. Pick everything deliberately with an idea to how it will be used and how effective it will be. Reliable electric lanterns and glowsticks take the place of candles, giving you brighter light, less fire danger, and other benefits.

As for the "bag" itself, it doesn't have to be a bag necessarily. Frankly, I have the camping backpack and bins of camping gear. In about two minutes I can have those in my truck with a minimum of fuss. The risk assessment I've done for myself is that if my house burns or collapses, I will have somewhere to go to supply those needs. Otherwise, I'll have sufficient warning to pull the camping gear. Although the skeptics will rightly point out I might be screwed by this approach if my house burns down after the end of the world.

A compromise for someone facing potentially inhospitable conditions is add in the bare minimum of outdoor survival items to your bag. For those in cold country, I'd add a compact survival bivy bag, a space blanket, handwarmers, and matches or a lighter. Potentially stranded folks who have to wait for rescue I'd add water purification tablets, a water bottle, and dense, high calorie food for 24-72 hours.

# 10 Minute Plan

- Wildfire emergency evacuation.
- Flash flood.
- Industrial disaster.
- Nuclear fallout.
- Looter gang sighted on the outskirts of town.

If you have ten minutes, what you can pack up increases. This is long enough for adults and mature children to pack a proper suitcase with a week's worth of clothing and necessities. The packing won't be neat of course, but it doesn't take much time to shove stuff in a bag. Given ten minutes and the expectation that I'm not returning home again, I'm filling up my suitcase and tossing all the clothes that I can reasonably grab into the hamper. This is predicated on your vehicle being available to transport everything.

Now in ten minutes you aren't going to be packing up random things around the house. This is bag packing with a purpose and in a hurry. A little bit more time gives you a little luxury of being able to select things and pack in more depth than a single backpack. You also may get a chance to rummage around the house for personal items or things that will give you greater comfort.

If you have warning, suitcases and any items that you're gonna need during an evacuation to restart your life should be in the car or pre-packed. If you can't pack it or load it, have it out, accessible, and pre-staged as far as possible. Your "go" bags should be in the car or by the door. This will reduce your time in a panic thinking of what to grab. Survival situations would mean that your survival gear is already set out or loaded up.

Again, you often have some forewarning of impending disaster. Flood warnings go out in advance of storms, fires are visible on the horizon, and other situations that might entail leaving on short notice announce their threatening presence earlier. A "head for the hills" disaster might see you putting the long-term food buckets in the car along with the guns and ammo. Psychological preparation can begin early as well. It costs you nothing to get your family mentally ready nor is it a waste of time to unload the vehicle for a crisis that didn't come.

Having some, but little warning, is probably the worst place to be in. Not only do you have to hurry and pack up, but you have to deal with all the emotions that come with an emergency evacuation. Some will outright panic. Children and spouses may need to be scared and comforted. Grief, fear, and nervousness may hinder your ability to think clearly. Mental and actual preparation is key to sidestepping the danger of emotional paralysis this could bring.

Most evacuations are going to be more than just sudden, between the one and ten minute types. So yes, a tsunami may be bearing down on you, but if you live two minutes from a hill tall enough to be safe, versus the guy who lives 30 minutes from safety on a barrier island, two minute guy has time to make extra trips to the car.

The major difference that more time gives you is greater quantity of things taken, better and easier survival (should that be called for), and more comfort items (either directly related to daily living or sentimental items). Contrast this with the one minute plan of the clothes on your back and the bag you were lucky enough to grab.

The best way to know what you can take in 10-60 minutes is to practice. Start with five minutes of packing to see what you can bag up and put in the car. Fill up the whole ten minutes. That will give you a baseline of what you can do and grab. You really won't have a way to replicate the psychological aspect or having to deal with children as these are unpredictable variables.

I cannot stress enough how important it is to have as many critical need items pre-staged. I keep camping gear in plastic tubs so that I can just grab and go. It helps organization in the garage and getting out to the field. In an emergency, all I'm doing is loading, which I've already done if I have some forewarning. The same can be done with emergency food and water supplies to a degree. Household items and heirloom type things can be packed and staged or loaded ahead of time as well.

## One Hour to One Day Plan

- The dam may break.
- Short-notice SHTF relocation to a bug-out location.
- The warlord's army has told you to get out tomorrow or die.
- A hurricane is coming.
- The state is closing the border.
- Planned relocation to a bug-out location.

Let's say that you know you have to get out soon, but it is not an immediate evacuation. You have at least an hour and up to a day. It's not enough time to properly relocate to find a new home and fill a moving truck, but enough to take most of your life with you. This is more than the basics but short of the furniture. This includes the important and the irreplaceable in case your home or your stuff isn't there if you return or you still have it at your new location.

Here you actually have time to pack carefully instead of throwing things in bags, grabbing containers, and just stuffing things in the car. Item selection can be deliberate. Packing can be neat. You can take time to box things up around the house, like taking the contents of the pantry with you instead of only those buckets that are easy to handle and stow in the car. Heirlooms can be taken as well.

This scenario is predicated on having a large vehicle like a pickup bed that you can fill up, preferably a trailer, *and* somewhere to go. The having somewhere to go is important because you aren't going to be hauling half your stuff around from refugee camp to refugee camp like *The Grapes of Wrath*.

The focus here is first on survival items and things you're gonna need where you're going. Again, if the world has already ended what you're going to need on the run will be far different than if you need to spend two weeks at Grandma's while the streets are cleared and the utilities restored. What you load your vehicle up with for a few days to a few weeks will be different in the case your home is burglarized or destroyed.

What you can take with you is predicated on how well you have organized your life to begin with and your evacuation practice. If you know what you need to take, where it is, and it is ready to go, then the actual steps of packing up is very uncomplicated. People with a lot of experience moving themselves or others will understand what I mean.

A person who has their things in boxes already will on moving day only need to add those items of daily living that were in use until that morning. Someone who is totally unprepared will have done nothing, so the movers are left putting wet shampoo bottles into a cardboard box and wrapping drinking glasses in bubble wrap. Be the movers that are done in an hour because all they are doing is lifting and carrying.

Of course not every scenario is going to be so neat that you'll have the opportunity to be neatly packed. Living organized is the alternative to this. Taking neat piles of gear off shelves in the garage and loading them into the car is much longer than crawling in the attic looking for crap. Using plastic tubs that are labeled makes packing a loading operation rather than a search and decide one.

## When you *must* evacuate

In any emergency evacuation, there is a fine line between getting out in time ahead of the crowd and being caught behind the curve. Most people want to avoid looking crazy by getting out too early yet no one with any sense wants to be stuck in traffic with the panicking hordes. At the far extreme, the guy who moved to the woods in the '80s definitely went too early and probably was more nuts than forward thinking. On the other hand, the people trying to get out of the big, blue cities in summer of 2020 wished they had relocated earlier.

Using the pandemic as an example, the folks that were stocking up and masking up back in January and February 2020 probably seemed crazy as well. Remember it wasn't until late February when people *really* started to get worried and preparing for the pandemic was cool. By the week ahead of "two weeks to slow the curve" toilet paper wasn't on store shelves and a fair number of people thought they were going to die.

I've made the example before but evacuating for a hurricane days before the evacuation is called for is prudent but will probably get you fired for deserting work. However, if you wait until the day when the governor proclaims the evacuation and work lets you go, you're stuck in traffic for 12 hours trying to get inland.

There will be situations when it is practically impossible to "bug in" at your suburban home, no matter what your options or preparations are. Even if you have nowhere to go, some disasters are awful enough that living as a refugee is better than dying at home. Some examples are:

- Genocide.
- Use of nuclear, chemical, or biological weapons that have contaminated the area.
- Before the arrival of open, combined-arms warfare.
- If an ultimatum to stay/leave is given and you have an intention to leave.
- Long-term failure of the water delivery system.
- A long-term failure of electrical or gas utilities *and* the heat or cold will kill you without heating/cooling.
- A long-term fuel shortage will prevent you from evacuating if things get worse.
- Your home becomes uninhabitable and you cannot relocate locally, but you have someone to take you in (vs. becoming a refugee).

Relocate or consolidate with relatives or close friends, if you want or need to be with them, and communication systems fail. Such as if the Internet and cell network experiences a long-term failure or will not be restored for an undetermined amount of time, get out. For example, if you live out of state working remotely from your brother and his wife, and your end-of-the-world plan is to move in with them, go to their home. Assume you will not be returning or anything you leave behind will be stolen.

This is not a last-minute thing to do if you want to take much with you or have a good chance of survival. Sure, you can cut it close and be successful but there are plenty of tragic stories of dead people who *didn't* make it out in time. Awareness and realistically appraising the situation is what will keep you alive, not stuff. Jews in 1930s Germany might have had all the money and preps they could buy, but if they didn't get out of Europe while they could, the Holocaust was their fate.


## Awareness

Timely intelligence is a matter of survival. In 2017, I was sitting at home one evening when I saw a tweet come across my Twitter feed from a guy who listens to scanners. He reported a brush fire starting up in the foothills. Since it was extremely windy, I turned on my own scanner to listen to the emergency response. As the hours ticked by, the fire exploded in size and was unstoppable.

Late in the evening I heard the operations officers discussing where the fire was going next. A particular foothill neighborhood in the city of Ventura was expected to be the first "major" impact. This seemed ridiculous at the time because the fire was roughly eight miles away. Except the wind was blowing up to 70 miles per hour directly towards Ventura. The fire fighters were expecting the fire to arrive at the first housing tract in two hours.

Two hours' warning was all that a *very* attentive person would have. At the time, the local news media wasn't covering the story, even though it was unfolding fifty miles west of Downtown LA. The local paper hadn't anything out online yet. The only people who knew were a very small subset of hobbyists and their followers on Twitter. Evacuations didn't begin until after that time, which for many was too late.

Nearly half of an entire neighborhood was burned to the ground. Few of the residents had any early warning. Official evacuation orders came far too late to do much more than run. One high-ranking sheriff's deputy lost his home with little more than his vehicle and the clothes on his back. He wasn't the only one to suffer such a personal tragedy.

The point is that planning for worst case scenarios is not enough. You must understand the hazards of where you live and be up to date on your intelligence gathering. With natural disasters, the weather report, news, and emergency service radios are enough. We discuss this in detail in *Suburban Defense*. A wider awareness of what's going on in the world and the nation is also vitally important to understand the signs of the times.

You shouldn't be relying on your bug-out-bag to just get you through the worst few days of your life. In the above example, two hours would have been a lot of time to pack up, even enough time to call a friend in town to come over. Most people wouldn't have the inclination to tune a scanner to the fire department nor would they really conceive of their house burning to the ground. That's really asking a lot.

On another note, if nuclear war were to break out, when would you find out? We might learn a half hour after the fact that North Korea launched a nuclear weapon when cable news breaks into coverage, but if you know where to go online, you can find out quite quickly. But before this, are you paying attention to the world? How would you have reacted in October of 1962 during the Cuban Missile Crisis? Or how did you learn of "the coronavirus" and when did you start buying emergency supplies?

The goal is to be well ahead of the curve. Understand what's going on so that your first notice of, say a tornado, is the forecaster announcing a possible chance of tornado weather a week out. Don't wait until the tornado watch is set for that afternoon or when the siren blares. At that point, you're running scared like everyone else.

A proper evacuation preparedness mindset is both readiness—having the capacity to respond—and awareness or knowing that you may need to respond before you *have* to. Every step you can get ahead of the storm, so to speak, puts you in a better spot. Having the emergency supplies, having an overnight bag, having critical things pre-packed is half of the game. Anticipating disaster allows you to start making better decisions and preparations to put you in the best position possible.

Forewarning—accurate forewarning—is what enables you to get out early with a lot of your stuff and not look stupid doing so. It is the key to a heavy-laden and comfortable evacuation.

# What Authorities Can Do

I wrote my first novel *Hard Favored Rage* partly as a missive to my compatriots in law enforcement to demonstrate how government could continue on in some beneficial capacity after a high impact, low probability event like an EMP. Early versions of it contained *way* too much detailed information on how to perform basic bureaucratic tasks. There's a whole draft chapter out there about commandeering stationary from a office supply store. Emergency management is something of an interest of mine, let's say.

The preparations discussed here are not for the average disaster, but major catastrophes that will likely break government responses. Examples are nuclear war, EMP, or a world war that involves crippling cyberattacks on local utility infrastructure. This can also be used as a framework for a partial governmental collapse in the face of civil war or economic collapse.

The consequences of societal failure are huge and the devolution of modern society will be largely the loss of all the basics of daily living we rely on. Local emergency services and governments can't do anything about supply chains, but they can alleviate some of the problems that will make or break life at local levels. Within their abilities, local emergency managers and agency administrators need to plan for unthinkable disasters.

The public will be looking to government to provide relief, and if the government can't do anything to help the public, public servants will lose all authority. Public agencies and officials will lose all credibility and the power vacuum will be picked up by those who *can* provide those services. A capable person or group that can restore security, water, food, etc. will accumulate public support, even if this is bad actor.

## Public works

## Water distribution

Determine where emergency water supplies will be drawn from; wells, lakes/ponds, streams, creeks, or rivers, etc. Proactively identify these areas and determine what resources will be needed to utilize them. Keep an up-to-date hard copy directory of well drilling companies in the area.

Establish emergency water supply points that fire trucks and water tankers can access with preferably high volume and flow direct from the aquifer or other water source. It may be desirable to prohibit direct public access to these points to avoid interference.

Ensure that municipal pumping stations can pump on auxiliary power, or that filtration systems that preclude gravity feed can be easily bypassed in an emergency to revert to gravity feed. Work with water departments, engineers, and manufacturers to ensure that in an emergency, normal well operation can be bypassed to utilize low-flow pumps to draw from the borehole.

Maintain a stockpile of auxiliary powered pumping equipment, large and small scale. Maintain a stockpile of piping or hoses of varying length and dimensions for water pumping or distribution. Perhaps retain worn out and surplus fire engines or tanker trucks with minimal functional maintenance to be used solely as an emergency pumping system. For example, the British Auxiliary Fire Service maintained for decades obsolescent Bedford "Green Goddess" pumpers for use after a nuclear war. These were intended as not only reserve fire engines, but to pump water over long distances including engines acting as booster pumps.

Maintain a number of portable water tanks, sufficient to place one for every half a square mile of residential areas. Tank size should be one gallon per person based off the average population density. Maximum practical size will probably be below this at one or two thousand gallons. A larger number of smaller tanks can be utilized and placed next to each other in lieu of a larger tank. Except in locations with low population densities and large tanks, multiple refills a day will be required.

## Water supply/transport

Have tanker trucks (or large tank on trailers) to refill the distribution tanks *and* sufficient fuel stored or available to enable the trucks to make their runs. Miled-out fire department water tenders are perfect for this duty. Specialist equipment can be obtained on the cheap if second or third line gear is purchased for contingency use or bought as military surplus.

For instance, the Ventura County Sheriff took delivery of a 6,000 gallon semi-truck towed water tank from the military surplus DRMO program. In addition, the county also received three 3,000 water bladders and trailers to transport the bladders. In January 2020, this was used to supply a mobile home park when the water main failed. While this was envisioned as a short-term, limited area program, it could be used in disasters of much greater scope and impact.

An alternative would be one to two hundred and fifty gallon trailers. Such smaller trailers could be moved by trusted civilian vehicles. Horses or even manpower could be used, but keep in mind that a full tank would weigh between a half and one ton

With many distribution points, the need for engines or generators to run pumps, and return trips this will be a fuel intensive operation. Larger vehicles may be more expensive but they can haul more, allowing more economical deliveries as they have to return to the water supply point less often. Water drops and routing should be established in advance to plan for equipment, manpower, and fuel needs.

Water requirements are based on one gallon per day which should be considered the minimum necessary for survival. On average, an active person will require a gallon of water to properly hydrate in warm temperatures. Three quarts for drinking and one for cooking or sanitation is the healthy minimum, although up to a gallon alone could be drunk.

Encourage the public to buy containers that can be easily taken to a water distribution point. These should be between one and five gallons and easily carried or moved by hand with common wheeled items like a wagon or wheelbarrow. These should be wide-mouthed for rapid filling and have securely locking lids to prevent spillage in the event they are dropped. Encourage the public to buy water purifiers and tablets. Provide education on purification techniques and basic sanitation to avoid waterborne contamination.

Law enforcement needs to plan to maintain guards at water supply points and water distribution points (water drops). This is to prevent exploitation of the resource for personal gain and to ensure equal, safe access. Water wells have traditionally been contested spaces and vulnerable locations for women and children who are drawing water. Security escorts may be needed for water deliveries.

Authorities and the judiciary should be ready to immediately and severely punish anyone attempting to monopolize water resources or those that engage in depredations on users.

### Sanitation

Ordinary garbage collection will cease. In major cities and suburbs, this is a problem because garbage dumps are often across a county or metropolitan area. The two garbage dumps I went to as a kid that were 20 minutes away are now closed. Waste is trucked to two transfer stations in warehouses in different cities, dumped, and then trucked across the county. Rural citizens may be familiar with driving their trash to a local dump. Suburbanites and city folk will end up with mounds of trash on the sidewalk if the trucks stop, just like with garbage strikes now.

So with SHTF, garbage will pile up in the cans in the street to get the stink away from the house. Some will burn their combustible garbage. The smart will compost some. Many will take to dumping garbage anywhere that is convenient for them. Mounds of garbage will appear first near businesses' and public dumpsters, which will probably attract further dumping as people desperate to get rid of their trash follow the lead.

Public health and sanitation officials need to designate proper dumping facilities that are easy to reach. Open land well away from homes or any water sources should be designated as dumps. Parks or schools remote from homes may need to be sacrificed. Large pits should be dug and the garbage buried once it reaches a point where this is efficient. Combustible garbage should be burned and it may be desirable to have a large-scale composting program.

Garbage sites should be easy to get to and require little to no supervision. Sites should be within a ten minute drive of urban populations or within an hour's walk if dumping by hand. People should feel that the effort of getting the trash to the dump is worth not having it piling and stinking up their neighborhood. Failing that, more local pickup points where people can wheel their trash bins by hand to a few blocks away for centralized collection may work.

As for the dead, people's fear and revulsion of corpses will work to good effect to motivate people to dispose of their dead properly. Mass burial sites will be the most efficient even for individual deaths. Large scale die-offs will be a problem necessitating mass burial. Facilities remote from water sources and preferably homes will need to be turned into cemeteries.

If provisions aren't made, the dead will be buried in backyards and public parks, which may cause friction with neighbors who do not want a grave so nearby. These will need to be somewhat removed from people, but also convenient to get to as the dead may be delivered by hand and not by vehicle. Sites should also be chosen with care as to future memorials and use once things have stabilized for survivors to visit their loved ones.

Bodies should be identified with corrosion resistant metal tags secured by chain or non-degradable cable to the body like dog tags in the event of future exhumation. It will probably be impractical to label individual graves, but plots should be marked and the general location of the dead that can be identified for survivors.

**Note:** the burial of the dead is covered in more detail from another perspective in a separate chapter.

## Criminal Justice System

### Detention

In my fiction novels, I portray a collapse of the jails and court system because of an overreliance of technology and an inflexible system unwilling to recognize that society instantly regressed a few centuries. The courts essentially decide that since things cannot go on as they have been accustomed to, that they cannot go on, and inmates must be released. Pre-trial inmates are simply released with little recourse to try or jail them and sentenced inmates are released due to "cruel and unusual" jail conditions.

Due to a lack of evidence, case information, habitable courtrooms, or fuel for staff, attorneys, and parties to get to court, trials and hearings can't go on. This sudden collapse and the damage to both safety and morale make it impossible for a suitable workaround to be implemented. I also hint at such workarounds being declared illegal, unconstitutional, etc. because they don't conform to the byzantine world of modern legal practice.

In my EMP novels, the jails are uninhabitable due to no air conditioning leading to high temperatures and poor ventilation. Without running water, toilets can't be used and drinking water has to be supplied manually by deputies. Food preparation and service is seriously impacted. Security is also difficult as doors and cells must be unlocked manually; our jails have very few sets of old fashioned keys. Movement would be a *major* issue without electricity.

Alternative jail facilities that don't require intensive technology use should be planned for. This most likely would be in the form of expedient detention facilities such as tent cities or conversion of warehouses. Military police field manuals describe how to construct these. National Guard military police corrections and POW units would be excellent resources.

### Data retention

Inmate booking data, court cases, and police reports should be backed up locally on air-gapped hard drives. In the event of an EMP or cyberattack, at least some of the records will be recoverable as long as computers are stored in protection as well. Total digitalization is great until the system goes down for like a week, which happened to my department not too long ago. Paper copies are decreasingly common and in a lot of cases paper case files no longer exist.

The means to create paper files should exist. At a basic level, paper forms need to be kept in storage. A working copy machine and lots of paper can take the place of an old fashioned print shop. And pencil and pens, lots. Anyone who has been in law enforcement long enough remembers the pencil, pen, and paper days.

### Avoiding lynchings

Involvement of the criminal justice system, trials, and punishment will need to be swift and flexible to avoid lynchings. A saying goes "When there are no police, the punishment for crime is often death," meaning victims will kill the suspect or mobs will lynch them. As one law professor said eloquently:

"Well, we'll see a lot of vigilante justice. And

what are people gonna do about it? Call the cops? Remember, in the end the police aren't there to protect the public from criminals, they're there to protect criminals from the public. Communities dealt with crime long before police were invented, usually in rather harsh and low-due-process ways. The bargain was, let the police handle it instead. No police, no bargain."[38]

The public taking justice into its own hands will erode any authority the criminal justice system might retain and complicate efforts to restart a fair system once order has been restored.

Basic constitutional tenants should be respected but modified for the current reality. Such as juries of fewer than 12 persons, departure from procedure when necessary due to the catastrophe, using any lawyer to act as defense counsel, etc. In essence, trial practice would be returning to less formalized days of centuries past.

Juries should be convened whenever possible with voir dire reduced to eliminate obvious cases of bias, rather than allow either side an "optimal" jury selection. Tales juries, which is persons rounded up by deputies, could be utilized if the jury duty system is non-functional.

If a lynching is unavoidable, authorities and judges should work with the crowd to ensure *some* form of due process and defense for the accused. Historical examples show that in many cases lynch mobs and vigilantes were willing to listen to a defense and take votes. Not in every case, but many times, an innocent person was let go or a guilty person sincerely confessed.

While such an unorthodox "trial" may seem like condoning mob rule, it should be framed as reinforcing due process. Some due process is better than none at all and such examples can be used

---

[38]   Glenn     Reynolds,     Instapundit.com,     6/30/2020,
https://pjmedia.com/instapundit/384041/

to remind the public of the legal system. It sure beats allowing a mob to simply kill a man without giving him a chance to defend himself.

Local sheriffs need to plan for expedient executions which should ideally be conducted under the auspices of their office after a guilty jury verdict, a death penalty, and judicial review. Universally executions are handled by state authorities at prisons whereas in the past and on the frontier many executions were done at the county level.

Even an unconventional trial and execution that has some due process, public involvement, and carried out by an impartial official is better than uncontrolled mob rule.

## Alternative punishment

Law enforcement many need to revert to ancient and third-world systems of punishment such as corporal punishment and beatings *en situ* rather than issue fines and citations. With no judicial system or one that can enforce such minor punishments, the only effective penalty is the incapacity to reoffend. Typically this is done through incarceration, which may be impractical or impossible, or death.

With no money, or if it is worthless or impossible to get, a fine is not a deterrent. Confiscation of goods should be avoided as a penalty in times of scarcity. A person may view this as theft, not punishment, and may actually have their survival imperiled by this. Taking of goods by authority figures also has historical support for allowing excessive taking, such as the biblical narratives of greedy tax collectors. Alternative sentencing such as public labor is a better alternative.

It may be that court systems fail entirely and lynch law is the only law. If police are still functioning, they may find themselves in the role of judge, jury, and executioner where they must investigate, establish guilt, determine a punishment, and execute that punishment. In such a case, officers and deputies should look to the surrounding public to testify, vote on guilt and sentence, and for their support for both guilt and punishment.

In such situations where police must act as the whole criminal justice system, extreme care must be exercised not to abuse power or engage in excesses. Police will have to exercise extreme discretion and good decision making to avoid being seen as oppressors or suffering reprisals for abuse. I recommend police in this role as they have been vetted and trained for impartiality and investigation, something a hot headed victim or crowd won't have.

The public, even if a small crowd has to be rounded up, can hear both sides of the story, hash out guilt and responsibility, and decide the if and how of punishment. The officer acts as a referee during the proceedings and can present what his investigation revealed. If he disagrees with a "guilty" verdict, he can veto the crowd's decision. If any punishment is to be handed out, the officer can execute it in a manner that will not cross the line into excessive cruelty or retributive barbarism.

Police are generally trusted to be impartial, thorough, and fair. In spite of 2020, for the most part police are all these things and many Americans still trust the police. Huge numbers of the public's first instinct in a dispute, fight, or when in danger is to call the police. Officers are trusted to settle disagreements, break up fights, hunt down criminals, and investigate crimes. We demand that they do this fairly, professionally, quickly, and efficiently. For the most part, officers do strive to do this. If cops can investigate crimes, collect evidence and testimony, and usually arrest the correct culprit, they can be trusted in a compromise situation to be more than just the guy with handcuffs.

Public opinions and pressure can work to influence post-SHTF police to be as fair as possible, even if they have to dish out beatings instead of booking a suspect. In fact, the public is vital to keeping super-empowered police in line. Such a combination of duties is a dangerous risk of authoritarianism or exploitation to the public. Citizens will have to ensure that officers do not abuse their roles if they are granted a magisterial role in addition to keeping the peace and arresting offenders.

Such power must be immediately relinquished as soon as practical. In fact, such power would likely be temporary even in the most catastrophic of scenarios as a reconstituted judicial system would be reestablished at some point (the sooner the better). Remember that humans had courts, prisons, jails, and fines as the direct ancestor of our modern system for centuries and cruder systems dating back to the beginning of civilization.

This last bit is mostly a hope and fantasy on my part, I do admit. Trust in the police has taken a nose dive in the last two years and passing decades thanks to the media blowing issues out of proportion. I expect that in any major SHTF situation the rule of law will eventually disappear entirely. Police will desert, disband, and generally look out for themselves. Mobs, gangs, and victims will mete out punishment as they see fit. Only once the dust has settled and people are sick of the chaos will they work to establishing a trusted justice system.

## Public Safety Agencies

### Communications

The major issues for agencies in a catastrophe will be staffing, communications, and consumable resources. Without people, without communications, and without replacing the stuff that gets used, the system breaks down.

Modern emergency services cannot function without timely communications. Without phones, the public cannot contact first responders without physically summoning them. This dramatically increases response times, decreasing the efficacy of these services to levels not seen in nearly a century. The public simply does not have a way to remotely summon official help without phones.

Police cannot be dispatched in time to stop crimes or apprehend criminals in/shortly after the act if people cannot call for help as it is happening. Fire detection might as well be putting a fire fighter in a tall building with a whistle to blow when he sees smoke. EMS in the most critical moments won't even be summoned until it is too late for them to do good.

The first step to maintain communications is having spare radios. An EMP may disable radios that are deployed. Store spare and last-generation radios with their batteries and antennas removed, preferably underground and/or in a Faraday cage, in the event of EMP. Simplex radio systems and frequencies should be maintained and not abandoned entirely when trunked or digital systems are implemented. Keeping the old radios just in case is cheap.

If communications without repeaters are not possible over your region (typically county or city level), create a local relay situation where traffic from distant stations or units can be relayed to their destination by intermediate stations. This will involve manual retransmitting. More powerful local transmitters (base station radios stored for contingencies) and even spare antennas may be needed to accomplish this.

Make relationships within the local ham radio community beyond ARES/RACES. Develop a "phones down" reporting system where a dispatcher or ham liaison can field emergency reports from local amateur operators. Work with local hams to publicize knowledge of this system so that in a crisis hams can radio in emergency reports or serve as a point of contact for the public to summon help.

Certain GMRS and CB radio frequencies should be designated as emergency only channels that public safety agencies monitor. These radios are quite commonly owned and ownership could be expanded in a crisis easily without knowledge of radio theory. If the agencies cannot receive the help call, other users can relay the call. Relays will likely be needed as many of the radios the public owns are low power.

## Employee retention

Major factors in desertion will be conservation/gathering of resources and personal/family safety. A fire fighter is not going to want to burn 10 gallons of fuel he may not get back driving forty miles from the high desert to downtown LA. Likewise, someone who is struggling to find enough food to keep his family from starving isn't going to want to divert the hours necessary for that to perform a job that isn't guaranteed to put food on the table.

Public employees in the emergency services or critical public works should be relocated to staff facilities and stations as near their homes as possible. This will reduce transportation expense and time should fuel sources, etc. be constrained. Employees will also feel that their efforts are more related to the survival of their families, friends, and themselves if they are working in or near where they live.

Police will not want to leave their loved ones to fend for themselves while he provides security for strangers; the officer would rather stay home and provide direct protection than trust some other officer who might or might not be there for him. The officer might not be guarding his house, but if he's not far away, he can respond home and also provide area protection that benefits him, his family, and his community. Simply said public servants care more if they feel they're working for their neighborhood.

First responders will not put their or their family's survival behind that of the public. The safety and survival of families are as vital of that as the officers, medics, and fire fighters for an agency to continue to be viable post-catastrophe. Families need to be welcome to shelter at stations with their loved one or in a specialty shelter set aside for that purpose. Though not all employees will have relatives who will want to use an official shelter, a good baseline is a family of four for each employee. This will create very large numbers in some situations.

A regional station at my department had in its emergency plan an invitation for families to shelter at the station with provision for feeding them. This was a large station that could support a lot of people (more if the jail was repurposed). The smallest station could have over 100 people if everyone was camping out there. One idea is to have the station distribute food and necessary supplies and only provide family shelter while the employ is on duty, in order to limit the number of persons present at any one time.

An alternative is an off-site location staffed by emergency and local government personnel. Those essential workers who may not come in for duty due to concerns for their family, or even their own safety, can be centralized in a guarded shelter, with creature comforts, food and water. Smaller locations won't be overwhelmed and this economizes on resources.

Such a facility should be remote, out of the public view, and well guarded. Though public employees would be working on behalf of the public under difficult and austere conditions, the public may resent officials having it "better" than they. One cannot count on the public understanding that without these accommodations, the emergency services become non-functional. Additionally, such a concentration of personnel and resources would be a tempting target to malign actors.

Public safety agencies need to take it upon themselves to invest in large quantities of long-term storage food for their employees. Emergency managers are capable of looking far ahead and investing in low probability, high impact events. That's their job. On a long enough timeline, the outside contingency they planned for will come to fruition. However, individuals aren't so good at this, even cops and fire fighters.

Having more than just casual experience among them, they are just like every other citizen. One guy might be so clueless he doesn't understand why there are no turkeys left at noon on

Christmas Eve and another guy might have a decade's worth of freeze dried holiday meals packed up in plastic tubs. We in the emergency response community are just as guilty of everybody else of assuming that tomorrow will be just like yesterday.

If public agencies want their employees to keep coming to work, paychecks aren't going to be enough. Money is used to exchange for necessary goods and if the stuff you need can't be had for any sum of money, your paycheck is no good. Even in severe shortages an employee isn't going to be willing to devote time he could be using to find food, etc. just to earn a check that can't help him.

At the most basic level, employees will have to be fed while they are on duty. I would also suggest sending them home with at least a meal for them and their family. Many of us have heard the stories of kids taking home their school provided lunches to share because it is the only food that the family would get that day; such will probably be the case for public employees. An employee might work under duress if he knows that he can eat and minimally feed his family. This could be made part of a crisis pay package or substitute entirely for money if things are so bad money doesn't have meaning anymore.

Non-essential employees will need to be excluded from such schemes to conserve resources. Only those who directly contribute to the maintenance of public safety, public health, or utilities can be protected by crisis supply and shelter systems. Non-essential bureaucrats have to be sacrificed in order to keep essential government systems working. If this alienates the office workers, so be it. Once things are restored they can come back to work. Otherwise paper-pushers can be found anywhere.

But who is non-essential? I don't have a good answer. Teachers, social workers, the people who issue permits, the tax people, human resources, etc. are non-essential to basic survival. Emergency and public works agencies have many "civilian" employees who handle administrative tasks. Often the critical workers are fond of the secretaries, clerks, etc. One has to carefully determine who is truly essential and who isn't. Sergeants can double down and do human resources work, freeing up one mouth for the scheduler/timekeeper, but the records supervisor might be a volunteer in the emergency operations center. A vehicle mechanic is not a front-line worker but is crucial to long-term operations.

### Fuel and vehicles

Local authorities need to have secure fuel supplies that are under their control. I was fortunate to work for an agency that used county fuel points, meaning that we didn't have to rely on commercial gas stations. Most fuel pumps were at secure locations that in a crisis could be easily locked and guarded to prevent theft. I can't imagine the underground tanks were anything more than a standard service station, but at least we weren't competing with every other motorist.

Many municipalities and emergency agencies rely on commercial stations and fueling cards. This system works well when fuel supplies are plentiful. As soon as a shortage develops public entities are in trouble and it is compounded when there is no alternative available. As seductive as it is not having to worry about long-term fuel contracts, building and maintaining fuel pumps, and having the ability to gas up anywhere there is a card reader, this can be a major trap.

Should a community rely on fueling its public vehicles from commercial sources, at least one emergency alternative fuel supply should be established. Motor pool facilities, public works yards, or municipal garages should have some sort of fueling point. If an underground tank and pump is out of the question, a very basic solution would be one to two thousand gallons in an above ground tank with an electric pump for both gas and diesel. This would ensure at least a few days of basic operations in a crisis before resupply and the fuel can be easily rotated.

Having police cars and fire trucks that run is absolutely critical. Cops aren't going to walk foot beats over large areas on the off chance that they are going to stumble on a crime. A fire truck without fuel is a lot of shiny paint and metal. American emergency services cannot provide any sort of modern service without running vehicles.

This is not beyond possibility. Imagine a future war with China and/or Russia where cyberattacks have disabled fuel pipelines and the payment/distribution systems for gas stations have been targeted too. Oil tankers, refineries, and major storage facilities may be targeted by kinetic attacks. Fuel and oil infrastructure has been targeted in past wars and will in future ones. We cannot assume that the homeland will always be free from attack.

# Water; the Most Important Resource

Where does your water come from? No, not the tap or the refrigerator. What is the source? For those in the northwest or outside the cities back east, this isn't a critical question. Those who are on their own wells don't have to worry much either. But for the average city dweller, especially those in the southwest, water supply is a matter of life and death.

Los Angeles is a perfect example. When the city was first founded on the banks of the LA River, it was easy for Spanish settlers to draw water from the river (more like a big creek). Wells could be dug as well. As the town grew, water had to be supplied via the *zanja madre*, or mother ditch. Groundwater supply for the booming city got to be a critical issue by the turn of the 20th century. Like Rome and its aqueducts, Los Angeles reached out into the countryside for water.

The most notable water source for Los Angeles is the LA Aqueduct that winds its way down from the Owens Valley of the eastern Sierra region in central California, hundreds of miles away. While much of the aqueduct is gravity flow, it requires electric pumps to clear the Transverse Ranges that separate coastal Southern California from the desert. Water then goes into reservoirs and is piped to the taps of Angelinos.

Other water districts bring water from the Colorado River, all the way from the Arizona border across the desert. From both distant and local sources, interconnected water systems allow surplus water to be sold to other water districts. This water is known as imported water.

Most water systems are now entirely dependent upon electricity. Even if a gravity flow aqueduct brings the water in, almost everywhere needs pumping and booster stations to get it to your kitchen. Government regulations have mandated filtration systems that need high pressure to get the water through the filtration elements that gravity flow alone can't supply the hydraulic head, so pumps push the water through. Many older systems have been retrofitted.

In one of my novels, I feature the city of Thousand Oaks, a city of 120,000 just outside the San Fernando Valley, an hour or so west of downtown LA. To oversimplify, the city sits on a plateau with a broad valley to its north and the Santa Monica Mountains to the south. No rivers flow through the city and there are no natural lakes. This is Southern California so rainfall is sparse.

Thousand Oaks developed the Conejo Valley, once a rich farming and ranching community. Wells and their windmills dotted the landscape. It looked like an old western because a lot of the old westerns were literally filmed right there. Farmers drew up groundwater that was highly mineralized. Local groundwater there doesn't taste very good. It was enough for farming and even the small town.

Over time, the city grew. Today, there is one active well which is not use for potable water. Many of the old well sites have been capped or totally abandoned and buried under suburbs. The city is entirely dependent on imported water for survival. Bard Lake, a reservoir at the north end of the city, is filled with purchased and imported water. It is a finite resource.

Las Vegas isn't any better. Though the Colorado River runs not far from the city (now submerged under Lake Mead) the water situation is tenuous. When Lake Mead was conceived and the water treaty negotiated between the western states, Nevada had a tiny population in the desert and received the smallest water allotment from the river. Las Vegas and environs are pushing that allotment to the limit, forcing conservation limiting growth, and officials are even contemplating a water project to transport groundwater from central Nevada.

Hoover Dam and the resulting lake were planned on a faulty understanding of long-range weather patterns. The period of the late 1800s and early 1900s was studied to gauge how much water would be available. This was an extraordinarily wet cycle, meaning

278

the predictions of rainfall over the Colorado watershed was exaggerated. As time went on, the predictions did not match reality and now the southwest is in a drought. Contrary to climate change hysteria, drought is an entirely normal and natural state in the southwest. Lake Mead is currently as low as it has been since it filled.

Also dependent on the Colorado River (besides Southern California) is Arizona. The Central Arizona Project transports water hundreds of miles to Phoenix. While the local prospects of water are better in Phoenix, both cities are still entirely dependent on electricity to supply water. Gone are the days of artesian wells and simple pumps bringing gallons to the surface. These metropolises with their millions cannot subsist on what is under their feet.

As long as water is flowing, you can collect it and purify it as necessary. Examine what threats you are facing and what will happen to the water supply in your area. In the arid southwestern cities, if the municipal water system goes down, we're doomed unless it comes back on. I plan for two weeks. Two weeks is enough time to replenish what you've drunk, repairs to be made, or FEMA to get its act together.


## Emergency municipal water supply

In my EMP series, I look at the worst case scenario. With the loss of electricity, no water can be pumped or imported. This means that taps run dry very quickly. Even if you have a well in your neighborhood, that water must still be pumped to you via electrical means. A well is just a hole into which a pipe is inserted and has to have its own pump to draw water to the surface.

If you have a well at home, you are familiar with this arrangement. Perhaps you are lucky enough that your water tank is gravity-flow assisted and you don't need a separate pump to get water to the house. But some force has to get the water to the surface.

Old windmill wells worked when the wind blew the windmill and brought water to the surface. Calm winds weren't very dangerous because the water would be pumped into a tank and it was just a single farm, plus the livestock, using it. Increase demand, and you need to increase the supply. More supply needs a pump capable of constantly pulling up enough water, and intermittent wind can't do that for a city.

In arid areas, the water table is often hundreds of feet down. Forget digging a well by hand and dropping in a bucket. Many farms went under because demand sucked the aquifer dry and the technology at the time couldn't get water that retreated several hundred feet down.

Poor Thousand Oaks is left with no water and a clock running out before authorities can no longer supply emergency water brought by tanker. In my other books, public works officials rig up contraptions on wells to pull water to the surface. Because I'm not familiar with the anatomy of a modern well, I left the details vague, but all are low-flow pumps powered by wind or solar. Someone who knows what they're doing could tear apart the well equipment and rig up a little pumping system.

In my books, these pump systems supply a few gallons a minute, but that's enough for a person to fill up a container for their daily water needs. Many of these people walk or bike miles in the heat to fill up everything from purpose made containers to recycled soda jugs. They are coming back, day after day, to get water. This happens all the time in the third world, but it is a huge shock to the fictional denizens of Ventura County.

In the real world, I would bet that local government would be unable to get hasty pumps rigged as I wrote. First, the government would be paralyzed by inaction and no one having any idea of what to do. Then whoever had the idea would have to convince the city or their boss to let them destructively tear off pipes, pumps, and equipment to rig something up, probably with equipment scrounged from other city property. How many bureaucrats would refuse this because, if and/or when things went back to normal, the cost to repair it would be high?

If everything goes as planned and water flows, people have to come and get the water. Many will not be physically able to do this if cars aren't available. Police then have to guard the well against those idiots who would damage the new pump mechanism, but against gangs or whoever might try to monopolize it. Just imagine you are someone with no morals and you control the water source for miles around. You could use that to get whatever you want.

For those in the deserts or arid west, a grid-down emergency and loss of water would be a massive problem. It might even kill you. Where does your water come from? Where does water flow naturally on the surface? Do you know of a spring? I have one less than a mile away, but these days it's mostly irrigation runoff from lawns. That creek in the middle of town? As soon as the pumped water stops flowing, the runoff from lawns and landscaping sprinklers stops and so does the creek flow.

Other cities are better off. Many cities have a river running through downtown. My great-grandparents had a creek on the other side of the neighbor's pasture. My grandmother grew up in a town that still has water flowing through the old Mormon canals. Some of you live in cities with creeks, streams, and rivers in and around town. In those places, water is just a walk away. The chore is hauling and purifying.

Do you want to collect rainwater? Better hope it rains a lot. In the southwest, you are going to have a tough time of it. Winter rain is chancy and monsoon season is inconsistent. In between are long dry times. But let's look at rooftop collection anyhow.

First, your whole roof needs to be guttered and you should have downspouts in each corner with collection barrels underneath. To calculate how much water you can get, you need to do some research and math. What is the square footage of your roof? How much water (volume) can the gutters capture and deliver to the barrels? How much rain falls in your area on average to calculate rainfall per square foot? You need to then calculate how much water will fall on your roof and if your gutter system can capture it all. Here's an example from my first book:

> "Finally, the catchment system that diverted the rainwater which would be otherwise lost down the rain gutters could more than replace the evaporated water. Mr. Palmer installed it when water rates went up during the drought and the city offered a rebate on the system. The math was simple: 1 cubic foot of rainwater equaled 7.48 gallons. The area of the roof used for catchment was about 2500 square feet of Spanish-style tile, which unfortunately has the worst coefficient of collection at about .9. So 2000sqft multiplied by 1.3 feet of rain (15.5 inches was the yearly average) times the coefficient of .9 meant 2,340 cubic feet, or roughly 17,500 gallons of water."

That's 17,500 gallons of water, but can your gutters capture the amount of rain that comes off of the roof in a typical rainstorm? Do you have storage for that much water? What about the pool? There are tens of thousands of gallons in there!

Drinking pool water isn't a great idea, but doable if necessary. It shouldn't be a first plan. Do you want to be drinking water with diluted chlorine (lots of it), muriatic acid, cyanuric acid, and even pee? Think about all the sweat, lotion, sunscreen, dirt, bacteria, and feces particles that come off your body into the pool. On top of that, there is algae and bacteria from the environment fouling the pool. At minimum, the water must be purified to avoid intake of pathogens.

Now as far as the chlorine, it is usually highly diluted. Pools with correct chemical balances have about 2 PPM (parts per million) of chlorine and you can safely drink double that amount. To keep the water from stagnating, you will need to continuously add chlorine and maintain your pool. Is this something you do yourself, or does the pool man come? How much chlorine do you have on hand? Don't forget the pool filter won't clean debris out of the water if there is no electricity.

## Water transportation

How are you going to get your water home from whatever source you have? Water is not light. A gallon of water weights 8.3lbs. The absolute minimum drinking water needed is two quarts/liters (basically the same volume). On a hot day if you are active, you can drink twice that much. Now take another gallon for cooking and another for cleaning. That's 25lbs. How much will your family need?

One gallon of water is the comfortable bare minimum for both drinking and minimal cooking/sanitation. Three gallons a day will probably be more than enough for a person. Three days of water is a minimum, two weeks is better. If you have water problems, store as much as you can. So at three days, we have 9 gallons per person, or 36 gallons for a family of four. Two weeks worth would be 42 gallons per person and 168 gallons for a family.

Remember not to buy all water bottles. Plastic bottles degrade over time, especially in heat. Ever drink water and get a harsh, plastic taste? That's the bottle breaking down into the water from heat. It won't kill you, but it tastes bad and isn't good for you. Washing and cooking out of 16 ounce bottles isn't going to be fun and storing them will be annoying.

Freezing is also another concern. Is your water going to freeze in the winter? If so, it needs to be in a container that can flex as the water turns to ice and expands. Plastic bottles survive this and even if dropped while frozen, can withstand a blow. Other solutions, better for cars and bug out bags, are juice-box water and pouches of water. If you have to defrost them, a smaller container can thaw faster than a larger one (larger containers have more thermal mass and resist temperature changes because it takes more energy to thaw them).

Water storage and transportation go hand in hand. Static water storage, the stuff you have at home, doesn't need to be very mobile. Large five-gallon containers just need to be moved across the room or into the garage. Almost anyone can manage that. As containers grow larger, it becomes harder to move them. Think of filling a moving box with books; you can put a lot of books in a big box, but the weight makes the box hard to lift. So if all you're doing is running a hose to a 55 gallon drum, you don't have to worry.

Moving a 55 gallon drum of water isn't easy. A full drum weighs over 450lbs. We had to rotate the emergency water supply out of the station to drain it and we almost killed two cadets and two inmate workers in the process before someone thought to get a hand truck. Are you going to buy a specialty curved hand truck to take your drums down to the river and haul them back home?

Big drums are great, but they are not going to be transported for refill. Smaller containers are a better idea. They're easier to handle and transport. My choice are five-gallon cubes with spigot attachments. They weight about 40lbs full, can be moved by one person, and can easily dispense water. For drums, smaller 15 gallon drums come with handles and are much easier to move and roll on their edges. Don't forget the bung wrench to open up the caps on the top and a pump to siphon the water out.

These can all be filled with tap water but must be treated with sodium hypochlorite to prevent bacterial growth inside. When filling, it is recommended you use a drinking water safe hose and not just your garden hose that probably has spiders living in it. You can also use specialty hose to create a shower or camp sink. Keep stored water in a dark place so light and heat doesn't encourage stuff to grow.

Some people advocate washing out two-liter soda bottles or juice bottles and reusing them. That's a possibility, especially if you are frugal, but the containers have the ability to retain flavors or residue that can contaminate, taint, or flavor the water. Careful washing and selection are important. Purpose built containers can be properly resealed to be water tight.

After an earthquake, one of the things we've always been told to do is fill the bathtub with water in case the city water lines are broken. There are problems with that. First, bathtubs aren't always clean, maybe for a couple of hours before someone plonks their dirty body in it. When you do clean it, what kind of chemicals are you using? Do you want to be drinking 409 and Ajax? Don't forget your body hair, stubble, and the soaps and shampoos that end up in there.

A better solution is a purpose built plastic container that attaches to the tap and uses the tub itself to provide structural strength. These things are just big, tough plastic bags with a pump on them that protects your drinking water from the nasty things in the bathtub. One brand name is waterBOB. This can give you up to 100 gallons of water. Until they are used, the bag folds up and is stored in a small box, perfect for apartments.

## Water purification

After an earthquake, a water main break, or some failure at the treatment plant, boil water orders are issued. Usually it's out of an abundance of caution, but just in case some bug got in the water, the water people want you to kill it with heat. Boiling water will kill any pathogen in it, unless you're drinking the water from those hot springs at Yellowstone with the colored bacteria that love high heat.

For those of us lucky enough to have running surface nearby (and not salt water—if I have to tell you not to drink that you deserve to die), water supply is not a problem. The problem then becomes chemicals. Luckily, most rivers and streams that suburbanites have access to in wet areas are fairly clean these days. The river in Cleveland doesn't catch on fire anymore. Contamination from factories is not common, but if you live in an area with heavy industry, find out what is in your local water source now in case it is present at a harmful level.

Local streams will probably be fairly clean. Runoff from roads will carry oils and irrigation runoff will bring fertilizer and lawn chemicals. In a survival situation, this will have to be accepted. Most chemicals diluted in water won't hurt you if you rely on the source for a short time but can't be easily filtered out or purified. I'd rather drink water diluted with car juices than die.

Since urban water ways are popular with the homeless, check upstream. Is someone defecating into the water? Check for garbage or rotting things. In rural or wilderness areas, check for dead animals upstream. Always draw from clean, running water, never discolored or stagnant, algae filled water (if you can help it).

Filter cloudy water through a clean cloth, paper towel, or coffee filter. Boil it for at least one minute, unless you are at high altitude, then boil for 3-5 minutes. Boiling longer than necessary is a waste of fuel. Let it cool before drinking it. Properly filtered and boiled water is safe to drink without chemicals. To improve taste, swish it between clean containers (to put air back in) or a pinch of salt per quart/liter.

Sodium hypochlorite is bleach. It is a clear chemical, with a slight yellow tinge and an obvious and familiar sharp scent. It is sold as a specialty product to purify and preserve a given quantity of water, such as a 55 gallon solution in a bottle the size of an eyedropper. It may be best and easiest to treat storage water with solutions sold for this purpose.

If using bleach to purify water for drinking, be careful what you're using. You don't want fancy bleach, just the plain boring stuff your grandmother used. Use bleach that is between 5.25% and 8.25% chlorine. Do not use bleach that contains dyes, other additives, or is scented. Use five drops (using a clean eye dropper) per quart/liter or ¼ teaspoon per gallon. Double the drops if the water is cloudy, colored, or cold.

Mix thoroughly and wait at least an hour before drinking. It should have a slight odor of chlorine, but not an offensive smell or cause burning or discomfort on drinking. To improve the taste, let it stand for a few hours or pour back and forth between clean containers. Remember, jugs of bleach will degrade over time and will no longer be chemically active as bleach, so buy fresh.

Water purifiers are great tools to have. Usually campers and backpackers use purifiers, but larger models are available for purification of greater quantities. These are almost always manually operated and the filters can remove most bacteria and viruses. Other models rely on gravity feed through filtration elements but do a lesser job of filtering out bugs. These usually are for taste and clarity of well water, which is generally free of pathogens. Your countertop and refrigerator "Brita" style filters are for taste only and will not purify water. Don't use them!

## Summary

In conclusion, for those in areas with limited to no surface water or domestic wells, store at a minimum of two weeks of drinking water. More is better to survive and give yourself time to establish a new water supply. Have a means to purify and transport water home. Encourage your municipal and water authorities to develop alternative local water sources and methods of water delivery in a superlatively catastrophic disaster. Encourage your local emergency services to purchase drinking water tanks and tanker trucks.

# Appendix: USMC Improvised Explosive Device (IED) guide

**Author's note:** *this appendix is taken from a Marine Corps document (MCCS IED 1001/1002, Improvised Explosive Device (IED), undated) and provided in largely its original form.*

## TERMINAL LEARNING OBJECTIVES

1. Given a tactical scenario with an Improvised Explosive Device (IED) threat training aids and an IED lane, **visually identify IEDs to ensure identification of ground emplaced IEDs, Suicide Vehicle-borne IEDs (SVIEDs), and Suicide Bomber attack IEDs are confirmed** in accordance with the references.
2. Given a tactical scenario with an IED threat training aids and an IED lane, **conduct immediate actions in response to an IED to ensure the tactical effects of IED(s) on mission accomplishment are mitigated, in order to meet the concept of operations and the commander's intent**, in accordance with the mission order and the references.

## INTRODUCTION

Improvised explosive devices (IEDs) account for the majority of wounded and killed military personnel in combat situations. As an emergency provider you are one thousand times more likely to encounter injury from conventional explosives than from a chemical, biological, or nuclear attack. It is important to consider some basic tactics, techniques, and procedures (TTPs). Understanding the TTPs will allow you to survive in an IED environment.

Knowing what to look for and where to look is a starting point. Understanding how to move, as part of a patrol or resupply element, for example, will give you an edge on the battlefield. It is important to remember IEDs are not the enemy; the people using the IEDs are the enemy. They can be defeated by being observant and looking for IED indicators. IEDs can be produced in varying sizes and can have different types of containers, function, and delivery methods. IEDs become more difficult to detect and protect against as the enemy becomes more sophisticated.

## 1. IED TERMINOLOGY AND COMPONENTS

Terminology

Improvised Explosive Devices are those devices that are placed or fabricated in an improvised manner incorporating destructive, lethal, noxious, pyrotechnic, or incendiary chemicals and designed to destroy, incapacitate, harass, or distract. They may incorporate military weapons but are normally devised from non-military components.

Booby Traps are explosive or non-explosive devices or other materials, deliberately placed to cause casualties when an apparently harmless object is disturbed or a normally safe act is performed.

Mines are explosives or materials, normally encased, designed to destroy or damage ground vehicles, boats, or aircraft, or designed to wound, kill, or otherwise incapacitate personnel. They may be detonated by the actions of its victims, by the passage of time, or by controlled means.

Components - IEDs can vary widely in shape and form. IEDs share a common set of components that consist of the casing, initiating system, and main charge.

Casings can range in size from a cigarette pack to a large truck or airplane. The container is used to help hide the IED and to possibly provide fragmentation. Countless containers have been used as casings including soda cans, animal carcasses, plastic bags, and vests or satchels for suicide bombers.

Initiating systems cause the main charge to function. It can be a simple hard wire (for command detonation), or a radio frequency (RF) device such as a cell phone or a toy car remote control. The initiator almost always includes a blasting cap and batteries as a power source for the detonator. Any type of battery can be used (9-volt, AA, or car batteries). Initiating systems are triggered in three ways – over time, on command, and by the victim.

Time - timed IEDs are designed to function after a preset delay, allowing the enemy to make his escape or to target military forces which have created a pattern.

Command - command-initiated IEDs are a common method of employment and allow the enemy to choose the optimal moment of initiation. They are normally used against targets that are in transit, or where a routine pattern has been established. The most common types of command-initiated methods are with command wires or radio-controlled devices, such as cordless telephones and remote car openers.

Victim - victim-actuated IEDs are initiated by the actions of the victim(s). There are various types of initiation devices to include pull or trip, pressure, pressure release, movement-sensitive, light-sensitive, proximity, and electronic switches.

Main Charge

High Explosive main charges are the most common encountered in theater. Common explosives used are military munitions, usually 122mm or greater. These items are the easiest to use and provide a ready-made fragmentation effect and multiple main charges together over long or short distances for simultaneous detonation. Common hardware, such as ball bearings, bolts, nuts, or nails can be used to enhance the fragmentation. Propane tanks, fuel cans, and battery acid can, and have been added to IEDs to propagate their blast and thermal effects.

Chemical - a chemical IED is a main charge with a chemical payload in conjunction with an explosive payload. Chemical IEDs are fabricated to kill or incapacitate victims with a chemical, rather than explosive, effect. Some indicators for chemical IEDs are smaller blasts, odor, gas cloud, and liquid on or near the suspected IED.

## 2. PRIMARY INDICATORS

There are many ways to detect IEDs. The best means of detection is your situational awareness. The primary indication of an IED will be a change in the baseline (something new on the route that was not there the previous day). Vigilant observation for these subtle indicators can increase the likelihood of IED detection. Some examples of possible roadside IED indicators may include:

- Unusual behavior patterns or changes in community patterns, such as noticeably fewer people or vehicles in a normally busy area, open windows, or the absence of women or children.
- Vehicles following a convoy for a long distance and then pulling to the roadside.
- Personnel on overpasses.
- Signals from vehicles or bystanders (flashing headlights).
- People videotaping ordinary activities or military actions. Enemies using IEDs often document their activities for use as recruitment or training tools.
- Suspicious objects.
- Metallic objects, such as soda cans and cylinders.
- Markers by the side of the road, such as tires, rock piles, ribbon, or tape that may identify an IED location to the local population or serve as an aiming reference for the enemy triggering the IED (such as light poles, fronts or ends of guardrails, and road intersections).
- New or out of place objects in an environment, such as dirt piles, construction, dead animals, or trash.
- Graffiti symbols or writing on buildings.
- Signs that are newly erected or seem out of place.
- Obstacles in the roadway to channel traffic.
- Exposed antennas, detonating cord, wires, or ordnance.

- Wires laid out in plain sight; these may be part of an IED or designed to draw friendly force attention before detonation of the real IED.

## 3. LOCATIONS OF IEDS

IEDs may be placed anywhere enough space exists or can be created to hide or disguise the IED. Whenever possible, devices are located where they can exploit known US patterns, such as the use of a main supply route, or vulnerabilities, such as soft-skinned vehicles or chokepoints. Common areas of IED placement may include:

- Previous IED sites.
- Frequently traveled or predictable routes, such as roads leading to bases and along common patrol routes.
- Boundary turnaround points (pattern).
- Medians, by the roadside (usually within 10 feet), or buried under the surface of any type of road, often in potholes and covered with dirt or reheated asphalt.
- Trees, light posts, signs, overpasses, and bridge spans that are elevated.
- Unattended vehicles, carts, or motorcycles (attached or installed in them).
- Hidden inside guardrails or under any type of material or packaging.
- Potential incident control points (ICPs).
- Abandoned buildings or structures (sometimes partially demolished).
- Hidden behind cinder blocks or piles of sand to direct blast into the kill zone.
- Animal carcasses and deceased human bodies.
- Fake bodies or scarecrows in coalition uniforms.
- At the edge of town.

Vehicle Borne IED (VBIED)/Suicide VBIED (SVBIED) – a VBIED is a parked vehicle in a high traffic area with the intent of causing the most damage. An SVBIED is when the driver is willing to give their own life in the process of detonating his explosives. These are very successful because the enemy is mobile and is able to choose a time and place with great flexibility. This unpredictability makes them difficult to identify.

Driver Indicators:

- A lone male driver is the historical standard for VBIED operations; however, there could be any number of people in the vehicle if an unsuspecting person is driving the VBIED. Some VBIEDs have two to three people and females are sometimes used as a distraction.
- Ignoring orders to stop, attempting to circumvent a security checkpoint, or attempting to maneuver too close to coalition assets.
- Unusual appearance. The enemy may be uncharacteristically clean-shaven and have very short haircuts. Cutting the hair is part of the purifying ritual that many follow prior to an attack.
- Age in mid-twenties. The average Middle Eastern suicide terrorist is about 24-25 years old, but this may vary in each unique situation.
- Driving erratically; driving too slow or too fast.
- Wearing inappropriate dress for the environment.

Vehicle Indicators:

- Noticeable sagging of the vehicle.
- An additional antenna for radio-controlled devices.
- Darkened or covered windows to conceal either the vehicle's contents or actions of the driver.
- Recent painting of vehicle to cover body alterations.
- Crudely covered holes made in the vehicle to hide explosives.
- New welding marks.
- No license plates.
- Escorted by unusual security detail for type of vehicle.
- New tires on an old vehicle.
- Anything unusual in factory-build compartments.
- New or shiny bolts and/or screws.
- Unusual scratches, possibly made by screwdrivers, wrenches, or similar tools.
- Signs of tampering, such as broken parts or bent sheet metal.
- Areas and components cleaner or dirtier than surrounding areas.
- Wire and tape stored in the vehicle.

Situation Indicators:

- Camera crew in the area.
- Observing the same vehicle more than once.
- Absence of normal routine for the Area of Operation (AO).
- Odd traffic patterns.
- Person(s) observed conducting reconnaissance.
- Vehicle testing local defenses (i.e., drives at a high speed towards traffic control point and then breaks off).

Suicide Bombers (Personal Borne IED (PBIED)) – most suicide attacks involve SVBIEDs, and include casualty rates from tens to hundreds. There has been an increasing trend for suicide bombers to attack with an explosive vest, belt, or baggage. U.S. and Coalition Forces have been attacked within the perimeter of a base; civilians have been attacked at polling stations and police recruitment drives. With better techniques being used to reduce the effectiveness of VBIEDs, the potential for the enemy to adapt to using suicide bombers increases.

PBIED Design – if the charges used by bombers are effectively packaged and concealed, a suicide bomber could carry up to 45 pounds of explosives; however, most suicide belts are designed to hold smaller amounts, up to 12 pounds. It should be noted that fragment producing materials are often incorporated into the design of these belts/vests.

Indicators of a potential PBIED attack include individuals who deliberately ignore orders to stop or attempt to circumvent a security checkpoint, those wearing too much clothing for the prevailing weather conditions, one with suspicious bulges in his/her clothing, carrying packages/bags or wearing satchels/backpacks, and an individual handling wires, switches, an actuator, or a "dead man's" switch.

## 4. EMPLOYMENT TECHNIQUES

IEDs can be used in a variety of ways. There are some TTPs that the enemy has used in order to hinder the mobility efforts of coalition forces, though enemy TTPs constantly change and adapt in an effort to stay ahead of coalition TTPs. The enemy also incorporates the use of small arms fire in conjunction with the IED attack to harass forces and increase the lethality of attacks.

Disguised static IEDs have been concealed with a variety of things (trash, boxes, tires, etc.) and placed in, on, above, or under where potential targets appear. Multiple IEDs have also been daisy chained, or linked together with detonation cord or electrical wire so that all charges detonate simultaneously, in order to achieve simultaneous explosions.

Thrown or projected IEDs (improvised grenades or mortars) have also been used against coalition forces. One TTP targets convoys as they drive under an overpass, attempting to drop IEDs in the back of vehicles as the pass under. Convoys must be aware of the 360-degree threat while traveling. Changing speeds and dispersion will help mitigate the threat to some extent.

Another example of how IEDs have been used is the hoax IED. These include something that resembles an actual IED, but has no charge or fully functioning initiator device. A fake IED along a given route and seen by the lead vehicle in a convoy will cause the convoy to come to a stop. Stopping for the hoax IED may leave the convoy in the kill zone of the real thing. Hoax IEDs are also used to learn coalition procedures, monitor time, delay or harass activities in support of the mission.

Other techniques used that are less specific include:

The Basic IED Attack - in the basic attack, the enemy will place IEDs along routes on either side of the road awaiting foot patrols or convoys to approach in order to cause the most damage to personnel or vehicles.

The "Broken-down" Vehicle Attack - this attack uses a simulated broken down vehicle placed on the side of the road to cause convoys to change their intended route. The broken down vehicle is staged along either side of the road, blocking one or all of the trafficable lanes. This causes the convoy to be directed between the broken down vehicle and an emplaced IED.

Coordinated Attack - numerous enemies work together to emplace an IED along a route, usually in an urban area. The enemy is usually located where they have the best escape route to not be seen or caught. Once the IEDs have been detonated, the enemy breaks contact and blends in with the population.

Ramming Convoys - the enemy has been known to ram their vehicle (possibly an SVBIED) in the rear of a convoy or to the side as they pass in order to get the convoy to slow or come to a complete stop.

Motorcycles - motorcycles are used by the enemy in areas of decreased mobility in order to harass convoys and possibly throw IEDs or grenades in the rear of vehicles.

## 5. OPERATIONS IN AN IED ENVIRONMENT

In order to counter the effects of an IED, there are several things that can be done. Wearing all personal protective gear available, to include ballistic eye protection, Kevlar helmets, body armor with plates, and hearing protection is the most basic. Other simple, but critical, force protective measures include wearing seatbelts when moving and ensuring all personnel have as much of their body inside the vehicle as possible to reduce the possibility of being struck by shrapnel or being exposed to the initial blast.

Pre-movement Rehearsals - operating units must be prepared to react quickly and efficiently to any attack. Study updated maps, as a significant number of IEDs are set up in the exact same location of previous attacks. Remember that IED attacks may be just one part of a complex attack. The unit must be prepared to react to any threat after the IED detonates and move out of the kill zone as quickly as possible.

Patrolling - one of the most important things you can do to protect yourself and your unit is to limit your predictability. Vary routes, movement techniques, and your TTPs for dealing with different situations. Never forget that the enemy is always watching.

Patrols should change direction and speed at seemingly random intervals, especially in areas of previous IED attacks.

## 6. MITIGATING TACTICS TO COUNTER ATTACKS

There are certain things every member of the unit can do to counter specific attacks. Every member of the patrol should be alert and constantly aware of the situation around them. They should also know the authorized Escalation of Force (EOF) and Rules of Engagement (ROE). The actions listed below will help limit your vulnerability in specific situations:

Counter VBIED/SVBIED Techniques - the key to surviving a VBIED/SVBIED attack is standoff and cover. Know that an SVBIED can come from any direction. Units have been attacked by vehicles turning into a patrol from oncoming traffic, moving in a convoy, or in firm base attacks. Maintain an aggressive security posture and have a plan for dealing with civilian traffic. When dealing with VBIED/SVBIED attacks, it is important to:

- Have a plan to deal with approaching vehicles. Decide if they will be allowed to pass or not and have a plan for the EOF [escalation of force].
- Be aware of danger areas/choke points such as turnoffs that force patrol to slow down.
- Watch merging traffic as VBIEDs have been used near on and off ramps to get close to coalition vehicles.

Counter Suicide Bomber Techniques

- Evacuate the area immediately. Safe distances will depend on the mass of explosives carried by the bomber and the amount and type of fragmentation used.
- "Close and negotiate" tactics **should not be attempted**, as suicide bombers are usually trained to avoid surrender at all costs.
- A "fail safe" cell phone or radio-controlled initiator could be used in the event that the bomber is incapacitated or hesitates. This tactic would normally involve a second suspect with a line-of-sight view of the bomber and should always be considered.

- If a "deadly force" response is taken, bullet impact may initiate/detonate the explosive charge(s). Firing on the suspect should only be undertaken from protective cover.
- If the suspect is neutralized and there is no explosion, **do not administer first aid**. Wait for EOD [Explosive Ordinance Disposal or "bomb squad"] to render safe the explosive charge.

## 7. ACTIONS AT HALTS

If a patrol or convoy must stop during movement avoid clustering vehicles and vary the vehicle interval between elements; establish your own local security and employ techniques to create standoff. Most importantly, do not remain at one site too long and conduct 5 to 25 meter checks as described below.

5 to 25 meter checks – depending on the length of time of the halt, the area to clear varies from 5 to 25 meters. At every halt, no matter how short, the crew must clear 5 meters around the vehicle while still inside the vehicle. For extended halts, teams must clear 25 meters around the patrol or convoy.

5 meter checks:
- Identify a position to halt.
- Visually check the area 5 meters around your vehicles.
- Look for disturbed earth and suspicious objects, loose bricks in walls, and security ties on streetlights or anything out of the ordinary.
- Start your search at ground level and continue up above head height. Then conduct a physical check for a radius of 5 meters around your position. Be systematic, take your time, and show curiosity. If the tactical situation permits, use a white light or infrared (IR) light at night.
- If in an armored vehicle, remain mounted during your 5 meter check to take advantage of the vehicle's protection.

25 meter checks:
- Add to the 5 meter check when the patrol or convoy leader decides to occupy an area for any length of time.

- Once 5 meter checks are done, continue visually scanning out to 25 meters.
- Conduct a physical search for a radius of 25 meters around your position.
- Look for IED indicators and anything out of the ordinary.

## 8. ACTIONS ON CONTACT

Should you be part of a patrol or convoy that finds an IED, the five "Cs" will help to ensure that the situation can be dealt with quickly and safely. Remember, an IED that is found is still an IED attack. By finding the IED, you have just disrupted the enemy's attack. Do not forget about the enemy's other forms of attack, RPGs, small arms fire, mortars, and secondary IED. **Enemy IED site = Enemy ambush site. You are in the kill zone!**

IED's Found Before Detonation - a simple set of guidelines that you should use when you encounter a suspected IED are the five "Cs":

Confirm - you should always assume the device will explode at any moment. From a safe distance, look for IED indicators while attempting to confirm the suspected IED. Use all tools at your disposal, to include moving to a better vantage point and using optics to look for tell-tale signs of an IED. Never ask civilians to remove an IED and do not attempt to do the job of Explosive Ordnance Disposal (EOD) or engineers.

Clear - evacuate the area to a safe distance (terrain will dictate) but do not set a pattern. Keep in mind some threats require more standoff than others. Assess whether your distance and cover is adequate and direct people out of the danger area. Sweep the area for any secondary devise or trigger person. Once scene is safe, question, search, and detain as needed. Do not allow anyone to enter your cordon other than those responsible for rendering the IED safe (EOD).

Call/Check - let your higher headquarters know what you have found. When you move to a new location, all personnel should conduct 5 and 25 meter checks for secondary IEDs. Always assume a found IED is bait and the real IED is near your "secure" location.

Cordon - establish blocking positions to prevent vehicle and foot traffic from approaching the IED. Establish 360 degree inner and outer cordon to secure and dominate the area. Most likely, the enemy is watching and waiting to make his move.

Control - control the area until EOD arrives. Clear and set up an entry control point (ECP) for first responders. Do not let others go forward to "inspect" the IED. Make contingency plans for coordinated attacks.

IED Detonation - immediate actions differ when an IED is actually detonated. The enemy may often combine the IED attack with a direct fire ambush to increase the lethality of the attack. If an ambush does accompany an IED attack, the priority shifts to address the direct fire and then conducting the 5 "Cs". It is important to keep several things in mind when dealing with IED detonation:

- Respond quickly and aggressively in accordance with ROE
- Immediately scan outward. The biggest mistake Marines can make is focusing inwards toward the site of the IED detonation and forgetting about the enemy.
- Move out of kill zone
- Search for additional IEDs
- Treat/Evacuate casualties
- Report situation
- Expect follow-on attacks

Chemical IED - coalition forces have had several encounters with IEDs also having chemical filler in conjunction with the explosive. Due to the complexity of manufacturing exact payloads, the chemical effect is difficult to achieve. Units must be aware of the capabilities and know what to do in the event of a chemical attack. Specifically:

- Move upwind, to high ground at least 240 meters away from release point.

- Normal combat uniform provides some protection; individual protective suits, masks and gloves will provide additional protection.
- Detectors will alarm, but best warning comes from your sense of sight and smell.

### What NOT to do with Suspected IEDs

**Never approach a suspected IED.** Establish standoff by using binoculars and spotting scopes from multiple angles to confirm the presence of an IED. When in doubt, back off and call EOD.

**Do not pick up detonation cord.** Detonation cord is an explosive and the presence of it alone is enough to call EOD. Do not trace or pull on det cord.

**Do not directly trace command wire (CW).** The enemy has placed trip wires and other IEDs under/in the vicinity of command wires. When a CW is located, rather than walking parallel to or over the wire to locate the initiation point, work in an "S" pattern, crossing the CW until the initiation point is located.

**Do not focus on the "found" IED.** An IED, once found, is not going to move. Conduct secondary sweeps (5 to 25) and set in cordons. Always think a couple steps ahead and have a plan for any possible encounters that may arise. Again, once positive IED indicators are found, move to safe distances and call EOD.

## About the Author

Don Shift is a veteran of the Ventura County Sheriff's Office and avid fan of post-apocalyptic literature and film. He is a student of disasters, history, current events, and holds several FEMA emergency management certifications. You can email him at donshift@protonmail.com.

This book is a non-fiction follow-up to **Suburban Defense**: *A cop's guide to protecting your home and neighborhood during riots, civil war, or SHTF*. Fiction works include the Ventura Sheriff EMP series, *Hard Favored Rage* and *Blood Dimmed Tide*, where deputies must survive after a devastating electromagnetic pulse destroys the electric grid. *Late For Doomsday* and *Limited Exchange* are novels of surviving and evacuating after a nuclear attack.

All works explore the realities of emergency planning and personal survival in the face of low probability, high impact events that highlight the shortcomings of a technology and infrastructure dependent nation.

While this work is free from profanity and crude or offensive humor, some of my other works do feature such elements and may not be appropriate for sensitive readers. — Don

Made in United States
Troutdale, OR
04/01/2024

18862692R00168